Flippin':
Filipinos on America

Edited by
Luis H. Francia &
Eric Gamalinda

THE ASIAN AMERICAN WRITERS' WORKSHOP • NEW YORK

Flippin': Filipinos on America

© 1996 by Luis H. Francia and Eric Gamalinda
Library of Congress Number 96-078962
ISBN 1-889876-01-1

Design by Wendy Lee
Cover art: Manong, by V.C. Igarta,
photographed by Archie Reyes
Distributed by Temple University Press, 1-800-447-1656.
Printed in the United States of America

Publication of this book was made possible through the generous support of The Rockefeller Foundation and The Lannan Foundation.

The Asian American Writers' Workshop is a not-for-profit literary organization devoted to the creation, development and dissemination of Asian American literature, and is supported by the National Endowment for the Arts, the New York State Council on the Arts, the Department of Cultural Affairs, Jerome Foundation, Bay Foundation, Greenwall Foundation, Axe Houghton Foundation, New York Foundation for the Arts, AT & T, Anheuser-Busch, Avon Corporation, Consolidated Edison, and Two St. Marks Corporation.

Flippin': Filipinos on America

Table Of Contents

Poems

Myth, Memory, Myopia: Or, I May Be Brown But I Hear America Singin'

By Eric Gamalinda

Something stirred in the dark. It was the wind, miasmic and oppressive on this humid June night. Private William Grayson, a volunteer soldier from the Kansas Regiment, cocked his rifle. A group of men were coming up the bridge. He aimed his rifle and called, "Halt!" But the shadowy figures kept advancing. He fired one shot. And then, suddenly, something whizzed past him—he was being fired at! Immediately, other soldiers from the regiment scrambled to back him up. Shots rang out from both sides of the bridge. It was a brief, intense exchange. When the firing stopped, a few Filipino *insurrectos* lay dead on the bridge.

Thus began the Philippine-American War in 1899, less than a year after Commodore George Dewey's fleet sank the antiquated Spanish gunboats docked at Manila Bay. One hundred years after the incident at San Juan bridge, however, the circumstances surrounding that war remain murky—even the name of the man who fired the first shot or his regiment has not been definitely established. It is not surprising, then, that the war is still largely regarded as a footnote in America's history. In fact, until recently, as far as history textbooks in both the United States and the Philippines were concerned, the Philippine-American War, which inexorably altered the destiny of this archipelago in the Pacific, never happened at all.

There is something Borgesian about a time lapse in history such as the Philippines experienced. Within those years a surreal transmutation happened. The country leaped from feudal possession to commonwealth to fledgling democracy. It adopted a Western educational system that was available to all— unheard of under Spanish rule, when most *indios* (as the natives were called) were nothing more than slaves. And it changed its official language, from Spanish to English. Indeed, so massive was the change and so successful the transformation that until the PC police said otherwise, for close to nine decades Filipinos believed the American moniker for them, "Little Brown Brother," was an expression of fraternity.

For Filipinos, America *is* Big Brother, though not always in the Orwellian sense: it is looked up to variously as mentor, exemplar, traitor or refuge. In the Philippines, America still looms as kingpin, destiny-maker, economic manipulator, and, until the last U.S. military bases were rejected by the Philippine Senate in 1991, a colonial master with a serious image problem, thanks to its support of Ferdinand Marcos' 21-year dictatorship and the nationalist backlash that accompanied it. It is easy to see why Filipinos have viewed their stormy relationship with America as something like the popular childhood game of *Jack en Poy* (scissors, paper, stone—again imported from America). American policy seemed determined by chance, and not infrequently by prevarication, and democracy came like a super value meal with all the trimmings: education, culture, rambunctious politics, a dictatorship, military bases, economic impositions, a shared war, citizenship (or promises of), and even a fourth of July independence day.

The United States, nonetheless, is second home to close to two million Filipinos—one of the largest immigrant populations in the U.S., and predicted to become the largest Asian minority by the next millennium. And because Filipino immigrants are especially proud of being "Americanized," they assimilate as though by birthright, blending into the landscape with little effort or recalcitrance. Filipinos are everywhere, but you don't hear of Filipinotowns. Perhaps because of the fractiousness of the "community" or the regional diversities within it, you won't hear of a Filipino million man march anytime in the near future. Filipinos are America's invisible minority, a status that until recently many Filipino Americans seemed comfortable with. Only a handful of academics and students, for instance, are aware that Filipinos settled in America long before the Mayflower pilgrims did, when they abandoned Spanish galleons and settled in California or New Orleans. Not many know that one of the founders of Los Angeles was a Filipino, or that the roots of the California orange industry can be traced back to the Manila-Acapulco galleon trade, when friars stationed in California grew the fruit and handed them out to sick sailors as an antidote to scurvy.

And yet, in the Philippines, America is a presence as huge as God. Every Filipino is expected from the first day of school to acquire an exhaustive knowledge of America the Beautiful—its language, literature, history, and culture—

and, irrationally, everyone expects America to reciprocate the gesture. Imagine the shock of the first-timer in the United States who is asked where in Latin America his country is. Americans have no clear knowledge of their country's relationship with the Philippines, primarily because when the U.S. was colonizing the archipelago—brutally, the way they eradicated the Native Americans—the U.S. government imposed a news blackout. Only a handful of Americans, such as Mark Twain, spoke against American imperialism.

Today, America's multinational role is perceived only from the viewpoint of recent history: Korea and Vietnam remain vivid in the hearts and minds of U.S. war vets, but those who fought in the Philippines are as dead as Jesse James. As the late Alfrredo Navarro Salanga, a poet who had obstinately examined the Philippines' relationship with America, succinctly put it,

> The only problem is
> they don't think much
>   about us
> in America.

Generations of Filipino writers have questioned not only America's presence in their own country but also their people's infatuation with it. Filipinos, in fact, have a term for it: "colonial mentality," which punsters have corrupted to the more derogatory "mental colony." It's a schizophrenic love affair to begin with. American TV shows and Top 40 music are extremely popular, but to say that American culture is superior to one's own earns one special tenure in the mental colony. Yet Filipinos' affection for things American runs deep, and these values are generally carried over by immigrants who take domicile in the United States. Many Filipino Americans still regard their own culture as inferior (that is, compared to America's), which further reinforces the Filipino's invisibility. It is no wonder that second- and third-generation Filipino Americans feel they are neither here nor there, perambulating between a culture that alienates them and a culture they know nothing about, or are ashamed of.

Filipino American literature has found itself in such a limbo. For decades Filipino writers have sporadically earned some degree of recognition in the

United States. Most notable, perhaps, were Carlos Bulosan and Jose Garcia Villa. Bulosan, a migrant worker who found his calling as a writer in the United States, lived a life as though it were tailor-made for a Hollywood script: he struggled his way through California orchards to publishing success, but eventually ended up destitute, infirm, unknown. Yet his works remain valid and relevant to this day, a reminder of the unchanging conditions not only in his country but in ethnic America as well. Villa, on the other hand, has played the quintessential bohemian, living since his youth in New York's Greenwich Village, hanging with Edith Sitwell, W.H. Auden and e.e.cummings, giving classes to generations of budding American writers, and writing poetry so rarified (and, retrospectively, so experimental and ground-breaking) it could not be pinned down to a specific geography (hence his absence in this anthology).

In recent years, more and more Filipinos have seen their works in print, and the success of writers like Jessica Hagedorn may have helped spark interest in Philippine writing. Names like Ninotchka Rosca, NVM Gonzales, Bienvenido Santos, Peter Bacho, Fatima Lim-Wilson, and Evelina Galang come up in current discussions of Filipino-American literature. Yet the general reader is not aware that there is an existing body of Philippine literature. It is perhaps inconceivable to think of a people coming from such a tiny archipelago to produce a substantial body of literature, but the fact is that Philippine writing remains one of the most vibrant in the world, an on-going tradition that can no longer be contained by the strictures of language or even of geography: for Philippine literature is a complex, multifaceted, multilingual organism, written in various dialects (and in English) in the archipelago, in Australia, in Europe and in America, by people who have never seen America, people who have never seen the Philippines, or people who have seen one or both, but who feel continually called upon to make sense of this unique and sometimes flabbergasting culture.

Collectively, these writers challenge preconceptions from both America and the Philippines. Through these voices, the myths about America, so rampantly propagated by mass media in the Philippines, are seen with an unflinching eye, while the myths about the Philippines—savage, ridiculous, too poor to have an interior life—are supplanted by a closer, more sympathetic and ultimately more enlightened point of view. By shattering the myths, one rearranges memory: history as a series of revelations. In this manner, a country, especially one still struggling to deal with its postcolonial identity, puts on corrective lenses to counteract the myopia which afflicts most modern histories.

It seems significant that literature should attempt to set the record straight on a colonial relationship that may have been occasioned by the language barrier. When America decided to colonize the Philippines, the U.S. regiments had not been more than a year in the archipelago. Filipinos still spoke little English, much less understood it. According to recently available documents, the Filipinos tried as much as possible to avoid war with America, while America kept looking for an excuse to colonize the islands. The skirmish at San Juan bridge was that excuse. But would the war have been averted if Private Grayson shouted "Para"—the Spanish/Tagalog for "Halt"?

All told, this is not a historical anthology, but as Robert Frost (not a Filipino) said, it was well worth preliminary mention. This anthology took shape on its own, after Luis H. Francia and I sent out a general call for submissions in the U.S. and in the Philippines (we also received inquiries from London). Although a few works deal with the Philippines' shared history with America, many deal with topics universal to all people, be they transplanted or not: family, relationships, nostalgia, survival, home, faith, loss, joy. These are the values that define a people, and with which they mark their place in the world the whole gamut of human experience, but seen through the eyes of those whose lives have been shaped and defined on both sides of the earth, by cultures that have often conflicted with one another. This conflict is at the heart of every Filipino, and writers have been doubly burdened by questioning it. In the end the search for identity is also a literary quest, and the answer, or fractions of it, can be found here.

The Other Side of the American Coin

By Luis H. Francia

You think you know us, but our outward guise is more deceptive than our history.

—*Carlos Bulosan*

What makes this anthology both appealing and necessary is the universality of its private histories: the stories and poems here embody, elucidate on, allude to, the person at the center of events, whether these relate to intensely intimate revelations or to larger narrative and poetic frameworks. They remind us of the crucial role the creative spirit plays in reclaiming what is never quite the past— because it will always be with us—and in asserting an identity, difficult and perhaps impossible to define, but one that is unquestionably distinct. More than the grim landscape of ideology, beyond the dry discourse of academe, this collection gives us flesh and blood in a communion of words, illustrates history not as lesson but experience, and commands our imagination. Along the way we realize how the notion/nation of America, a common thread linking Filipinos in their diaspora, is full or paradoxes, cornucopia and Pandora's Box all at the same time.

I recall having heard someone say once that "America" was essentially a catch-all term, a repository for ideas and races originating someplace else—positing a limitless There as background to a limitless Here—the world swept up in one word, a mantra that everyone on the planet was capable of uttering and probably had at one time or another. Indeed behind its heroic self-portraits, its dominant ethos, America notoriously appropriates on a global scale, with the sweep of a humongous discount shopping mall (the U.S. as K-Mart of the world) but where exactly, on what shelf, do we find particular selves? With expediency in lieu of accuracy, with stress on mono- rather than multiculturalism, various storekeepers excluded much in constructing a paradigmatic New World that is a deconstructionist's wet dream, with a fluidity of identity possible only in a place that, sans irony, simultaneously confirms ands denies the existence of borders even as it consumes them voraciously. Whole histories, sensibilities, aesthetics, communities, most notably those of nonwhite non-Eurocentric peoples, get chewed up. (Of course this trope of a New World disregards Native Americans; try telling them, or African-Americans for that matter, that this is a nation of immigrants.)

Because or in spite of our having been the objects of colonial and imperial desire, many of us resist participating in this assimilationist trope. Still, wherever we may have been born and wherever we choose to live, America can never be a neutral subject for Filipinos. Dealing with Filipino-ness is to deal with this condition, with a fall from grace, when the twin-headed snake of Spain and America seduced us with the promise of boundless knowledge—we too could be white gods!—even as we reposed in an unimaginably beautiful garden. So it is that the West has insinuated itself over the centuries into the national character. Hence, the continuing preoccupation, to distinguish between a presumed utopian precolonial self and the confused dystopian mongrelized nation-state that we have allegedly become. In the postcolonial world, however, newer than the New World (what Guillermo Gomez-Peña terms the "New World Border") hybridity rules while purity, in a decade where ethnic rivalries have been revived violently, has acquired a fatal taint. Unity Divides, Difference Unites, could very well be the chant of the approaching millennium.

As Filipinos we move about easily, for the most part unself-consciously, through this amalgam of borderlands; we've been hybrid so long we don't usually remark on it. Such calm self-recognition is often mistakenly interpreted as passivity, an indifference to our status in the larger society. Make no mistake; that status retains a largely neocolonial cast, abetted, it must be said, by Pinoys, who reside in a "mental colony," quick to yield for instance to claims of primacy by other cultures, whether this be in the context of art or marriage. And so it has been commonplace among Filipinos to talk resignedly about being forgotten even in a secular "paradise." But that tells only half the story. To forget implies an unconscious process, absent volition. Our insistence on forgetfulness lets America off the hook, as though we were making excuses for a doddering but essentially benevolent uncle. Ignoring and denying: not quite the same as forgetting.

Consider the transformation, by the U.S. War Department, of the Philippine-American War to the "Philippine Insurrection": by such simple sleight-of-word does an official ideology reduce the conflict between a newly formed republic and an emerging empire to the violent refusal of some malcon-

7

tents in accepting their continuing roles as slave/workers on the farm. With that label, the Yankee colonial adventure in the Philippines, as Eric Gamalinda points out, ends up either as a footnote in formalist discourses on America or as a desaparecido. Count history among the victor's victims.

Is it a surprise then that, consistent with its popular do-gooder mythology, America denies an imperialist past? That denial goes hand in hand with a deepseated schizophrenia, eloquently described by Mark Twain (honorary Filipino) in his powerful essay, satirically titled "To the Person Sitting in Darkness." When in 1898 President William McKinley wanted to Christianize a country that had been Catholic for three hundred years running, Twain surmised what Filipinos must have been thinking:

> The Person Sitting in Darkness is almost sure to say: There is something curious about this—curious and unaccountable. There must be two Americas: one that sets the captive free, and one that takes a once-captive's new freedom away from him, and picks a quarrel with him, with nothing found on it; then kills him to get his land.
> The truth is, the Person Sitting in Darkness is saying things like that.

Half a century later, Carlos Bulosan and Bienvenido Santos, my spiritual manongs and, I suspect, of other Filipino writers in America, quickly recognized this malady in their writings. The young men they described in their stories were handsome, cocky, naive, hooked on a quasispiritual vision America preferred, and wanting only the chance to prove themselves equal to any other participant in the American enterprise. But the America they encountered, of racism, exclusionary laws, of violence against people who were different, ground these men's spirits relentlessly. It is a tribute to them that at the end they stood proud, sadder, yes, even bitter at times, but unrepentant in their sense of being Filipino, hair still slicked back.

This book is for them as well as for us, their sons and daughters. It asserts our existence, our history, our difference, our refusal to stand in a light that wounds rather than heals. We insist on our redemptive darkness even as we form part of that Rushdiean empire writing back. We return a borrowed tongue, to use poet Nick Carbo's apt title of his recent anthology of Filipino poetry. This is about flippin'—getting out and flippin' the pot over, about taking "flip," the slang, derogatory term for us who would insist on the primacy of our selves, and yes, flippin' it. This is about flippin' out: losing our minds and composure, in order to rediscover them.

Turn the page, fellow traveller, and find the Flip side of the American coin.

Stories

from *The Man Who (Thought He) Looked Like Robert Taylor*

Bienvenido Santos

— *What good that green card do you?*

— *Now I can get better job. I kiss you beautiful green card.*

— *Kiss my hass. What's wrong with dribing a cab. You make good money. Like I do.*

— *Guess I'm tired, that's all. Besides, all I see here are color people. Bet they think I'm color too.*

— *Of course, you har. I look like a white man beside you.*

— *O, quit it! We're Pinoys, we're not color, we're not white. But Jesus! I come to this country to enjoy, you know, blondies, hitting the jackpot, money in the bank, happy happy, but I'm surround by Africa. Oh, I know there's nothing wrong with 'em, but they're too big like they're gonna crush me any time. And I can't breathe. I get my lungs destroy smoking 'em out. Maybe I go to another state.*

— *You're crazy. Where you gonna go? They're everywhere. In the White 'ouse maybe? White 'ouse my dick. One day they're gonna call that place Black 'ouse. I like that. I like 'em black people. They'll be kings of the world, a black world. You know why? They don't die, that's why. I mean they don't die like they get sick. They live porever, that's why they shoot 'em.*

— *They make trouble, that's why.*

— *You know what's wrong with you? You're scare. Like that time I take you to this Pinoy party, lots of heats and so porth, but you don't wanna stay. You're scare of your hown people.*

— *But those are different Pinoy. They're educated, they're rich guys.*

— *Rich guys? Didn't ya see 'em heating with their 'ands, talking with their mouths pull of pood? Didn't ya see 'em licking their pingers like they gonna heat 'em too?*

— *Yes, but...*

— *And the girls, their faces like masks, smelling like broads, scratching their be'inds. I know where they hitch too. And some of those guys they're crazy about 'ave wives back 'ome who write 'em sweet letters. I miss you, darling. They pray God keep my 'usband well. And their 'usbands har pucking around.*

— *Ha! You're envy.*

— *Me? Enby? You know why I left 'ome. Don't ya porget that. No more Philippine girl por me. Too much expense. Too many tears. In this country, no problem. You want a woman. You get one. Por kilo. Bang. Pinish, You porget.*

— *What's to forget?*

— *Besides, those Philippine girls are nuts, 'ave you talk to 'em? They always hask what cha doing 'ere? I can't say just pucking around, they'll scream like I'm raping 'em. If I say I'm a cab driber they make like the talk is pinish unless they wanna ride my cab por pree. So I don't say. I make like there's mystery story. Like I'm Mississippi gambler with lots of money. They see my wrist watch, the rings on my pingers. They see the debil in my highs. I can get 'em. But I gotta marry 'em pirst. Who like that?*

— *Guess you're right. But those parties ain't for me. Like I don't belong, like they know I ain't high class. And they use different language with some English words like it's Pilipino with American accent.*

— *'ear! 'ear!*

As soon as Sol received his green card immediately after the war, he knew that for him there was no more going back to the Philippines. He was, legally and in fact, a U.S. Permanent Resident. Again, fate had spoken. Now there was one thing he had to do: master the English language as a way out of the many difficulties that plagued the lives of his countrymen in America. True, his accent would be there always, like his complexion, but a conscious attempt to improve his English was imperative. His mastery of the language was to be part of his survival kit. Read. Read. Listen. He would listen to everything, pay close attention. When he talked he must articulate well what almost amounted to ridicule from his friends and fellow workers in the munition factory outside Washington. They called him professor. What the hell, they were plain envious, that's what. What do you know, the natives were green with envy.

He was young. He had all the time in the world. *Time was of the important* as he was fond of saying. How strange that even in his mind the ungrammatical structure of this particular thought should strike him as quaint and not too harsh sounding. Cute perhaps, but sincere in the way platitudes were not and serious, the way the rhetoric of lost causes didn't seem to be. Not to him, in any case.

Once long ago as a newcomer in this country, when asked whether he dreamt in English, he was quick to answer, yes, apart from dreams without dialogue. Yet afterwards he was not too sure. Not until he had begun to listen to his own thoughts. Then he knew without doubt that his answer summed up the truth of both his predicament and his intent.

Many years later, that last time out of Washington, he vowed to keep clear of such concerns and involvements that drained him of every ounce of emotional energy and henceforth live it up in words, instead, get drunk with language not only at every opportunity, but to create such opportunities as allowed him to sense in words the heady vintage of his second language. Although the language as the Americans he knew spoke it was a world apart from the language of his favorite American poets, he would, nonetheless, plunge headlong into the mainstream of current speech and writing, breathe into the lungs of his being all the clichés that polluted the air of sensitive purists who wasted time, precious, golden time, watching the pollen count of what was trite and overused to death. He would take in all those cliches and add to them the flavor of strangeness. Why, even his accent wasn't bad, not bad at all. The girls, especially those on the night shift, half asleep most of the time, loved it. When he pronounced their names, like this girl's, named Barbara, she put her covered head on his shoulder and touched his cheek gently with her gloved hand, which smelled of oil. "Say that again," she sighed, and when he did, she practically swooned in his arms in a gesture of complete, absolute surrender.

The language, his accent, not to mention his good looks, would make up the sum total of his personality, his charm. Now he found himself speaking in English to his own countrymen even when they spoke to him in the dialect. Once in a while, when he tried to speak the dialect, he would pause in the middle of a statement, groping for the right word, a turn of phrase that had once been familiar, and revert to English in a strange paraphrase.

Sol decided to attend night school. When he began to make inquiries about going to school nights, some of his friends told him frankly he would be wasting his time. What did he want to be, a politician? Go back to the Philippines and run for senator? His boss had other ideas.

"What you wanna go to school for? You think you earn more? Nah! You gotta be smart here," he said, touching his head with a greasy forefinger. "You don't learn that in no school. Besides, you miss the time anahuff on the night shift."

Instead of getting discouraged, he became determined more than ever to resume his studies. This guy with his illiterate English would be no better than a factory boss all his life unless he became a crooked operator and joined a big time gang. No, he wouldn't listen to him. And what did he care for time anahuff?

The first night school he attended proved to be a mistake. It was an adult class, mostly of aging aliens, who spoke very little English, and attended the class to prepare for U.S. citizenship. He could be their teacher. What he wanted was something else. Regular college night classes.

He applied for admission to a freshman class in English in the extension department of the American University, but he was turned down at first because he didn't have any credentials. He claimed that the high school in the Philippines where he graduated was burned down during the war. All the records were burned with it. But he was willing to do anything to prove that he was eligible for college work. Sign an affidavit. Swear on the Bible. Anything. Did they want to examine him? He was ready.

The admissions official had a baby face and looked amused when Sol said that he was ready to be examined.

"It's the honest truth, professor, I'm a high school graduate. It isn't my fault that I have no credentials. Blame the war." He wanted to say, blame the fucking war, but he was afraid he might be sent up to graduate school for using such language. He was not yet ready for that.

"Let's see. Your case deserves study." Baby face still wore that amused look. He appeared delighted, listening to this young man talking like a book. His blue eyes seemed to say, go on, say some more, I'm listening.

"Some of my teachers were Americans. They're still there. And I'm here. They were good teachers. It was from them that I learned to love English. I've read Edgar Allan Poe, William Cullen Bryant, Henry Wadsworth Longfellow, John Greenleaf Whittier. I know some of their poems by heart. I have won in a declamation contest, interscholastic. I recited Poe's 'The Raven.' Do you want me to recite some..."

"That won't be necessary," the professor said, a pink smile spreading on his cherubic face. "To tell you the truth, I couldn't follow you... I mean, I couldn't understand much of what you were saying, at first, that is. But later... now, I do get the drift of your speech."

"A speech, sir? Did I sound like I was delivering a speech?"

"Oh, no, no!"

"I'm very strongly moved to ask for your consideration, that's why, sir."

"I know. Perhaps we can admit you as a special student."

"What's so special, sir?"

"Not so special. Special. A special student is allowed to attend a class and pay a minimal fee, but is not entitled to a certificate or degree like regular students in good standing."

"Ah, a visitor."

"Not exactly. Auditor would be more like it."

"Auditor?"

"You know. Audit. To hear. Auditor. Hearer."

"Oh, I thought for a while... I mean, we have an auditor general in the Philippines, but that's not it, I guess."

"Oh, no. That's a different auditor."

"In this class I might be allowed to attend, as you say, what do I do? Just sit and listen? I wouldn't be allowed to recite?"

"Of course, you would. You would be a member of the class. Recite when called upon, do the assignments, take examinations, if you wish, and you could have a grade."

"Special. Auditor. The name isn't really that important, is it, sir? I just want to improve my English."

"Your English is fine, it's excellent. Even your accent. After a while, it's fine."

On that fine note, he attended night school. Now he showered twice every day, once on waking up in the morning and again upon arriving home from work. He changed into a clean shirt and a well pressed suit. Well-scrubbed. Spanking clean. Compliments he loved to hear from those who noticed him. He had a natural fresh-from-the-shower look about him. No amount of menial work or hard physical labor, hunger, deprivation, seemed to alter the youngness of his face, the silky texture of his palms so that whenever he shook hands, with girls in particular, they often asked, was he an artist, a pianist maybe, his palms were so soft and he had such beautiful fingers. And he would quite candidly say whatever he was at the time: cab driver, stevedore, laborer, janitor. Surely, they would say, he was joking.

His first class was a disappointment. Grammar. Diagramming. Rules. He didn't want any of these. All he wanted was to learn how to write correctly and speak well. The rules be hanged.

But he suffered it all. Stoically, he said to himself, wishing someone had heard him and had asked what the word meant. How impressive he would sound in his knowledge, terribly limited such as it was, of etymology. Stoic, from the Greek Stoikos, a philosophy of indifference and unfeeling (almost) to either pain or pleasure.

But he was not a stoic. That was the trouble.

The class met three times a week. Sol was present every time. Winter presented problems like transportation. He had no car and waiting at the bus stops on the coldest winter nights, he kept himself from freezing by jumping up and down and swinging his arms about. One night during a blizzard, he stayed home only after he was informed that classes were suspended.

During oral recitation week, he volunteered to speak. He was afraid he might not be called if he simply waited. It was their last meeting for the week.

"What will you talk about?" the instructor asked. He sounded like the actor Edward G. Robinson and looked like him, too.

"Many things," Sol answered confidently, feeling he had prepared for this moment, the moment of truth no less, the hour of unburdening. He was the cynosure of all eyes. There were a few pretty girls in the room and they had fellows waiting for them after class. No matter. He would make them forget their boyfriends.

"But you have fifteen minutes only at the most, maybe ten."

"Just stop me, sir, when I've eaten up my time."

He began talking haltingly, apologizing for his accent and the very personal nature of his talk.

"This is all about me," he began. "I come from the Philippines where I finished high school. It had always been my dream to come to the United States. As you can see I have realized that dream. Perhaps you would want to know whether the reality is anything like the dream. The answer is yes and no. But I won't go into all that. I have only fifteen minutes at the most."

"Never mind the time," seemed to be the meaning of the audible murmur that broke the silence briefly and the look in his classmates' eyes. This gave him added assurance.

"In the Philippines my American teachers taught me to love the works of American poets, but, alas, nobody knows them here. Some recall their names, Longfellow, Poe, Bryant, and the rest, but very few remember their works. And I thought that as soon as I touched American soil, all I had to do was mention 'Evangeline,' 'Hiawatha,' 'The Raven,' 'Annabel Lee,' 'The Death of the Flower,' 'Rhodora,' and every door would be open to me. Not that doors have been shut in my face because I have tried to quote lines from these poets, but I have been stared at with eyes that seemed to say, 'What a pity that one so young could be so crazy already,' or words to that effect."

There was tittering from girls in the back row. He glanced towards them. Their eyes were applauding him. Maybe they no longer remembered the guys outside waiting for them to be dismissed. Edward G. Robinson's double was doubling with silent laughter somewhere in the rear of the room.

"I should have been discouraged, but I was not. I knew that one day I was going to find an audience receptive to the beauty of the poems I carried with me like a treasure. So I went about my way, throwing around my favorite passages from these poets, waiting for recognition from anybody, any group who would throw back at me a similar bouquet of lovely poetry. But they only threw me surprised glances. Some actually suggested I must be drunk. Oh yes, I was. I still am. Drunk with words, with the sweet, musical words of the American poets whom I loved, but none of my acquaintances in America knew well enough to understand the nature of my insanity, if insanity, indeed, it is. But tonight, I believe I have found the audience I have been looking for."

The class was in a mild uproar. What had he said? What were they trying to tell him? His time was up? He looked towards the instructor, who was smiling and nodding as he leaned towards a group of students who must be asking him to allow him to keep talking. He had just begun. Finally, he could distinguish some of the things the class was saying.

"Recite the poems!"

"We don't know those poets."

"You don't?" he asked. It was incredible. "Really, you don't? You mean to say you haven't memorized such lines as: 'This is the forest primeval, the murmuring pines and the hemlock...'" and he went on and on, leaping from verse to verse and poet to poet by simply saying, "And this from 'Annabel Lee,'... and we loved with a love that was more than love, I and my Annabel Lee... and the moon never rise but I see the bright eyes of my beautiful Annabel Lee...' Or this from the 'Rhodora', 'If the sages ask thee why, this beauty is wasted on the earth and sky, tell them, dear, that if eyes are made for seeing, then beauty is its own excuse for being.' Don't tell me you haven't memorized these lines."

"No, no. But go on!"

And he went on, like a fool, he thought later, unburdening himself of all the beautiful lines he had wanted to hear himself say all of the two, or was it three, years he had been in America.

He regaled them with anecdotes. Once when he told a girl he liked, "Your breath is as sweet as kine that feed in the meadows," straight from 'Evangeline,' the girl refused to see him after she found out that kine meant cows.

Still they kept asking for more. So he went beserk. Soulfully, dramatically, he intoned:

"The melancholy days are here, the saddest of the year,
Of wailing winds and naked woods and meadows brown and sear,
Heaped in the hollows of the grove, the autumn leaves lie dead,
They rustle to the eddying gust and to the rabbit's tread."

"And listen to this. My favorite teacher, a Miss O'Malley from Boston, read and reread to us, 'Snowbound' by you know whom..."

His classmates looked at one another.

"Well, Miss O'Malley, around Christmas time, did nothing but read from 'Snowbound.' She kept talking to us about snow. We had never seen snow. Our idea of snow was drugstore flakes on a Christmas tree covered with cotton balls or something like in the movies. And she would recite, homesickness in her eyes:

'No cloud above, no earth below,
A universe of sky and snow...'

while we sizzled in the classroom."

After class, the only thing his classmates didn't do, which he hoped they would, was ask for his autograph. But perhaps they were afraid he didn't know how to write. A joke, a joke, a joke!At their subsequent meetings, however, the class reverted to diagrams and worse, punctuation and spelling, and a record cold spell stayed too long in the Washington area. First, he missed a class, then another. About the end of the term—and thoroughly ashamed of himself—he attended class. He looked around self-consciously, ready with an excuse should someone ask why he had absented himself so long, had he been sick or what? To his surprise and his disappointment, no one seemed to have missed him. The instructor gave them the subject for a theme, due the first meeting after the Christmas break. Subject: My Philosophy of Life.

Now he had a rather strong motive to resume attending class. He was going to show them he could write as well as talk. Could he, though? He had never tried writing. Besides, what was his philosophy of life anyhow? Honesty is the best policy? Cleanliness is next to godliness? That's not a philosophy, that's sanitation. So. What did he believe in?

He believed in Fate. In lives that are extensions of other lives. Like his and

Robert Taylor's. That their lives followed some sort of pattern, running parallel but close, so close they touched at certain points ever so lightly but palpably, like pure coincidence–and mystical because unnatural. But this was mere belief, strong as it was, but not philosophy.

He went around, asking at every chance he got, "What's your philosophy of life?" hoping that by listening to others, he would learn how to formulate his own. The guy with whom he often shared the same seat on the bus said, "Philosophy of life? Workers of the world, unite. You have nothing to lose but your change–loose change." The man chuckled, completely pleased with himself.

Others gave out with mottoes he had heard of before and didn't sound like anything nearly close to what he was looking for. He wanted something with an impact. One of those statements that hits you between the eyes, something memorable, a blow below the belt, a kick in the groin, at the least, a tingle. Like what for example?

Like this picture of an old, ragged man, kneeling on the floor beside a sagging bed, saying, God, remember me?

Another picture: of a man in pajamas, unshaven, his eyes still heavy with sleep, talking to himself as he stares at his face in the mirror: "What mistakes are you going to make again today?"

"Life is but an empty dream..." —Longfellow

"Roses are red, violets are blue
I'm still beautiful, but what happened to you?" —Anonymous

Seriously now, what philosophy? It's better to receive than to give. Any time. Merry Christmas!

There were scribblings in the men's room at the World Trans-Lux in downtown Washington:

See Wanda Supple, 69 4th St. S.W., after 5 pm if you wanna good fuck or a blow job

And right below, in red ink:

For your spiritual needs, Call on JESUS, Address:
Heaven. Open: Night and Day

Obviously written in a different hand, also in red ink, underneath all these was a P.S.: May I call collect? (Signed) John Leland Scrooge.

None of these came close, most of them were just intended to be funny. Could he not, however, extract an essence out of these various texts and pictures and formulate a philosophy of life? Perhaps. But it would not be his philosophy of life.

The truth was he had none. That is, nothing that he could spell out like a rule on punctuation marks.

The new year found him without anything written down. His thoughts were as vague and mixed up as ever. Perhaps he would have to tell the instructor frankly that he couldn't do it, he didn't have any philosophy of life, nothing original, exclusively his own. It didn't have to be, though. He could borrow from his favorite poets, but they sounded so sad. Longfellow's "Life is but an empty dream" was more like an elegy for all losers than a philosophy of life.

When classes resumed he didn't show up. The term was almost over. He had paid all the required fees. What did he learn in class anyhow? What a ham, what an ass he could make of himself, that he could be funny like a clown? Shit!

Crossing Over

NVM Gonzales

Our boat, a freighter with sugar from Negros and hemp from Albay, was to dock at San Francisco; but a longshoremen's strike, we learned, was in progress there and we had to proceed to Oakland instead.

"Isn't there anyone in this bright winter sunshine, anyone I might know?" I said to myself, seeing a little crowd gathering twenty feet below where I stood on the deck, leaning over the railing. I felt as if I needed a miracle.

Someone tapped my shoulder from behind, and said: "Oh, here you are. This is for you."

It was the purser, with a long, light blue envelope for me. And at once I knew where this had come from: the foundation that had awarded me a fellowship. To set foot in America and to be looked after like that was beyond my wildest dreams. An omnipotence had brought me over and would keep watch all the way.

The letter could not have been more reassuring. It did, in fact, have a hundred-dollar check to tie me over until my regular stipend arrived. Proceed directly to Stanford Village, in Palo Alto, it said.

On the other side of the bay was the big city that I had only seen in pictures—in the midst, a rise of skyscrapers aglitter in the cloud drift of sunshine. To the far south, shrouded with fog, would be Palo Alto.

These distances and directions had remained fixed in my mind for so long, how could I not know them now by heart? But how does one get to Palo Alto from the Oakland pier? It seemed quite an insurmountable problem. At the same time, it did not faze me. My self-confidence was of course without foundation. Down below, on the dock, things were utterly at a standstill on account of the strike.

I did see a pickup pull up close, and the thought occurred to me that it might not be a bad idea to try to get to San Francisco on it.

Did I, perhaps by telepathy, manage to send that message to its driver? He was a middle- aged fellow; a second look, and it seemed he was in fact smiling at me.

In the meanwhile, a tall gray-haired woman had come up on our deck and, with a smile even more welcoming than that of the old man, she said she'd be happy to give anyone a lift.

She was fifty or so and wore a flouncy skirt and a loose-sleeved blouse weighted down by shell shards and glass beads. A large comb stuck out at the back of her head, keeping in place an ample knot of hair. Over her shoulders was an alpaca shawl. "A witch...that's who this is," I told myself.

"Isn't San Francisco where you are going?"

Her offer should fool no one, I warned myself.

"If it's a ride you're looking for..." she tried once more.

"Friends are coming to fetch me," I said—which was a lie, of course.

"Taxis are also on strike."

It did appear so, although no one on board had told us about this. "My friends are coming anyway...with their own transport," I assured the woman.

Words which, I figured, could impress if spoken confidently, which I did— and just about then two men and a girl turned up.

"Oh, I see," said the old one, stepping aside. "Here they are."

But friends of mine, they most certainly were not.

Let me pause here to say that I had not been the only passenger on that freighter. There had been two others, Filipino students like myself—Visayan girls, in their early twenties—and such poor sailors, those darlings. They had been so seasick that I had been cabin boy, deck hand, and brother to them most days of the voyage.

It took some convincing to have them quit their stuffy cabin for the impoverished quarters that the captain let them have, an area on the starboard, adjacent to the bridge, where at least they'd feel less cooped up.

But this camping out invited attention. Hardly could the ship's officers avoid hanging around. My role as chaperone seemed predestined; I would have to be ever on the alert, lest an innocent invitation for a viewing of a breathtaking moonrise over the Pacific would become a not too unromantic scene. Being Filipinas, of their time and place, the two girls could not be exposed to casual friendships, let alone shipboard romances. They seemed to have understood this and they felt I understood this, too. That they had a compatriot seemed a godsend. Before me was a duty to be nobly discharged.

How I came of this foreknowledge and sense of obligation puzzles me today. At that time, I thought nothing of it. Shipboard adventures were the stuff of Hollywood movies, but my complicity in holding romance and life at bay—where did that come from?

Although a sword may hang too long as a piece of wall decoration, it cannot but fit as snugly as before into the tooled leather scabbard that, in the first place, had been fashioned for it. This I see now. But at that time, all I knew was that I aspired to no reward for my bother. Back of my mind, however, to be honest, I believe I had hoped that my being helpful could count towards something, although what this might be I had no idea.

The friends the old woman referred to were people who had come to fetch the two girls. How they had located the boat amazed me. In any case, they were no sooner on board than the two girls were gone, off with their two offerings of what some alleged to be the pristine innocence that I had been asked to preserve. And I felt considerable rancor over their allowing themselves to be whisked away like that. They might have offered to take me along—their friends had cars!—even only as a gesture. Or they might have asked how I planned to get to the city on my own. I would answer in some indeterminate way, but their show of interest would suffice. They could have easily made the effort, taking into consideration the fact that I was at least a countryman, if nothing more.

The hurt was there. At that time, I had no explanation for it, but perhaps now I have. They came from rich Visayan families, from some hacienda in the heartland of Negros, back home. I had been the sharecropper's son allowed to linger about the plantation house. My feelings of betrayal would have been beyond their grasp. If at that time I had already identified it and had somehow let on how it hurt, they would not have been amused.

What with these feelings and then the offer that the old woman made, it seemed I was being set up by the Fates. The old man had been waiting on the dock, in his pickup. As in folktales, it is shrewdness that often comes to one's rescue. In this instance, I had lost neither the peasant's talent for it nor that of the boy, whose place was the back porch steps of the hacienda house, that tin-roofed island in the sea of noble cane waving in the sun.

The old woman had disappeared, and the man in the pickup materialized before me in her stead. It was all I could do now to dissemble and assume an air.

I inquired what it would cost me, baggage and all, to be taken to the city. He named a sum that seemed reasonable enough. I did not try to drive a bargain.

We were on our way in no time. It would be only a forty-minute ride, he assured me.

He was talkative from the start. He pointed out the landmarks as if he were a regular tourist's guide. I did observe almost immediately that we had taken the lower deck of the Oakland Bay Bridge. Why not the upper one? I wondered.

Up till then I did not associate his ebullience with any plan of action, but I couldn't but think back on the events of the last twenty minutes: my rejection of the crone; and this man's waiting, his making a move only after the two girls had gone; and now my being utterly on my own—why, here was quite a stratagem. The old man could only mean harm. And, worse, the situation struck me as familiar. I had seen it in all the movies!

Instead of a clear and open view of the bay, as might have been the case had we taken the upper deck of the bridge, all that I could see from my seat in the pickup, with the man at my left, were girders, steel beams, and huge cables: hardly an introduction to America to be enthusiastic about.

Added to this was the thought that the old man could knock me cold and then toss me into the bay. The light traffic could make that a cinch. He'd have to rob me, I'd imagined. Well, he'd only find a few loose bills and the check. There was very little he could do, really. In his disgust, he'd panic. He had merely wasted time on me and would then have to get rid of me entirely, shoving me overboard at the first opportunity.

While his crime in all its heinousness shaped up in my mind, my fingers, seemingly working on their own, were busy fumbling for my name-card, attaching one to the inner lining of my jacket. Where I found a safety pin for this operation, on all accounts a not uncomplicated one, I couldn't say. But that was one handy safety pin all right! I took a deep breath to enjoy my success. Surely, my name-card couldn't come away or fall or get torn off, however my body tumbled off into the water. I would be fished out before the turn of the tide, as the newspaper account would have put it. The old man would read the story in his evening paper; right there before his eyes would be a picture of the body of his Filipino! And not just anyone, either. For this one had taken pains to leave his identity with no doubt. In the morgue, some witty coroner's assistant would have a ready tribute for him: "Ah, the guy knew! Identity, to him, was of the essence!"

This drama unfolded on a stage entirely all its own in my mind—while, on another level of actuality, I made small talk with the old man. I must have dropped words and phrases in the conversation that let on that I had come to America to study. As we drove on, I observed that he couldn't seem to have enough of me. He'd look me over from head to foot, as if he had to be certain that there was nothing more to this hapless hacienda yardboy he was taking into the city.

I did have in my suitcase a light pinstripe woolen suit, a gift from an uncle. The package had reached me in Manila just in time. It was a suit he might have worn for a Sunday stroll at Portsmouth Square or down Broadway. He was somewhere in the Pacific, though, on his merchant ship at that time of day, a mess boy answering his captain's summons to be served up his coffee and pastry.

Uncle had gotten no farther. He had written to say how sorry he was that we could not meet in San Francisco, but there would be a time for that. Anyway, he said, he was sending the double-breasted; I should look great in it. How amazing that all these sentiments could be conveyed in a postcard; the *Watsonville Mariner*, in color, held her bow proudly awash against the feathery crimson of a Pacific sunset.

This was the juncture when the man announced he must take me to his brother who was a tailor. It was a fortunate coincidence that, in a matter of minutes, we could get there. He'd have me outfitted right.

"But I do not need any clothes," I protested.

"Something warm...that's what you must have."

"No, I do not need any," I insisted.

"You forget that clothes make the man!"

He was indefatigable. We had left the bridge and now the flow of traffic took us into a narrow and bustling street. My anxiety mounted. It's here he'll do it! Even without benefit of the watery depths, or of shadows, or of darkness. Scenes of this kind abound in Hollywood movies.

"My brother's shop is only two blocks away from here."

But I seemed to be merely imagining these words. For things around seemed to have come to a standstill. In the street nothing moved; the buildings to the left and right of us stood square-shouldered in a frieze of concrete, glass, and graying sunlight.

Were it not for several quick flashes of red that crossed my line of vision, I would not have understood that we had stopped at yet another traffic light.

"I've this train to catch," I heard myself speaking.

The old man remained quiet and remote now. Only his hands and shoulders moved, as we rejoined the traffic.

What would come next I had not the slightest notion. Never once during the next few minutes did I drop my guard. One false gesture and I might have swung the cab door open and run to safety. I'd be among the pedestrians in the sidewalk and slipping into a crowded shop or escaping to freedom in some alley.

I began reading aloud the names of the streets we passed. This seemed to have created an impression on him of my level of alertness.

"Now, here we are!" I announced on seeing the railroad station at Townsend and Third.

He pulled up at the curb and let me go without a word.

A Man's Reward is in Heaven

F. Sionil Jose

Dr. John Robertson was refreshed when he woke up from his afternoon nap. The venetian blinds were up and he could see the shimmering blue of Manila Bay beyond the wide glass window. It was one of those translucent April afternoons and in the clear, cloudless horizon, he could make out—like small humps in the sea— the bastion of Corregidor, and, nearer, to the left, the white washed buildings of the Cavite naval base. A few ships sat in the harbor like gray ducks against the mirror-like calmness of the sea, and the neatness of the scene entranced him momentarily. He remembered the wrecks of merchant ships and destroyers that once stood like nightmares on the waters, reminders of a war that was past. Too, the once-magic, if not heroic, visions which Corregidor always evoked; now, Corregidor had become a tourist spot and everything around Manila had taken on the smugness of a land given to weeds.

For the last two weeks this scene had been framed before him and he had wanted so much to see another thing—that fabulous Manila sunset which he had heard so much about, when the mountains, strung across the bay in that velvet dusk, took on the shape of a reclining woman, and the air above the bay ignited like fireworks. But sunset meant cocktails or merienda with teachers, cultural groups and what-have-you and now, even on this his last day in Manila, he was denied the pleasure of seeing this sunset because he had one final meeting—a cocktail-dinner—to attend. Carlos Soler, his host, was an art patron of sorts and was easily the most prominent of the Manila promoters of culture.

Robertson idled to the desk where his portable typewriter was. He glanced at the notes which he had worked on when he arrived the other night from a party given in his honor by the president of the AAA (Atin-Atin Association). It had been a profitable evening although he had not really appreciated the food—the same round of Filipino dishes which he had for the nth time—and when he returned to the hotel he immediately ordered a hamburger sandwich and a fresh supply of alka-seltzer. A loquacious senator was present and he had rattled off on a lot of subjects quite alien to his cranium. This had amused

Robertson very much, for the senator had reminded him immensely of the types he knew back home.

He read what he had already typed on the roller: April 18, I'm now convinced that Philippine nationalism means more than just a desire of Filipinos to have more refrigerators and vitamin pills. A certain element of despondency has crept into it and this despondency is partially created by the intellectuals, particularly those who were educated in the United States, who now find themselves unable to change the social attitudes overnight. I speak now of the widespread corruption which a senator acquaintance blandly accepted as a synonym of the failings of democracy, the inability of leaders to show themselves as examples of service. I encountered today a rather outspoken fellow from the University of California (check his name and research material on political parties, local), who said that if the minor bureaucrats are stealing, it is because they assume that their superiors are stealing and they will be damn fools if they don't do the same. It's a chain reaction and if this reaction must be broken, it must be at the top. The writers admit now that although they did not like Magsaysay and his "lack of guts" in the face of American "pressure," at least Magsaysay was honest and his honesty was strong enough to seep down and pervade Philippine bureaucracy, infuse into the bureaucrats a sense of mission or a sense of doing things properly. This, while Magsaysay was alive...

The phone rang and Robertson picked it up. It was Carlos Soler and the millionaire's voice sounded more squeaky than it actually was. "Of course, Mr. Soler, of course, I'll come."

"It's been two years since you came to the house," Soler said. "I'm not taking chances and I'm sending you one of my men to fetch you, so that you don't lose your way. Sebastian Cuerva—that's his name. He writes, too. He should be there before five."

"Isn't that rather early?" Robertson glanced at his watch. It was almost four. "I thought the party wouldn't start until six..."

"You'll regret it if you can't come earlier," Soler said ingratiatingly. "The best of our writers... I've told you about them. Gomez, Tita Ramirez—all the rest. I'm not trying to make them look important. They are. And if it's a lively discussion you want they can give you that. It's so difficult to invite them—you are an American. Filipino First, you know..."

"I understand," Robertson said with a nervous laugh. "I'll be ready when your boy comes. Filipino First then."

A guffaw at the end of the line and Robertson placed the phone down. Well, even a slogan can be a good joke. For a while Soler was on his mind. The businessman, he quickly remembered, had been coarse and gruff most of the time—a congenital fault, no doubt. It's all right, millionaires can afford to be coarse in spite of their supposedly sincere avowals of patronage and interest in the arts and in literature. And he wondered again what Soler's gimmick was—he was a sugarman, a magazine publisher and now a champion of the arts and nationalism. There must be some profit in this, Robertson assured himself, basing his judgment on the general run of Asiatic and Filipino businessmen he had already met.

Before Soler hung up, Robertson had already made up his mind to make the most of this party. If Ramirez, Gomez and all the vocal people whom he had heard so much about were coming, well and good. Robertson, however, had a very low regard for newspapermen and columnists, and he had never for the life of him come to believe that newspaper people could really shape opinion. Somehow he felt a little piqued with Soler. The cultural impresario had impressed Robertson that he, the Asian director of the Foundation, had wanted to meet these characters, when actually he never made such a wish or even the slightest hint of it. That simply was not in his code. People should come to him. After all, he was here to give fellowships, not to engage in silly debates with those who were not interested in what he and the Foundation were doing.

These thoughts were in Robertson's mind and he dared not dredge them up. He did not want to think of the consequences and the harm that such thoughts might do to him and the Foundation's program.

And yet Robertson liked the Philippines sincerely, because here he was able to talk freely and there was no mistaking his capability to connect. That was his main difficulty—to connect. All over Asia his failure to do this had hampered him. Japan, particularly—ah, that country. He could not get anything from the Japanese, not even from those who had studied in America, in his own sunny California. They always seemed distant, withdrawn—and the women, they were always giggling.

It was not so in Manila. Still, though the Filipinos were usually vocal, they brimmed constantly with Asiatic reserve and politeness. It would be different this evening with the writers. The few whom he had already met he found articulate.

Robertson lighted a cigar from the box presented to him the previous evening. He then took long draughts of the wonderful aroma. These Filipinos, they make such wonderful cigars. What do they want to go into heavy industry for?

The phone rang and Robertson picked it up.

"Yes, good afternoon. Of course I remember you," he said jovially, but could not place this Sebastian Cuerva, whom Carlos Soler had sent. "Yes, do come up…"

This was one Filipino who was extra punctual. It was only five and here was Cuerva already. Robertson powdered his face with talc. In the mirror his face looked lean and tired and the rings formed around his eyes—too many damn parties. The knock on the door came sooner than he expected and he opened it to a young man with dark, deep-set eyes, shaggy hair and an emaciated look. His *barong tagalog*, the cheap ramie kind, Robertson quickly noticed, was frayed at the collar.

The Filipino paused at the door. "I was delegated to fetch you, Doctor," he said. "Mr. Soler's idea is that I should give you a briefing although I'm sure you are already familiar with the people coming tonight. I'm not really familiar with them. Just nodding acquaintances, you may say."

"I think I know them," Robertson said, guiding his visitor in. "You see, this isn't my first time here. And I enjoy Manila…" he found himself sliding back to the worn-out amenities and he checked himself. "Do you write, too?"

Sebastian Cuerva took in the American's features, the blue eyes, the distinguished crop of graying hair. "In a way," he said humbly, "but usually they are not literary things. I used to teach sociology. Then Mr. Soler hired me to write press releases." He sounded very apologetic. "It pays better than teaching."

"I see," Robertson nodded, quite disappointed.

"Some of the people coming were friends in college. Gomez was my teacher. The others—well, you know how it is. The intellectual circle in Manila is small."

Robertson was amused inwardly at the facility with which Cuerva used the word "intellectual"—the American had been exposed to it in his frequent conversations and was not pleased to find that almost everyone who had appeared in the "Letters to the Editor" column could be called an "intellectual." But he quickly regained his humor. "This is my fifth visit," he said. "Way back in 1946 it was reconstruction. Everyone was concerned with rebuilding, backpay, guerilla recognition and friendship with the United States. I've never seen anything like it."

"The Liberation," Cuerva sighed too, "nothing like it."

"Then, in 1949, it was the Huk scare. I was afraid even to go out of the city. Those were terrible times. By 1951, it was the rural areas, the barrios..."

Cuerva immediately got the drift. "And in 1959 it's nationalism."

The American broke into a short laugh. "Yeah, nationalism..."

Cuerva stood up. "I hope you won't mistake it for a fad, Doctor. It isn't."

"Of course, of course," Robertson assured him. They strode to the door and Robertson locked it. "I have never doubted its genuineness."

They rode quietly in the elevator and at the lobby the American spoke again: "I thought you were going to brief me."

Sebastian Cuerva smiled wanly. "Shall we sit down then? We have lots of time before the party."

They went to one of the huge upholstered lounging chairs near the desk. Cuerva continued: "There are actually only three important people in this gathering. Each has quite a coterie. There's Tita Ramirez—she is the president of the Writers Club—now idolized by college kids. Guilleng Santos is a big shot along newspaper row and Manny Gomez is a professor."

"Is that all?" Robertson was bored. He had hoped that this Cuerva would tell him a few spicy things, just as other informants had done—fed him with interesting bits of gossip about people he had never met and would never meet on this trip, perhaps, but whose names he jotted down nevertheless, because someday they might be possible candidates for a grant.

"Well, I may add," Cuerva said meekly, "they are all outspoken and quite anti-American."

"Nationalists," Robertson beamed. They stood up and walked to the parking lot, where Soler's car was waiting.

As the car sped on, Cuerva suddenly found himself tongue-tied and he had nothing more to say to this American who seemed to divine his thoughts and know all the answers. Around them the city, saturated with the last vestiges of the day's gummy heat, flowed by. Cuerva wondered if the party would break up early and wished it would. He was never at ease in the parties which Soler gave, maybe because all the time he was aware of his being Soler's special hack. If the party ended up early, he decided, I would pass by Ma Mon Luk and buy my wife a siopao or two. Why doesn't Soler have the courtesy to ask her along? He asked himself and laughed inwardly at the silliness of the question. A couple of siopaos would not cost much, but it was what they stood for which bothered him. What was it she liked best the last time? Green mangoes in December? Another mouth to feed.

Sebastian Cuerva shook his head and wished they were already at the party. He could use a drink now. It was never his habit to drink, but in these parties, it was the thing to do. Drink made it easier for him to withstand the prattle. It made him feel nice, too, made him feel he belonged, made him feel like an honored guest and not a member of the cheering squad.

It was dusk when they reached the Soler mansion in Quezon City and the lawn was already ablaze with lights. All the tall agoho trees in front were festooned with electric bulbs, and beyond the shrub of cherry vine near the pool were gathered Soler's guests.

Carlos Soler, comfortable in a white T-shirt and white pants, bounded across the green when he saw them come. He was short and squat, with unmistakable Chinese eyes and a firm handshake. "I didn't invite many, just a dozen or so — nothing but the cream for you. And I must tell you, I don't think you are in the market tonight; these people don't need fellowships."

Soler, Robertson knew, had not meant to be impolite. "I don't usually go around dangling fellowships before people," Robertson tried to hide his displeasure with a grin. "I merely want to meet real writers." He would have gone on explaining his point of view, but Soler was not paying attention and he was now beaming as he introduced his guest raucously.

Robertson saw two faces which he remembered—and, of course, Tita Ramirez, whom he had already met, a buxom woman in her middle age who had Negroid features and to whom he said warmly, "It's so nice to see you again, Miss Ramirez"; Guilleng Santos (he could write this down later), thin, lean, with a balding head, an aquiline nose and an asthmatic voice; Manuel Gomez, a political science professor, a barrel of a body with a rasping voice, and the rest apparently minor gods receding in the background, just as Sebastian Cuerva had told him.

His eyes sought Tita Ramirez again after he had sat down. Yes, that well-fed look had not changed. The eyes still flashed, the thick lips were still sensuous and moist. She was as usual with a new escort (Robertson could pick him out at once)—a tall fellow with a crew cut, who sat close to her — and this fact confirmed what he had already known: that, in spite of her flaunting nationalism, Tita Ramirez's partiality to Caucasian males had not diminished.

"We were talking about you, Dr. Robertson," she said when the amenities had subsided. She had raised her voice for all to hear.

"I hope it wasn't too uncomplimentary," Robertson said. "Americans aren't very popular nowadays and I hope I haven't contributed to that fact."

"I said that you are different—that you know Asia and the Asian mind, particularly the Filipino mind."

"Thank you," Robertson said with real pleasure. A white-uniformed waiter hovered by and Robertson ordered a gin and tonic. He did not get what Guilleng Santos (that asthmatic rasp) said, so Robertson asked him to repeat the question.

When Guilleng Santos spoke again he did so as columnist and editor and, as such, brimmed with cocksureness and that bludgeon-like certainty in which he wrote. "Is there really an Asian mind?"

"I'm not a scholar, mind you," Robertson said softly, "and I'm afraid I'll get lost in circles if I were made to define it."

"Well," it was Manny Gomez who spoke, his massive jaw thrust forward, his wide forehead crinkling in the soft light of the multi-colored bulbs, "how about the Filipino mind then?"

"I believe that Filipinos," Robertson neatly evaded the question, "can describe themselves better."

Hovering in the background sipping his second scotch, Sebastian Cuerva was quietly fascinated by the talk, the calculated belligerence which Gomez, the teacher, and Santos, the newspaperman, displayed.

"Well, let me tell you," Santos said in his high-pitched asthmatic voice. "The Filipino mind is a senile mind. It has been warped by fifty years of American mendacity. Not your mendacity, perhaps, but the mendacity of this rot, this democracy, freedom—all this myth when what it actually is, is naked American imperialism. That's the truth about the Filipino mind."

"I can only speak about myself," Robertson said, his face suddenly flushed, and the caviar-covered cracker which he was about to put into his mouth trembled slightly in his hand. "Mendacity is a strong word, an unfair word. I do not apologize for the meanness and the crookedness of some of my people, but, surely, to say that all Americans are mendacious or naked imperialists isn't borne out by historical fact, by records, by the Philippines itself."

And listening keenly to what Dr. Robertson said, Sebastian Cuerva thought: I'm not senile, I'm not senile in thought. God, I may be a lousy hypocrite, working for Soler. That's economics, nothing else. But I'm not senile. And listening now to Gomez, the teacher, speak about propaganda, how Americans hoodwinked Filipinos into thinking that freedom was already theirs, Sebastian Cuerva pitied Dr. Robertson.

It suddenly seemed unfair that he should be placed in the pillory. And what about Gomez and Santos? They wore their hatreds and their frustrations like decorations and he found himself loathing them, maybe because he himself was not as courageous as they. Courageous? He checked himself and pondered the word. And above the talk now of Santos about the meaning of nationalism, the usefulness of the past and the present, above the noisy rasp and the arid taste of the canapes, Cuerva remembered what Santos was. He had always written in his column about the rights of workers, about liberty. He had always brimmed with righteous indignation at the slightest infringement on civil liberties and yet when there was a linotypists' strike in his newspaper he was the first to approach the publisher and he had asked the publisher to fire the strikers. He, Sebastian Cuerva, knew this. The intellectual elite knew this. And now here was Santos, talking again about humanity, about the rights of the working class. And what about Gomez, the teacher, the champion of academic freedom, the bloated spokesman of the proletariat? Cuerva had listened to his lectures long ago and had believed in Gomez until he slowly found out that the teacher's greatest frustration was to be a creative writer. And now, after thirty years of teaching, he had not written anything of value. He had been a failure, too, as a man, for he was incapable of procreation and his wife had fooled around with some of the teachers in the University and with Gomez's own students.

Gomez spoke stolidly in that faultless classroom manner of his: "One of the problems of nationalism is how to divorce itself from the notion that this country cannot progress without American assistance and tutelage..."

And to this Tita Ramirez, ever ready with the cliches, added sharply, "Remember, we lived during the Japanese Occupation — and we did not import anything from America..."

Sebastian Cuerva studied Tita Ramirez now. He had always regarded her with some awe, maybe because of her hugeness. He had once been able to have a brief talk with her and she had held his hand, pressed it, the warmth and the insinuation of that warmth coursing through him. He would have appreciated the gesture, but he had to look at her closely, at the big flat nose, the overripe and sensuous lips and the hungry eyes, and he was sorry that Tita Ramirez did not look as beautiful as her writing. Once upon a time, Sebastian Cuerva recalled now with quick intensity, in those gay, halcyon months that followed the Liberation, he saw her lining up for ice cream at the old PX store in the corner of Azcarraga and Rizal. He was then working inside as a waiter and he had caught a glimpse of her, holding on to this blond lieutenant as if he were the last American on earth. And later, so he learned from the writers' grapevine, the romance had ended rather dismally. The lieutenant was not after culture and Tita Ramirez had aborted, was left in the lurch to hate that vile refrain, "Hanggang Pier."

"I think we are foolish," she said, shaking the ash from her cigarette, her left hand sliding to the hirsute arm of her Caucasian companion, "we are indeed foolish to prove ourselves with anything we do. The time has come for us to assert ourselves, to cut the umbilical cord that ties us to our Spanish and American past—to be ourselves."

"Ourselves?" Guilleng Santos, the newspaperman, asked with a mocking laugh, his thin lips arched in derision.

He is going to curse, Cuerva told himself, hoping to hear any moment now the famous Santos invectives. Ourselves? That was all he said and, unable to say more, he spluttered quietly.

"Unfortunately," Robertson said seriously, "the desire to be ourself is not limited to Filipinos. I, too, always try to be myself, to understand more the necessity of individual—if not national—differences."

"How thoughtful it is really of the American race to be imbued with such nobility of spirit," Gomez said.

Dr. Robertson stirred in his seat, cracked his knuckles. He always did that when he was excited. But when he spoke again, his voice was calm and it did not betray the nausea which was starting to rile him. "Well, gentlemen, I do admire your frankness. Isn't it too bad for the whole world, the Philippines in particular, that Americans, who are such lice, happen to have so much money, so much nobility? I am sure you can use our dollars and I'm sure you have been using some of it already." He rose, his six-foot frame towering over the crowd, and to his host he said gravely, "I think I have to fix myself a stiffer drink," and, with a knowing smile, he bowed to the group and headed for the bar at one end of the glazed swimming pool.

"We are senile people," Santos said lamely.

Up to this day, Sebastian Cuerva could not recall why at the mention of the word senile he spoke aloud for all to hear, "Well, Mr. Santos, thank you for your confession of senility, but I beg your pardon, I don't think I am senile like you."

Guilleng Santos, disbelief all over his pallid, ascetic face, turned to his tormentor. "Who is *he*?" he asked contemptuously.

"One of the Filipino people objecting to your label," Cuerva said. "Perhaps some people get real pleasure calling themselves inferior, perhaps some people want to prove their superiority with their crass manners."

"Do you mean us?" Gomez blustered.

"That's strange," Cuerva said, his blood singing, "I was thinking of this gathering, yes, this gathering." He gazed around— to Tita Ramirez, to the teachers, to the writers and to his own frowning boss, who had now returned with Robertson to join the group. And then, in one lucid moment of insight, he found out the reason these people were what they were. He wanted to bury the thought, but he could not, because he found himself saying aloud, interrupting Santos with—"Enough of this self-depreciation. We are not before the confessional of before commissars. We are among ourselves."

"Ourselves?" Guilleng Santos shot back. "Ourselves?"

And Cuerva found himself standing on his own, glaring back, barking, "I don't know to what dung heap Mr. Santos has relegated himself, but I still belong to the human race. I don't know why you should spread hate when you should spread love and pride in your country instead."

Tita Ramirez shrilled. "This is an insult. Have I ever said I hated my country?"

But Cuerva was undaunted. "Hate takes on many forms. The true believer hates the past and the present because he feels that only the future matters and he knows the way to this future. Sacrifice, sacrifice—this is the catchword. And yet, what have you to offer and what have you to sacrifice? What were most of you doing ten or fifteen years ago? What did you do during the Occupation? What kind of lives do you live now?" He trembled with rage. "You preach hate... you don't really care for the people. Within yourselves, you are selfish, afraid, lonely, defeated—and you take out your frustrations, your hatred in creeds and slogans..."

Soler caught the gravity of the situation then and, in that crisp, authoritarian voice of someone speaking to his menial, he motioned to Cuerva: "Enough of this now, Cuerva. I think you can help instead with the drinks. Do bring a tray of martinis over here..."

Back in his hotel, Robertson remembered clearly several other things that happened in the party: Sebastian Cuerva—his guide and Soler's lackey—going to the portable bar, lingering there, then returning with a tray of martinis and passing the tray around, his ashen face expressionless; in his puny, lonely presence, all talk had stopped. He remembered the tasteless dinner and Cuerva nowhere to be found. He remembered, too, how quickly Gomez, the teacher, had offered him a ride back to his hotel, since he was going that way, anyway, and somewhere, along the nameless streets, as they drove quietly, Gomez had become coy. But Robertson had dealt with so many people and Gomez, he found out with great relief, was no different, after all, from the host of characters he had met in other Asiatic countries which he had already visited. The only difference was that Gomez had more finesse. He said it jokingly, of course, but Robertson knew that the professor was very serious. How did he open up? America, said Gomez, was not spending dollars properly. There were people like himself who could use a trip to America, to finish their unwritten books. The more independent-minded a fellow was, the more he should be assisted and respected. Independence was the basis of mutual respect and if America wanted respect of the Filipinos, America should give them independence and assistance to follow their individual pursuits...

The proposition was too pat and Gomez was too glib. He had but a few minutes to make the pitch and he did not miss it. Yes, he had a manuscript on

Philippine political development but, as yet, it could not be published because it was not complete. He needed materials, the time to research in establishments like the Newberry Library or the Library of Congress. Would Dr. Robertson like to see the work before he left?

Yes, Robertson had said, I must see it. Bring it over first thing in the morning. I am leaving around ten.

And now, in the silence of his room, Roberston finally admitted that Gomez was a smart cookie indeed. He would not be surprised, too, if any moment now Gomez would burst in, his manuscript in hand. So, when the phone rang, Robertson was annoyed, particularly since he already knew what he would tell Gomez. He was not an American for nothing.

He was surprised, however, that it was not Gomez at the lobby downstairs but that clerk Sebastian Cuerva. Robertson felt that his privacy was being intruded upon again, but he could not dismiss Cuerva perfunctorily. "Do come up," he tried his best to be jovial. They will try everything to be noticed, even make speeches and bootleg visits, Robertson smiled grimly.

In a while his visitor was at the door. Robertson opened it and found Cuerva looking disconsolate and forlorn in the dimly lighted hall. The Filipino held a crumpled paper bag with smudges of oil. "Come in," Robertson said. "Would you like a drink or something?"

"No, thanks, Doctor," Cuerva said, still standing in the foyer.

"Come on, take something."

"I don't need anything, really," he said.

"Not even a Coke?"

"No Coke, please," Cuerva said.

Cuerva started feeling his way. The siopao was getting cold and his wife would not want it too cold. He must say it quickly. "I hope you enjoyed your stay here, Doctor," he tried to sound matter-of-fact although there was a tightness in his throat.

"I always enjoy Manila," Robertson said. Then, soberly, "That was quite a speech you made. You shouldn't be as blunt as that in polite company."

"I don't know. Maybe I drank a little too much, but I assure you my mind was very clear. And come to think of it now, it was not the liquor really." Cuerva smiled wanly. "I'm tired of it all." He was tired of himself, too, of his own weakness. Who was he to talk about righteousness and dignity when he had deserted the University for the salt mines of Soler— when he wrote not treatises but press releases extolling the virtue of the sugar industry and the contribution it was making to the country's economy? Economy, he concluded, was my personal economy—my wife and three children and the future that is bleak and, perhaps, will always be.

"I'm tired, too," Robertson said with feeling. The drinks which he had ordered came in and they sat down, the American with his nightcap and the young Filipino with his morbid thoughts.

"And besides," Sebastian Cuerva said nervously, "I felt I had nothing much to lose—except my job."

"I'm sorry," Robertson said. "I suppose Soler will do something for your spoiling his party."

"Mr. Soler can't stand being embarrassed," Cuerva sighed. "If I'll be an additional figure in the unemployment statistics tomorros I wouldn't worry too much. It's not difficult for one like me to get a job—my price isn't too high, for one. There's always some advertising agency that will take me—or some firm which needs a hack—or I can free-lance for a while to keep my family from starving. But I must not trouble you with my personal worries. Forgive me, I must not do this…"

Robertson suddenly felt compassion for this young man who had borne the malefactions of his generation on his conscience silently, until tonight. He must do something for Cuerva before leaving Manila. "Tell me, Robertson said eagerly, his blue notebook in his hand, "Have you ever done any scholarly work?"

"Of course, Doctor," Cuerva said matter-of-factly. "I've done some studies on our religious minorities for my master's degree and now I'm working on 'Islam in the Philippines'—a pastime of sorts, but it isn't important." And looking down on his battered shoes, Cuerva went back to what he had come to say. "I hope you will not consider your experience tonight as your sole criterion of Filipino nationalism. This so-called anti-Americanism among the intellectuals, it's not pervasive. The general mass of Filipinos—the provincianos—they don't share this sentiment. Almost everyone has a distant relative in the West Coast. Almost everyone has a pleasant memory of the Liberation. I had an uncle who was in the Philippine Scouts and to me—and in the village where I come from—he typified success and all that is benevolent and good. He died in Bataan, but I don't regret his death too much. He was sold on the idea, you know. I'm sold on it too, but I don't go around shouting about it..."

Robertson found the line familiar, but the way it was said, the sincerity of Cuerva, touched him. "I must thank you for your interest in my welfare," he said, glossing over the words with infinite care. "There's such a rash of anti-American sentiment in Asia today that it's a real pleasure to hear a Filipino speak kindly of Americans."

"The important thing," Cuerva said humbly, "is for you to remember that we want to run our own affairs and to build our country with our own sweat without some outsider claiming the credit. That is, of course, a difficult thing to do. I am tired myself of hearing the Philippines referred to as America's show window. We are our own show window..."

"Yes, yes," Robertson said benignly. "But have you ever been to the United States?"

"I haven't given it much thought," Cuerva said, "but I don't think my not having been there at all should deprive me of sanity in appraising America—and Americans..."

"Of course," Robertson said. He gulped his martini and leaned forward again. But Cuerva had stood up. "It's getting late," the young Filipino said. "I'm really glad that I've told you this. Don't misunderstand us, Dr. Robertson." He headed for the door.

"Wait," Robertson held him back. "I want to tell you something."

Cuerva paused before the half-open door.

"You really interested in research? You really are? About that study on religious minorities, that's a very good project. I'm sure of it. That's where I can assist you. I'm sure of that. Now, you said you have never been to America..."

Cuerva stepped back, shaking his head. His face burned. "I don't see the point at all, Dr. Robertson," he said.

Robertson grabbed his blue book. "I'm leaving tomorrow. We must finalize this." He started jotting down the name: *Sebastian Cuerva, religious minorities*. "We haven't got a lot of time. Let us settle this now. You must go to America," he pressed eagerly. "I can do that for you. Would you like to leave next month? Everything will be taken care of— your family, your schooling, your..."

Cuerva flung the door wide open and lurched out and on his face, before he turned away, Robertson saw affliction or was it bewilderment?

And above Cuerva's clear voice, above his simple, "I did not come here to ask for a fellowship," above the quiet tone of disillusionment, Robertson felt the whole roof crash down on him. And he who had always considered himself learned and wise in the ways of the world, he, Dr. John Robertson, Ph. D., Anthropology, wished he was not merely entrusted with the thousands of dollars that he distributed to these poor and struggling Asiatics. He wished he was instead endowed with a bigger, much bigger heart that would understand them.

Fortress in the Plaza

Linda Ty-Casper

That Friday morning there was a protest scheduled at Clark against the use of the American airbase in the Vietnam War, and Jess woke up as his father was trying to leave quietly. For the first time they talked—in the darkness and until the sun hung gaily at the window, like a curtain.

What Jess recalled of the long conversation that tried to make up for the long absences was his father saying, "I can't tell you what to do, Jess. I myself do not know a lot of things; but I am grateful you asked me." And what Jess wanted to say, but out of respect did not, was, "It's not a mortal sin to be wrong or to fail. Give me any advice."

Afterwards they had breakfast together, during which they spoke, not to each other but to Inay and his aunt Pura, who had come out of their rooms that early without being called. Jess felt they were sharing a feast as he listened to the three—such a tumble of recall and wish that almost made him feel he had no right to be present.

For the first time Jess sensed the love between his grandmother, his father, and his aunt, that relied not upon assertion but was of such intensity, like light at once calm and blinding, that it did not have to be declared. No rampage outside the three could destroy it, Jess thought. The next instant he wondered if he already shared it with them for they allowed him his silence. Carried away by the moment's intimacy, Jess thought that this love was what people achieved if they were lucky; that this was what bound the earth to the world beyond, this love which he longed for like a fugitive.

His father Miguel asked Inay and Pura to go with him when he returned to San Idlefonso, asked him, as well. Jess replied that he was going to Bulacan to help organize the fishermen but that he would proceed to San Idlefonso from there. They postponed taking their leave by making plans for the rest of the week. Miguel placed himself and his car at Inay's disposal, except for that Saturday when there was to be rally at Plaza Miranda.

"I want you to meet a special guest I'm bringing to the rally." Miguel led Jess to the backstairs that brought them to the lower floor. "I want you to meet Inay's brother. Yes, the one who went to America. Last week, I met, in Santa Cruz, someone I recognized from pictures but did not know. It was like meeting myself in the future. It was he. He will be glad to know you are coming with us Saturday. You will, won't you?"

Jess said he would and followed his father to the door which opened at their light knock, as if they had been expected.

"Come in. Is this Jess? I've seen him entering the house." Tadeo Illustre stood at the top of the three steps that raised his long dark room above the flood level of the estero at the back of the house. "This used to be the chapel, Jess. Our mother used to come down here and pray on nights she could not sleep. Come in. Take that chair."

The altar was still in place at the end of the room, but not the saints in their carved niches. Desks and chairs and wardrobes occupied the rest of the room with the malevolence of indestructible things that survived their owners.

"So! I've seen you once or twice, young man." Tadeo welcomed Jess a second time. "You look like your father, and he, like my father. The two of you are Ilustres."

"He resembles you, Tio." Miguel returned the compliment.

"Yes, the three of us are Ilustres," Tadeo answered, pleased. "Does Jess know I was the one who went to America?" He switched on the electric fan, directed the air toward Jess and his father, before sitting down. His trousers were neatly pressed, and he was wearing shoes.

Without knowing why, Jess thought that something about his grandfather appeared to have been wrenched.

"He knows, Tio," Miguel answered.

"That I was the one who embarrassed the family? But I was the youngest son. It was expected of me." Tadeo laughed. "However, I won't talk about myself, I heard that Jess..."

"When did you return, Tio?" Miguel asked, studying the old Philco cathedral radio beside his chair. "How long were you actually in America?"

"Let me see," Tadeo looked up at the ceiling which was twenty feet high. "I left before the Depression, years before it made poor men out of the rich and poorer the ones without. I spent two lifetimes there. In any case, I returned when it was too late to begin a third anywhere. I never picked up my life..."

"You're too modest, Uncle," Miguel protested. "You're still young enough to make waves. You're not seventy yet? I have more wrinkles than you."

"Seventy-two. A lot of things have failed to happen to me. Everything now depends upon you, and Jess. Would you like a beer? I have a few bottles of San Miguel in the old icebox."

"Later, Tio," Miguel refused gently. "Why don't you move upstairs? Room enough there. If you wish, take one of the beds in our room and give Jess company after I leave."

"No, I am settled here. Maxima wanted me to live upstairs too. When I returned, your mother had one of the rooms cleaned. I told her I did not want to listen to all the women talking because I would only be forced to take sides. How about a beer for you, Jess. Later too. It's not that I'm not grateful for the offer. My sisters spoiled me. You know that, Jess? They played mother to me. They wanted to marry me off to their best friends. One wanted me to become a priest; another, a lawyer; a third, an engineer; and the fourth, a surgeon." He counted them off on one hand. "I became none of those."

"What did you become?" Jess asked, claiming his grandfather because he saw something sad in the way the old one was giving an account of himself. Yet he sensed pride too; sensed the stubbornness that led to rebellion, that fed dreams.

"I was happy being myself. I didn't want to be anything. Anyway, I went to America and there hangs the story of my life. When I returned a few of my friends were still around. Unlike them I did not retire from a good position and a healthy pension—those marks of success—but Maxima gives me the rental from her property in Legarda. I can't refuse. She says she has no need for the income while I do."

"Why did you go to America?" Jess asked. Professor Ivy Millan kept after her proteges to go to America and write. "It's the only way not to become a cannibal," she told them, choosing words she meant to cut deep.

"Why?" Tadeo opened a pack of cigarettes and offered it before taking one. "I suppose I was running away. As simple as that. America is the farthest place I knew. Now, we have the moon." He laughed, turning the cigarette between his fingers before lighting it. It was Blue Seal.

The way Tadeo talked and dressed gave Jess the impression he knew nothing but the best—of some things.

"Tio Tadeo is a Hemingway hero," Miguel said. "When we were young and we cried, we were told that if we were not brave, when Tio Tadeo returned from America, he would be ashamed of us." He spoke affectionately. Running from death was farthest from Miguel's mind at that moment. What he wanted was Jess to know the strength in the men of their family; the strength that came to them in their moments of weakness and prevented them, at any rate, from falling all the way down. That was more important to inherit than money. He wanted to remind himself, too, of that strength. It survived deaths in the family, the way a country survived the deaths of its best sons. It was what was passed on. Some called it integrity. He hoped that Jess would recognize this for himself so he would not fall slave to anyone, even to his lesser self.

They lit their cigarettes from Jess' lighter.

"Last thing I remembered before leaving was Maxima leading me across the Colgante, to the church so we could pray for my salvation. She had been summoned to my school. I forgot what I had done. Our mother was too embarrassed to come herself..."

"An Uncle of yours overseas sent for you, didn't he?" Miguel spoke earnestly, culling facts from memory for Jess' sake. "You went to school in the States?"

"Not quite. I saw an ad for a pianist aboard one of the Matson Lines ships. I applied. I told my sisters I was going to a friend's hacienda for the grand vacation in the summer. I guess I've never admitted this to anyone before."

"Just like that, you left?" Jess asked, admiring his grandfather even more; almost envying the still handsome face, the cunning that probed them even as he was telling secrets.

Miguel smiled at Jess' surprise. Why not? If it had occured to him, he would have done the same. All a person needed was to be young in order to dare the world and not think of failure. But his next thought brought up his wife Arsenia calling to say, "It should have occured to us. The jeep had merely skidded. No one had shot at the tires. No bullet was found nearby. The wounds, the death...natural." But he did not believe that someone was not waiting for him to return to San Ildefonso so he could be the next mayor assassinated in the province. Arsenis was too ready to believe otherwise. It took him the assurance that he was a survivor, like Tadeo. "Those were the good old days, Tio when one could take hold of one's life."

"Yes, in those days, I thought after I acted; I did not wait for the Lord to speak." To himself, Tadeo admitted: I came to regret it immediately. Looking at the cigarette in his hand, he dropped his voice, "Society was stricter then." When he applied for the job as a pianist, he did not realize he was not going to be a passenger but an employee, the same as the Chinese crew and the Pinoy waiters who had learned to accept the rules. Discrimination. Parlor games were not for him. It was hard. He was used to mixing with the best people and, aboard the ship, he acted the part. He returned the tips for playing tunes requested by passengers. Yet though some passengers treated him as one of themselves, he felt he had been banished from his life by being treated as if he belonged in the steerage.

Somehow, Miguel heard Tadeo's thoughts, saw these in the way his eyes evaded them, in the fierceness with which he squashed his long cigarette in the ashtray. It was part of the ambiguity of life: people were more than themselves; and less.

"What do you mean?" Jess asked.

"There was a lot of sickness in the steerage." Tadeo stared at the ash lengthening on the cigarette he had just lighted. "Some of the Filipinos, of the class trying to escape poverty, tried to get some air by sitting on the steel ladder leading to the deck. Some passengers saw them, were offended and complained; so the hole had to be sealed. Food was slipped under the cover. Many died before Honolulu. The doctor came down only to separate the dead from the dying. . . " The ash started to shrivel. One of the survivors recognized him years later in Anchorage. They were both working in the salmon cannery then. The boom had gone out of his life.

Jess tried to hide the pity welling inside him. Pity never fed another's hungers. What difference had he been to the sacadas whose idea of a feast was to have dried sapsap with their rice? If he had lived with them, not to know how it was to be a sacada but to give the sugarcane workers a sign that God was alive in the world; not to liberate them from poverty but to remind them that Christ became a man and also suffered and that if He were still in the world, He would choose to live with them, he might not have despaired and left. They could not leave as he could. What good did it do to remind people of God so they could be drawn to Him, so they could love back God who already loved them when that God also presided over the inequalities of the world? How clear his mind was, Jess thought, that it could think that a Christian was one in whom God is encountered. It was love, not sacrifice that God wanted. Not holocausts from man. But that was enough, the whole of the Good News message?

It was sweaty in the room. Miguel went to the window but could not lift the sash. He stood there a moment, trying to look through the dusty panes. He had taken Jess down to Tadeo to give his son the idea of the unlimited possibilities life offered, if one knew how to seize them; and because he saw no darkness in Tadeo's heart that matched that in his own. "I will have to go. A caucus..." he lied. "Uncle, let's have another beer-and-crispy-pata session near the Monte de Piedad Bank. Before I leave, let's have Jess along, too. Jess?"

"Go ahead, Father. I'll stay awhile." There was that demonstration in front of the U.S. embassy but he would stay awhile because he felt closer to God thean he was to himself. Saint Augustine described as *Deus intimior intimo suo...*

At the door Miguel brightened up. "I remember Inay used to say that you could have been a brain surgeon, Uncle, because of your long slender fingers. Well, I'll go ahead."

Tadeo slipped his hands down, let them hang at his sides. They were warped, splayed at the tips by farm work. He wanted to explain that in those days in America, to be a Filipino on the West Coast was to be a Negro in the South. When police stopped them, his friends admitted to being South Americans, not Filipinos. He challenged their pride. After a few beatings, he also denied himself; he began hiding, sleeping during the day and gambling at night. Maxima sent him money through a cousin who worked in a bank. The monthly allowance kept him big in the eyes of others who did not have the same resources, so he did not realize, until it was too late, how low he had fallen.

"What kept you in America?" Jess asked after his father hsd left.

"It did not occur to me to go home," Tadeo answered, looking slwly about the long room like a hand feeling its way in the dark. "No. The truth was I couldn't. I was sick most of the time. I was forever trying to get better so I could go home. I didn't want to say any of this while your father was here. He's too old to go to America now. Let it be part of his good dreams. But you're young. You'll think of going, I'm sure. Perhaps it's much better than before, because of the Japanese War when we, the outcasts, volunteered to fight. But why should you believe these things from me?"

"I believe."

"For awhile there, I was numero uno with that bank mittance. Soon enough this changed. I've been trying to determine exactly when this changed. For the worse...."

They both looked at the empty altar.

"Some Filipinos, migrant workers, were found murdered. It looked like vigilante work and it occured to a few of us that it was something to avenge, so we all got in my car." Tadeo snapped the knuckles of both hands, as helpless in that gesture as in his inability to say exactly what his heart felt.

Jess became impatient to know, "And...?"

"To make a long story short, we were stopped on the highway by two police cars. They made us raise our hands while they rifled through our pockets, called us monkeys and told us to go back where we came from. They were large men with coarse voices. I could have done it all by myself, avenge the dead, had not the Pastor. . .he was the law student who was shot in one of our strikes, years later. . .Pastor hit back. At first with words, then with fists. At that the policemen fell upon him, hitting him with the butt of their pistols, kicking. Pastor could never stand erect after that When he fell unconscious, the policemen turned to Matias, no to Mateo, who was studying to be a surgeon, because he made a move to Pastor. When the policemen began working on Mateo, I suddenly ran. They were smashing his fingers with their heels when I ran, not to hide, but to draw the policemen after me so the others could get into my car and escape. That was on my mind. The police began firing at me. I got hit. Once in the chin. I passed out. The bone was shattered." Tadeo's hand went towards his face. "The bullet is still inside."

Instinctively, Jess looked away. He had wondered why his grandfather's face looked slightly off center. It was a handsome face, made interesting by that flaw to which one's eyes were immediately attracted, tempting one to pass him off as ugly until one saw the rest of his features, the smile that made his face gentle. Imagining hurt men, the smashed flesh of the demonstrators, the faces hit by truncheons at Rizal Park, Jess thought of the old woman calling out to them at Plaza Moriones: *Pagbutihin ninyo, mga anak!*

"... when I regained consciousness I was in a rundown chapel, just a roof on four uneven posts, the way you'd find chapels in the *poblaciones* during fiestas Even worse, for this was destroyed, was not damaged slowly by the elements.

Hate had demolished it. The Filipino chapel it was called. I suppose because it was ransacked every time Filipinos hid inside. It was open season on Filipinos all year round. Two brothers brought me there; took me along until I healed; while they harvested hops and lettuce around San Francisco, sugar beets and asparagus in Los Angeles, flowers in Lompoc, apples in Yakima. I wonder if the people whose tables those produce reached ever tasted our bitterness. But I got to see the country that way."

"What kept you there? Why didn't you leave?"

"Loyalty. I couldn't abandon those two after what they had done for me. They spent on me the money the money they had been saving to send their father, so the old man could buy back the land he had lost through *pacto de retro* sale. And sometimes, it was beautiful. Simple and beautiful to work to work, get tired, sleep and work again. The life of men who had lost all trace of God yeilds a moment of peace now and then, of simple wonder that one can see the earth grow, the sky become alive with stars. Sentiments certainly. Sentiments. But it's true. The sleep of tired men is something to envy, until he gets too tired to wake up and get to work in the morning. Until he begins to fall behind, to fall out. . .I began to have fevers. Right on top of what we were harvesting I'd fall asleep, eat my supper when I woke up the next morning. The seasons became one..."

"Are they still there?"

Tadeo shook his head. Then because he did not explain what happned, he added, "They're dead." Even that did not say anything though it said much. "The older brother, of a fractured skull received during a strike. Eman. The younger, of a social disease—that's how fine families called it, describing the result of lapses—acquired from dance halls. He could have been a fine horn player, the likes of Louis Armstrong. He strengthened his lips by blowing into a wall. Such powerful lungs. But such painful music. Pruning grapes, he and I talked about the band we would put together when he and I saved enough. When he had sent his father the price of the farm. Is that not funny, men thinking they could not start living until they had settled their accounts, fulfilled obligations? So we never did. There was always someone who needed what we managed to save. To get out of paying our wages, some growers sicked the police on us just before payday. On one such occasion, running, the younger brother got whacked across the face. His front teeth dropped like seeds from his mouth. He died too. America took more than she gave. Her West Coast was our graveyard."

"But you came back," Jess said, pronouncing victory for his grandfather.

"I came back. After years of being shot at in the fields, shoved off the streets, chased from public parks, barred from unions, beaten by gangs employed by Chinese and Japanese gambling lords, contracted away to canneries by Filipinos with diamond rings and thick money belts! All kinds of men fed on our bodies. There were lobbies against us in Washington. Relief agencies would have none of us. Not that our pride would not have kept us off their rolls. We had no rights we could relenquish, out of anger. I lived at the edge of the Mexican and Jewish districts. Dancehalls, bars, poolrooms and ransacked lives. I was no angel, Jess. People tend to think all victims are good. Pushed to the limit, I stole. We stole, fought each other, lived off those who still had jobs, hid in rooms so small you had to keep your arms at your sides when you yawned. And even *pensionados*, who came to America to study in her institutions of higher learning, were humbled in the streets. California was a urinal. You had any color on your skin, you were for the dogs. Urinal. Except for the trees. Apricot trees in flower, bees as wild and fierce as flies over a stripped carcass. I always think of those trees when I see the flametrees in Luneta. Then, I always thought of the flametrees when I saw the apricots and apples, the cherries. . . They should be called resurrection trees. Do you want your beer now?"

"Next time, Lolo," Jess said, getting up. It was too painful to hear anymore, like being accompanied by nightmares.

"Be careful, Jess. I heard that armed men are being hired. Those men will not be afraid to take lives anymore than the police were in the old days in California. Only here, we're doing it to each other."

"You did not have to tell me what you have not told the others, but I'm grateful." Jess wondered if, having shared his life with him, Tadeo would let his hand be kissed out of respect, but he did not ask or try.

"I couldn't say any of that when I returned home because I lied to the family. I lied again and again because they would not have believed I had not bought a house in California. That I had not raised at least one blond, blue-eyed child. 'Where are the pictures?' people asked me. When I returned after the war, '50's it was, before surprising the family, I had stopped to deliver a package. I think it was money. It just happened that the house was raided. Think of luck. Some Huks were caught. There was a store on the groundfloor. The government thought everyone in the house was a Communist. It was found out that I had worked with the Communist party in California, but it was the only way to be able to organize the unions. It was a matter of ideology. But I spent some years in Muntinlupa. The year I got out is the year I said I returned."

"No one will find out from me."

"Don't feel too bad about me, Jess. I achieved something in America. I had not taken advatnage of anyone. I did nothing for personal gain; nor out of fear, desert my friends." On his bad days, he ascribed those virtues to a stone. "Sometimes just staying alive is a miracle. Just wanting to stay alive, sometimes requires more courage than anyone has a right to have. Once, I had that miracle and that courage."

Jess walked to the door, tears filling his eyes. "Maybe, one of these days, you will go out with me." He looked down at the floor, at the hand he did not trust himself to offer for a handshake. He felt older than he was, as if his grandfather's years had been added to his.

Something's Got to Give

Bataan Faigao

After a day working on Marilyn's lips, after a couple of rounds of San Miguel, Manong ordered Chinese food to go. He ran into Beverly, tall, gaunt, her tough face white and pale. White, he thought, like freshly laundered linen. In the dark of Broadway, underneath the artificial sky of neon marquees and bright flashing lights, she looked like a wraith.

"Manong," she wrapped her frayed tweeds tightly around her, throwing her long, almost white hair back. "How did your day go?"

"O.K.," Manong replied. "It's comin' along."

She looked toward the billboard. "It's coming along? She looks simply divine. I watch you work from down here. I'd say she's mighty fine. The eyes though, you gotta do something about the eyes."

"What about the eyes?" Manong asked.

"Don't have that sleepy look, y' know." She mimicked Marilyn's eyes.

"Are y' comin' home soon? I bought some dinner.""Yeah, I'll be home soon. Soon's I get some business done. Won't be too long. Can you spot me some cash?"

Manong hesitated. "Aw, yer jes gonna pop it!"

Manong reached into his pocket, peeled off a twenty and handed it to her. "I gotta be crazy."

"Thanks, you're a darling, as ever. See you in a bit. I'll be with Miranda." She ran back to the Blarney.

Manong lived in a cavernous apartment on West 49th. Three rooms, two baths, sparsely furnished, dimly lit. There was hardly anything on the walls. He was not one to hang pretty pictures on the walls, except for a poster-sized repro of the M specs, which looked like a mosaic. After he ate his supper, he sat in the dimly lit living room, chomping on his cheroot for the evening.

Beverly came home with Miranda. They plopped themselves down on the couch. Beverly threw a packet of tin foil on the table and took off her jacket.

"Hello, Mira," Manong said.

"You want a hit, Manong?" Mira asked.

"Nah...Had a long day. And another one comin' up! Y' girls jes go ahead n' kill yrselves without me."

"We'll be okay, Manong. You go get yourself some sleep." Beverly kissed Manong and said, "Good night. I love you, Manong. I'll see you tomorrow."

Just before he fell asleep, Manong heard Beverly play her guitar—soft, woeful melodies that made him want to cry.

Dawn on Broadway. The street became alive again. The blue of the new day lit up the raggedy patch of sky. Manong crossed the street toward Duffy Square, a small triangular park enclosed in an iron grill, benches, a brush of greenery, pigeons and crumbs on the pavement, the usual bunch of men, some women, bundled up in their coats, smoking cigarettes, drinking coffee, standing still, trying to look as inconspicuous as they could. A small, hunchbacked person with a red woolen hat, dark glasses, who waved at him, jumped up and down, and flailed his arms. Felix, he said to himself. A man, who had been walking close to him, strutted past and set himself on a park bench. Everyone converged on the man. For a brief moment, they appeared huddled together, and all of a sudden they broke up, they stashed their packets of tin foil into their pockets, each going their separate ways in all directions. It happened very quickly, like the flutter of pigeons in flight as he walked. Manong, astonished, crossed the street and went to work.

As he finished up the panels of Marilyn's lips and open mouth, Manong remembered the dream he had. He was strolling the dirtways of the swath of Tondo slums in the Manila of his dreams. This beautiful woman walked past him. She said, "Wow, those black panthers and pink prostitutes got to my head," referring to a couple of cocktails she had at the Trade Winds, a nightclub by the bay. Shortly thereafter, Manong was making out with this woman in the back of a red top-down convertible. The woman turned out to be the great Marilyn Monroe herself. She was moaning beside him as he kissed her on the lips. He cupped his hands on her enormous breasts. His hands reached down to the soft hair between her legs. He felt her lips soft and wet. She cooed with immense pleasure. Manong found that she had worked her panties off and he had cum, gobs of it, white creamy gelatinous cum, all over his hands. There was a sink nearby where he washed it off.

The dream disturbed him. He did not know what to make of it. He felt strange about feeling guilty for desecrating the white goddess, especially in a dream. He remembered when he was a child, he used to hear stories told by the housemaids, of white fairies with golden hair who roamed the dark nights in the forests, abducting little children, especially little boys. These fairies would take their captive children to the overseer, a white goddess who ruled the forest night. The housemaids told these stories to scare the children into behaving themselves. Instead, he was fascinated by these fairies with white skin, white as milk, and the golden aura about them as they wandered the dark forests. Many times during the full moon, he would steal into the night and wander to the edge of the forest where there was a dry river bed, among the tall bamboo groves, hoping to encounter one of these supernal beings. But there was nothing, just the languid creak of tall bamboo spires. Occasionally, he would get frightened by dark hulking shapes among the shadows which turned out to be nothing but a water buffalo.

Remembering these, he felt sad. Feeling sad, he thought of Beverly. He could not erase the image of her curled up, helpless, frail and faraway, in some unspeakable ecstasy, her arms riddled with needle marks, dark and tender. She had to find a vein in her foot, she and Miranda, because their arms, with the shredded skin, could not possibly take another. How much longer could she last? At least he took her off the streets. Beyond that, he felt powerless.

Instead of his usual Blarney draft, Manong sipped a fine cognac and sniffed it in its snifter. He brooded over Beverly. He felt this tragic vein in her, from the very first time he met her. He had just finished having dinner at the Mabuhay restaurant on 45th Street off Broadway. The Mabuhay, where his friend Isidro worked, was owned and operated by Manny Casales. Manny used to be Frank Sinatra's personal valet. That's what it said there on the bill in front of his restaurant. Even got a picture of Manny serving Ol' Blue Eyes a ham sandwich. Manong was just finishing up his leche flan when this woman came running down the lobby restaurant. She was terrified, screaming for help, her clothes torn, her long blond hair disheveled. She was barefoot. She tripped and fell on an empty table with a terrible crash. A large burly man with a crew cut, dressed in a green Hawaiian shirt with yellow bananas, was close on her heels, yelling, "You bitch! You can't run away from me!" The man grabbed the woman with these huge pair of hands, his hairy arms bulging with muscle. The man dragged her out while she held on to one of the bamboo rafters.

Manong got up from the table. "What do you think yer doin'?" he yelled. "Leave the woman alone."

"Stay outta this." "I'm goin' to call the police."

"I said stay outta this, goddamned gook."

Manny and Isidro came rushing out of the kitchen. Ceding, Manny's wife, was screaming.

"Get the fuck outta my place or I'll call the cops," Ceding yelled. "Leave that woman alone and get outta here!"

"Fuck you n' mind yer own business. This is between her and me. You come with me, bitch!" Isidro joined in the fray and said, "Let go of her or I'll carve you up." Isidro, his white apron stained with the day's butchering and cooking, waved his meat cleaver wildly. The man barely flinched. Soon Manny came out of the kitchen, brandishing a kitchen knife. The woman yanked herself out of the man's grip and Isidro took a whack at the man's hands. The man pulled them away, while Manny whacked at him in his turn. The man backed and fled, screaming, "I'll be back motherfuckers! You can't fuck with me. I'll be back!"

"Who the hell's that guy, y' think?" Manny looked at Isidro.

"I don't know, U.S. Marines. Did you see his tattoo?" Beverly was badly beaten and bruised. Her eyes were black and her mouth bloody. Ceding cleaned her up as well as she could and Manong took her to his apartment on 49th Street to put her to bed.

On the day he painted the panel with the mole on her left cheek, took about four panels, Manong had a dizzy spell. He almost fell off the scaffolding down to the street, about 150 feet below. A whole bucket of black paint ran down Marilyn's cheek. He sat for a while against the cables, his heart thumped faintly. He thought maybe he should give up the cheroots and cigarillos. Go see the doctor right away. For a moment he though he was going to die, and that was okay with him. He thought maybe he was getting too old for this kind of work. Someone else could finish the mole on Marilyn's cheek, clean up the mess. His life was complete. It wasn't an easy life, definitely. But he wasn't called to any wars, world wars especially. He didn't own a house in New Jersey and have to slave away at a desk job from 9-5. He wasn't deprived due to poverty, debilitated by some terminal illness. He wasn't about to die feeble and soft-brained in front of the TV watching Beverly Hillbillies. He didn't end up in Attica or the I-Hotel in San Francisco. And he's had his fair share of brawlin', drinkin', and shootin' shit. He was satisfied, here, on Broadway, a refugee from Tondo, a nowhere place, dies on the left cheek of the goddess.

He looked down. People were walking briskly up and down the silent streets. The traffic snaked through the canyons of the Big White Way. He thought about Beverly, the only love he had ever known was dying, and there was not a thing he could do about it. He was sorry he never told her he loved her. There were times when he found a moment to confess his love, but each time he reeled back, thinking his love would diminish. So, he kept it to himself, smoldering beneath the veneer of his caring, his kindness and compassion for her. He thought that maybe he should, before it was too late. He took a cigarillo from his pocket and puffed on it.

He never dreamed that he would end up here, above the Great White Way. Not bad for a kid from the slums of Tondo. He came to the United States in the early 1930's as a migrant farmer, worked the pineapple plantations in Hawaii. There he learned the art of Kali. In the Philippines, this martial art became known as Arnis. He was lucky to run into guru Lucky Lucay-lucay, an old man from the Philippines who had come to the Hawaiian islands at the turn of the century. After several years working the pineapple fields and training with Lucky, he impregnated a white girl, a *hapa haule*, and had to leave.

He left for San Francisco, bummed around there for a while, worked as a dockhand. Then he had to leave again after getting into a nasty fight outside a bar in the Mission district. Bouncers kicked him out and pointed to the sign in front of the establishment that said: No Dogs or Filipinos Allowed.

He fled south, down to Burbank where he found refuge among migrant farmhands who worked the potato fields.

After a few years, when Manong thought the heat was off, he headed east and ended up in New York City where he lived for the next ten years, worked as an itinerant sign painter until he landed a job with Allied Advertising painting custom-made billboards. Always had a steady hand. The practice of Arnis helped with that. He'd done Lucky Strikes (the one with the smoke blowing out of a lady's mouth), Chesterfields, Florida Vacationlands, Coca Cola. He had come a long way and he had no regrets.

"It's no big deal," he said to Isidro.

"Hit me two," he continued, his hands held close to his chest.

"Three for me," Sam scratched the table with his cards.

"Three for the budding playwright. Possible flush."

"I'm okay," John said.

"Nothing for the Jewish Mafia. From the looks of his grin, he's got somethin' good. Where's Joani and Mark?"

"They're out in the Bahamas doin' business."

They quaffed from their mugs of San Miguel and chewed on their cheroots. "Hey, man, these cheroots are damned good," Sam coughed, "A little strong."

"It's like paint by the numbers," Manong explained, "I call ten. In this case, it's paint by the panels, square foot panels. I'm no Michelangelo. The tricky part is working the scaffolding. It's a good job, if you don't mind the heights."

"Yeah, like the Indians, man. They love to be banging out there in the sky," John said. "Like Jack, the riveter. Here's the ten. I raise you twenty."

"I jes got to make sure I'm present alla time, right there from moment to moment, doin' these panels one at a time."

"You're lucky, man. Damn lucky. Wish I had something like that," Sam said. "Then I can keep writing without having to starve. I fold."

"What are you working on these days, Sam?" John asked.

"Oh, nothing to get excited about. Jacking off, mostly. These days I'm totally uninspired. I'm trying to write this cowboy play."

"I couldn't believe it when my boss called me in one morning to give me the gig. I couldn't believe it! Paint the face of Marilyn Monroe on a giant billboard on Broadway. For him it's jes another job, like a Camel job. Calls her a dame, says, 'Manuel, we gotta do this dame here, some blondie, for her next picture." There she was on the spec sheet, golden hair and all, her dreamy eyes half-closed, and those big red lips. Took those specs home and tacked it on the wall'n I'd geta hardon jes looking at it. Beverly thinks I'm nuts. Let's see what that silly grin's all 'bout, man. Lay it down."

"How's she doin'?" Isidro slapped his cards on the table. "Sheet!"

"She's coming along, as y' can see. I got the picture all in my head. Oh y' mean

Beverly? Well, she's doin' okay. Well, y' know, she's shootin' junk. I dunno what to do wd it. A full house. Fuck, man."

John chuckled as he raked his winnings in.

Day by day he watched the face grow bigger and brighter. He was pleased with the way things were working out. From the corner table at the Blarney Stone, he would say to himself, to his friends, or to Charlie the bartender, "Hey Charlie, ain't she beautiful? An absolute doll," spitting a flake of tobacco from his cheroot. Jack, the Indian, came by and asked him if he wanted to score some really good dope. "What dya got?" Manong asked while Charlie brought a round of drinks for everybody and they raised their glasses to the great M.

The day he finished the painting, a bunch of his friends were gathering at Blarney's for a celebration. On the way he ran into Blind Man Johnson, parked on the corner of Broadway and 46th. Blind Man Johnson played a song on his blues guitar that Manong had never heard before.

Got me a woman, yeah
    got me the blues
Got me a white woman,
    got me the blues, yeah
Got me the white woman
    blues....

Several nights ago he had a fight with Isidro, after he worked on the eyes. They were both drunk and Isidro said, "It's no big deal to fuck a whore, especially if you're paying her rent." He decked him right off, in the chops. He dropped a twenty in the blind man's guitar case. "Go, Johnson," he said.

Reggie McCutcheon came, the Zulu-tall black man with the bald head, worked at the corner store on the block where he used to live on 109th, dealt nickels and dimes in the Little Korea area. "Sleepy told me about your gig man, just had to come by say hello."

Felix, the deaf mute, black Puerto Rican who lived in Central Park, grunted, snorted, gyrated, and pointed to the billboard and Manong knew exactly what he was talking about. Furthermore, he was saying, "Wish Roger could be here, man. Been on the lookout for him. Heard he's on the run though. He's probably out in the Bahamas tryin' to stay off the heat."

"Hey, Manong," John slapped him on the back. "I'd like to buy that shit. How much do you think it'll cost to buy that after they have to take it down?"

"I don't know man. I don't think it's for sale."

"What are they gonna do with it after the movie's over?"

"They'll paint over it, put another one on it. A Camel ad." Manong laughed.

"I'd like to buy it, hang it in my loft. It's a little bigger than my loft, but we can crop it. Take out the text."

"No man, it's there today, gone tomorrow. That's Art." Jack the Indian said.

"Who do I talk to, to get it down?"

"You can talk to my boss. But, no way, man."

"It'll fit perfect," John said.

There were all the Blarney regulars: junkies, bookies, whores, small time racketeers, hustlers.

Manny, Ceding and Isidro came too. Beverly was supposed to come, but had not arrived.

A big man with a crew cut, wearing a brown leather jacket with a fur collar, walked into Blarney's as it was about to close. The man cased the joint. His eye caught Manong. Then Manny and Isidro.

He walked straight toward Manong and with a fierce look in his eyes, demanded, "Where's Beverly?"

"What dya want with Beverly?" Manong asked.

"None of your fuckin' business."

"She's gone back to Detroit.""Listen, you don't fuck with me, you hear? I'm gonna turn you into chop suey."

"O.K. man, not here. This here's a respectable joint. Howd Charlie feel if you wrecked his place, man? He spent his whole life on this. It wouldn't be nice to ruin it."

The marine shoved Manong toward the exit in the back. Everybody scrambled. The man threw a jab at Manong which hit him square in the jaw and sent him through to the dark storage room. Manong sprang to his feet and took another blow to the chest. That one sent him reeling into the alley. The punch nearly knocked his breath out. He staggered back and recovered his balance. The marine pulled out a .45. In an instant Manong held the man's gun with his left and jerked the marine's hand with his right, one sudden instinctive movement he'd done may times before with a yantok, the wood he used for his practice with disarms. The gun went off to his side. The marine jabbed again. Manong dodged. He swept the marine off his feet and kicked the man, who was face down on the pavement, with a downward stomp on his lower back. He heard a tok sound, like the sound of the yantok hitting each other, just like Lucky said it would, and the man yelped like a dog.

Manong ran out of the alley into the neon-bright street. He heard the sirens from a distance, then closer in a crescendo that converged on the Blarney. The lights of Broadway blinded him momentarily. He saw the face of Marilyn all lit up. The lights of Broadway whirled and flashed around him. He ran up to his apartment on 49th Street and stepped into the dark of his home. It was quiet.

"Beverly," he called. He knocked on the bedroom door. As he was about to enter, Miranda, who was sitting and sobbing quietly on the couch in the dark, rushed up to him, held him in her arms, buried her head in his chest, and cried. "Manong, don't go in there."

Manong held her close, rocked her back and forth. "It's okay," he said. He felt life had been snuffed out, and he wanted to see.

The bed was empty. He noticed he had stopped breathing. The radiator hissed. The faint light of dawn washed into the window. The blinds were half-drawn, yellowed and stained with old rains. There was a smell of incense, strong and pungent. The closet door was ajar. Clothes hanging on the knob. The drawers of the chest were half-open, clothes sticking out. On top of the chest a votive candle burned steadily. He usually bought one for her from the Puerto Rican store. She always burned one through the night. A Coca Cola can, crushed. An oval-shaped picture frame with a sepia-toned photograph of her as a baby and her mother, both smiling. On the bedside table the lamp was dimly lit. An ashtray overflowed with crushed butts, a spoon, a lighter, matchbooks, cotton swabs, a couple of syringes wrapped in tissue, industrial blades. A dollar bill rolled up. A small face mirror. Strings of floss, mint-green. Wrigley's gum wrappers. Packs of

Lucky Strikes and Salems, crumpled. His heart started to beat heavily. Tacked on the wall was a child's drawing of a clown face done in crayons. Her daughter, she said. Her beat up guitar, patched with duct tape, was propped in the corner. The potted plant he bought for her when she moved in six months ago looked like it needed watering. He thought about giving it some water. The bathroom door was open. The light was on. He hesitated. It was getting brighter. Daylight was breaking.

Fugitive Colors

Ninotchka Rosca

You are hand-in-hand with the November sun on a quiet street in Manhattan when the voice strikes between your shoulder blades. "Move along now. Move along. I don't see you moving." The policeman, bundled and capped in matte blue, nightstick at his waist, arms akimbo, straddles the sidewalk. Eyes and voice, however, aren't aimed at you but at another boy, five paces behind you, younger, perhaps ten or eleven years old, in a jacket the color of a bullfighter's cape. He is black, Afro-American, his head a curt curl. Instantly, you wonder what he's done, what he's been caught doing. But he seems simply to have been taking a walk, much like you, and has wandered without premeditation into this street of brownstone houses with precise gray stoops. You feel you should say something but you're yourself only a few years older; to remonstrate with an adult is too big a responsibility. You must be careful to merge appeal and sub-servience, nudging the policeman towards the same shame and embarrassment assailing you. "He's just a kid," you say in a mumble. The eyes and voice shift. You know nothing; mind your own business; this is New York, not some paddy field and you mind your own business. Your knees buckle at this out-gush of malice. You shy away, outraged but frightened, because while you may be older than the boy and not as dark, you're still this shade of tan; your hair and eyes are black and your nose fails its valiant attempt to come to a point. The boy follows your quickening steps, the pulse of his. hurt a small wind at your back. You feel his need to have the pain eased but you balk and he turns left at the next inter-section, giving you up, giving up on you. You think: *they* are treated so badly, so very, very badly. For a second, you are the boy, the common judgment of your skin's unworthiness an incessant drip, drip upon your skull.

Jejomar Reyes' moment of knowledge on a Saturday afternoon in New York City shrivels his heart with regret. This autumn has barely turned into the sea-son for his liking where he lives, after 36 months of numbing homesickness. But what can he do, what could he have done, except to walk away, hurriedly, to van-ish beneath the desultory trees. He is sixteen now, old enough to sense the link between the nude branches overhead, clawing at the sky, and the earth's inexorable passage through the vastness of space. The thought grows huge as a cathedral. He leaps, legs scissoring through air, drops to the mica-spattered cement and hunches his shoulders forward, spine slouching, groin aggressive. He slides heel-and-toe, imaginary drums beating a staccato, in rhythm with the accidental chant rising from his spine to his eyes, spilling outward in a laser glare: *Pinoy-Kano, Pinoy-Kano...* He snaps his fingers, searching for a better coupling of sounds to define what he is, for a fiercer name, a unique handle. Instead, strange words leap into his mind: reticulate, ventilate, oscillate—remnants of the previous night's self-study, on top of his homework, because Jejomar is determined to improve his English, to pile words upon words, and thereafter never be at a loss when it came to arguments. He is slowly but surely memorizing his Webster. Reticulate, ventilate, oscillate... The rhyme brings him to a fruit-and-vegetable store, to the *greengrocer*, yeah, where Mr. Kim stands guard, whisk broom in hand. Jejomar gives the man his most engaging smile but Mr. Kim shakes his head. No work today, no work today; Wednesday, come back Wednesday... which is logical, Jejomar knows, because produce gets delivered on that day, boxes and crates and cartons of tomatoes, lettuce, grapes, apples—all needing that extra pair of hands that he, the upcoming one and only Filipino-American rapper of New York City, can offer. Flashes of green, red and purple tempt him but he shakes his head with regret.

He can't work Wednesday, of course. He has to be in school, where his parents expect him to be. They would not look kindly on his doing odd jobs during school days. How often have father and mother made it clear there would be no breaking of tradition where school was concerned? Students study. Except for light chores around the house, that's all they do back home. Parents work to keep their children in school. Parents should and will do just about anything for their children's education: mortgage the house, sell the family jewels, work two jobs and take on a third during the year's vacation, borrow money left, right and center, up and down, eat a mouthful of rice less each meal, even freeze their toes in New York's winter. This is not even open to discussion; it is simply a law, unwritten though it may be, but a law nonetheless for which children have to be grateful forever after.

But neither Mr. Reyes nor Mrs. Reyes, father and mother of the upcoming one and only *Pinoy-Kano* rapper of New York, could imagine the needs of a high school kid, especially when among the school population is first cousin, seventeen-year-old Gidget Reyes, she of the honey-brown skin, limpid dark eyes and mouth of perpetual petulance. She looks very grown-up, Gidget does, soft and firm at the same time, long-limbed and dazzlingly graceful even when just walking. She tacks in the wind as neatly as the hand-carved boats of Jejomar's island home, trailing a scent illicit with promise, excitement and revelations Thank god he's been memorizing Webster; otherwise, he would never know how to describe her to himself. At family gatherings, even the women follow Gidget with their eyes, measuring her, before bending heads together, whispering in Tagalog. "That one," Jejomar has heard his mother say in a voice crinkled with envy, "takes after her mother. Which bodes no good at all." He understands. Gidget's mother left without notice four years into her marriage with Jejomar's uncle. "She was black, you know," his mother would add, as though that was a revelation.

Jejomar remembers Gidget's child face at the end of a gauntlet of hostile, pinched and imposed-upon faces at the Kennedy Airport. Disoriented, throat parched and bones melting in the fatigue of the fourteen-hour flight from Manila, he had been relieved to see in the crowd two faces which, while not exactly friendly, were there at least for his family alone. His mother threw a bone-crushing embrace about her brother and when she broke away to wipe tears off her cheeks, Jejomar's father seized the man's hand in energetic greeting before introducing Jejomar and his sister. This was Uncle Fred and this was Gidget. Jejomar was happy to hear the names. It was bad enough that he and his sister had picked up their parents' habit of calling each other Mr. Reyes and Mrs. Reyes. Since the adults were all first cousins and the children all had the same surnames, there would've been Misters and Misses Reyes all around.

With a strangely melancholic fondness, Uncle Fred then presented Gidget, at which Mr. Reyes shoved Jejomar toward the girl, saying, "he's yours; turn him into a good American." Mrs. Reyes then remarked that the girl seemed well brought up and genteel but Uncle Fred demurred, saying, "Oh, I don't know. I think I'm closer to her than she is to me." Which was an odd thing indeed to say about one's daughter.

Mr. and Mrs. Reyes would not bother to question their closeness to or apartness from their children. That's a question reserved for another kind of feeling—

this kind now that makes Jejomar wonder whether he is closer to Gidget than she is to him. He wanders through the shadow-dappled Union Square park, heading eastward for the row of ethnic shops clustered like weeds around First Avenue giant hospital. She had always seemed oblivious, Gidget has, to the whispers about her, until summer this year, when she turned up in an in-your-face Afro-American style: purple and gold beads threaded through corn row braids, gold hoop earrings, seashell and leather choker and bracelet and inch-long amber-painted fingernails. A breathing stereotype, Jejomar was forced to conclude, though her blood-mix made her look softer, different, infinitely exotic.

The make-up and the get-up occasioned a terrible to-do between her and Uncle Fred, in the course of which it was revealed that Gidget had been wait-ressing at a diner to augment her allowance. Gidget yelled it was none of her father's business; the cosmetics cost him nothing, and so please stop already with this accounting of what she owed him, don't say anything more, fathuh! He did-n't, fetching her instead a hefty slap on the left cheek. Gidget fled, yelling child abuse all the way down fourteen floors. Child abuse, battering, domestic violence and other ugly imprecations. She disappeared, didn't come home that night. Hay, naku!!! Panicked Uncle Fred had to round up friends and assorted relations to mount a search through the Manhattan canyons.

She met Jejomar in the park, ambushing him from his MTV dreams as he walked home from the library. They huddled on a bench, sipping sodas he's bought to calm their nerves, smoking three unfiltered cigarettes each, one after another. He tried to explain how the slap was actually a sign of caring and affec-tion, and why battering, the very idea of it, couldn't apply to Flips like her father. A parent simply had absolute dominion over his children, at least until they were old enough for jobs. "Real jobs," he told her, "not make-believe, pass-the-time, make-a-few-bucks..." She snorted. "Career," she said. "You mean careers." She snorted again. "Thass probably what he did to my mom. Thass why she left." Twin plumes of smoke issued from her nostrils, as though anger and hurt had turned her into a small dragon. They lost some minutes there while she showed him how to do it. But once he managed a scraggy kind of dragon hiss, they were back to the problem. Patiently, he went over the thing again: the duty of parents to set their children on the proper path and that included all corrective measures. Spanking, a knock on the head, a shove, a push, endless nagging. "Before mongo beans became expensive, kids were made to kneel on them for hours. With arms outstretched, like this, as though crucified." She flicked the cigarette butt away. "Child abuse," she said.

For four weeks, the same scene played itself out over and over again in their conversation: Uncle Fred livid; Gidget in a fury; the slap, the shout, the thud of the front door. Only it seemed Jejomar watched from the front row while Gidget was backstage. He couldn't make her see the justness of it. "They've got you brainwashed," she said over and over again. Mr. and Mrs. Reyes were pressuring Uncle Fred, meanwhile, to call a family assembly—meaning, themselves, Uncle Fred, Gidget, and three or four distant cousins who'd drive in from Long Island and stay the weekend. Jejomar's sister, Linda Bie, rasped angrily that she should be included; she was family, after all, or did they all think she was already dead? That occasioned another great to-do, with Linda Bie setting their whole building trembling with her own silent fury. But once she calmed down, it was Gidget's turn to be outraged. "What have all these people got to do with it? Who're they? I met them once, twice, at parties; we got maybe thirty words between us. I don't know them. It's none of their business. Dis between me and my fathuh!" Pacing the park, under trees shaking their heads, Gidget kept switching from grammar to patois, her outrage erupting occasionally into a no, no, no, no, sirree, every line of her body taut, her hands making abrupt waves of dismissal as she perorated against the idea, the very idea, of a family assembly. "What family," she yelled. "There's only me and Dad!"

The park was the only place she would meet Jejomar, deeming it neutral, traveling there from an undisclosed friend's apartment whenever he whispered into the phone that he had a message from her father. Jejomar usually preferred a bench to walking about and he'd sit there, telling himself to be as patient as a crocodile cooling in the mud. He'd wait for Gidget's tirade to end before explaining once again that this was the way things were back home. "I'm home right now," Gidget countered in a thin voice, "he should go into therapy." Jejomar ignored her words. Problems, he began again, were examined, inspected and unbraided in gatherings of friends and relations; no one went into counseling. "Thass why you're all crazy!" No doubt. In the meantime, this was the way to do it because the thought of laying out one's most private concerns to a stranger, a paid ear if you will, was totally repulsive. "But it's okay to tell these cousins, these strangers. Not even trained, not even professionals! Simply meddlers. Meddlers!" Jejomar pulled out the sigh clogging his chest and began again.

The meeting did take place, though—reduced to Uncle Fred, Mr. and Mrs. Reyes and Jejomar himself. It was just as well since Gidget's fury so shrunk the living room of Uncle Fred's apartment Jejomar could hardly breathe. Gidget threatened to go to court and have herself declared a major minor. "Easy enough," she declared, "'cuz you're all aliens. Aliens!" That required explanations which provoked Uncle Fred into threats of physical violence—"you're not too big for a spanking, so help me God!" Mr. and Mrs. Reyes made soothing noises, trying to calm down this short balding man yelling from the depths of his throat. Uncle Fred suddenly covered his face with his hands and let loose with tears and sobs. "I'm not an alien," he said in a wee voice, "I'm your father." That terrified everyone, even Gidget, and healed the rift between father and daughter. To everyone's immense relief, especially Jejomar's. Gidget returned home, devastated at having caused the only tears of her father she'd ever seen.

Sideshow
from *The Gangster of Love*

Jessica Hagedorn

Milagros, Fely and Bas walk up the steps of the federal courthouse at nine in the morning. Reporters and photographers are already there, smoking cigarettes and drinking coffee. Fely happily points out a few Pinoys with video cameras, notebooks, and self-important airs. There is excitement and anticipation, an odd sense of camaraderie among the waiting Filipinos. All are here for the same reason, eager spectators at Imelda's daily sideshow. Rich or poor, clad in Gucci loafers or double-knit polyester, they know it's the best drama in town, and it's free.

Fely approaches one of the men. "What time is Imelda coming?" He is friendly and answers her in Tagalog. Fely hurries back to where Milagros stands, clutching her handbag and smoking. Beside her, Bas is carefully recombing his hair. "Maybe thirty or forty minutes *pa daw*. That's what the guy said. You want to have breakfast? Should we go in? Where do we go?" she asks Bas.

Milagros is curious. "Who's the reporter working for?"

"I think the *Filipino Inquirer* or *Philippine-American Herald*, I'm not sure."

Milagros is disappointed by Fely's answer. "Look! It's that guy from NBC." She nudges Fely with her elbow and points to a beefy young man with curly blond hair and a mustache. Bas wanders off to the Filipino reporter and introduces himself. Soon the men are laughing, and other Filipino men join them. Fely is annoyed. "Bas is always making tsismis with everyone he meets. Next thing you know they'll come back to the motel with us for dinner," she complains. Milagros gives one of her I-told-you-so smirks. Bas leaves the reporter and goes back up the steps to the women. "Where's the camera? Hurry up, Fely. Let's take a souvenir picture!" Fely hands him the camera.

"Let's pose at the top of the steps," Bas suggests. "And maybe when Imelda gets here we can pose with her." Milagros gives him a disapproving look. "What's wrong, Mila? Don't be a killjoy, *naman*! This is a herstorical event, *di ba*? Or maybe I should say hysterical." Bas laughs.

Milagros is furious. "How can you even think of posing with that woman?"

"Why not? She's famous!"

The three of them huddle, Bas in the center with his arms around both women, beaming. Milagros cringes from his touch. She has taken great pains to dress elegantly but simply for the trial, a strand of valuable Mikimoto pearls around her neck. The pearls were a gift from Francisco, before Milagros found out about his mistress. He'd won them in a high-stakes poker game.

You never know who might show up from Manila. Why, Patsy Lozano had called to say that she planned to come with someone whose name Milagros can't remember, someone who made a stopover in New York from Manila on his way to Rome. Just to see Imelda! The trial has become a major tourist attraction for most Filipinos.

There are rumors that today is the day George Hamilton will be called on to testify. Wouldn't that be something? Now there's somebody Milagros wouldn't mind standing next to in a photograph.

Her friend Patsy Lozano once danced with George Hamilton at one of those parties in the old days. When she isn't in Manila visiting her grandchildren, Patsy Lozano divides her time between a town house in London and another on the Upper East Side of Manhattan. She calls Milagros whenever she's in San Francisco. They meet at Macy's and Gump's and gossip while Patsy shops. Patsy always treats her to lunch, which Milagros finds embarrassing. "I'll see you at the trial," Patsy chirped the last time. Patsy Lozano considers long-distance calls, flights on the Concorde, and intimate dinner parties with Imelda and Doris Duke "no big deal," though Patsy Lozano also considers herself a staunch Aquino supporter. She was featured prominently in a cover story that the *New York Times Sunday Magazine* did on upper-class women in the Philippines aligning themselves with the People Power movement. Rocky sent Milagros the magazine, which Milagros saved in her trunk along with press clippings of Rocky's band and other assorted Rocky memorabilia. Milagros was amazed at how demonstrations and street rallies had suddenly become chic among Manila socialites. She knew half the women mentioned in the article and couldn't believe what she read. And there was her friend Patsy, absurdly glamorous in Cory-yellow golfing shirt and

Cory-yellow visor, immortalized in a photograph, shouting, "Cory! Cory!" at some pivotal rally held near the American embassy right before the Marcoses were forced to flee. Milagros almost fainted from excitement when she saw it. She was thrilled for her old friend, and also envious. History was being made, no matter how raggedy or chaotic. Yet she was so very far away from it.

"What's the difference between the Marcos regime and the Aquino government, ba?" Milagros had once asked Patsy. Patsy Lozano could easily get on Milagros Rivera's nerves, but she was too powerful and privy to all the latest gossip for Milagros to dismiss easily. Even more important, Patsy's ex-husband used to be Francisco Rivera's favorite golfing partner and visits him frequently now that he is sick. Because Patsy is still on good terms with her ex-husband, she pumps him for information whenever she's in Manila, then passes on to Milagros all the gossip she's gathered concerning Milagros's ailing husband. The only thing they never discuss is Francisco's son by Baby Guzman, who Milagros continues to call "that woman."

So? she would ask Patsy as casually as possible. Have you heard any new tsismis about that woman?

"That woman" is also what Milagros sometimes calls Corazon Aquino and Imelda Marcos. "Seems to me things haven't changed one bit. And from what people say, under that woman's rule, they've gotten worse."

"Excuse me, *lang*, but I happen to believe that Cory is progressive," Patsy Lozano argues.

"That woman doesn't run the country! The army runs it!"

"Ay, Mila! There you go again! *Puwede ba*, you've been away too long and you believe everything you read in the foreign press!" Patsy Lozano chuckles. "Put yourself in Cory's place, *naman*! She's expected to clean up an economic mess that's been going on for over twenty years."

"And why can't she? Because she's just like that other one!"

"You're being too critical. Just put yourself in her place and ask yourself what you'd do in a similar situation."

"A helluva lot more than those women!"

"Ay, Mila, *naman*! Change takes time…" Patsy Lozano deftly switches topics and tells her about a certain Manila matron who caught her husband in bed with the houseboy.

Fely, in sneakers and pastel sweatsuit, carries snacks wrapped in aluminum foil in plastic shopping bags into the courtroom. Milagros hopes Patsy Lozano doesn't see her enter with Bas and Fely. Bas and Fely are exactly the kind of people Milagros wouldn't have bothered with if she'd stayed married to Francisco Rivera in Manila. But being in America has changed things. As far as Milagros goes, her sister's life has been ruined by her marriage to the loudmouthed, smarmy Basilio Cruz. Milagros refers to him as a commoner. A gold-digging wife killer. But like it or not, thick-skinned, jokey Bas is someone she's forced to put up with in New York. Besides, Bas makes himself indispensable by renting a car and driving them around.

Fely is older than Milagros by four years, but people often mistake her for Milagros's mother. The image of a bewildered immigrant in perpetual culture shock, Fely slyly trails behind her sophisiticated sister when they are out in public. Rocky adores her and lovingly refers to Fely as "my no-bullshit aunt." Voltaire has said she should've been canonized when she married Bas, and he calls her Santa Auntie. Milagros can't live with her, or without her.

Basilio Cruz outdoes himself today in a seersucker leisure suit, which he wears with white nylon socks and white patent-leather Florsheims. "Just for Imelda," he brags. He keeps his counterfeit Porsche Carrera sunglasses on even indoors. Basilio's open shirt displays his diamond crucifix, and the brand-new Olympus that Fely has bought him hangs from a strap around his neck.

"Poor Tiyo Bas. He can't decide whether he's a pimp or a tourist," Rocky whispered to her mother when Bas drove up in the Cadillac earlier that morning.

Milagros stares straight ahead, following Imelda and her lawyers into the courtroom. She is fascinated by how Imelda's famous lawyer towers over Imelda, who is pretty tall for a typical Filipina. The cowboy lawyers reminds Milagros of ... is it John Wayne? Randolph Scott? Imelda, all in black, gives her fans and supporters a tentative, sad smile, the practiced smile, Milagros decides, of a martyr. Imelda glances in her direction. Perhaps she notices the genuine pearls around Milagros's neck. Milagros is sure that Imelda, at the very least, retains a good eye for authentic jewelry. Did she remember Milagros? There was a time when ... Milagros puts the thought out of her mind as she looks around for the best place to sit.

Bas has already situated himself in the press section, next to the Filipino journalist. He pulls out a small memo pad and ballpoint pen from his pocket, ready to take his notes. What nerve! Milagros shakes her head slowly. Fely puts on her eyeglasses and pats the space next to her on the cushioned bench. Milagros is relieved. At least they are sitting in the safe, pro-Aquino section, the second to the last row on the left side facing the judge. Patsy Lozano, a veteran spectator at the Imelda trial, has warned her that one's political sympathies are determined by where one chooses to sit.

"But what if it's crowded, and I have no choice?" Milagros asked her.

"Get there early then," Patsy Lozano advised.

Patsy is one of those powerful, in-the-know Filipinos. And no matter how Milagros feels about Cory, she certainly doesn't want to be mistaken for a Marcos loyalist. It's too...common and vulgar. Like the way Bas and Fely dress.

Milagros glances at her preening brother-in-law. What did Fely ever see in him? "Moocher" was practically tattooed across his forehead. Milagros was sure Bas was planning to one day poison her loyal, trusting sister for insurance money, just like he did his first wife.

Milagros spots another familiar face. Isn't that ex-Congressman Diosdado "Cyanide" Abad sitting in front of her? Definitely a Marcos loyalist, everyone knows that. Why is he sitting on the left side? Milagros panics.

The marshals usher more important-looking foreigners into the courtroom, slender women carrying Chanel handbags and balding Middle Eastern men whose various colognes perfume the stuffy atmosphere. Are these Khashoggi's people? Milagros wonders. "Who's that?" Fely whispers loudly. A bent man with white hair, a trimmed beard, and the gaunt, ascetic face of Saint Jerome is helped to his seat by a haughty woman who wears a hat. The old man is someone out of a more elegant era, with his impeccable linen suit, spats, and bamboo cane. Intrigued, Milagros forgets about Congressman Abad and Fely rustling her bags packed with Spam sandwiches and cans of Diet Coke.

Too bad Raquel couldn't come with them today, Milagros thinks. It would certainly give her something to write about. Maybe she could talk her into coming tomorrow. This was much too important for Raquel to miss. And if that companion of hers or whatever she wants to call him is too busy to take care of the baby, then what the hell, Raquel should just bring the damn baby with her. Ay, *dios ko*, Milagros sighs to herself. If things were different and they were back in Manila, she would hire a yaya to help Raquel take care of Venus. Then they wouldn't have to be bothered with any of this.

Three rows behind Imelda and her lawyers, a familiar woman fans herself and whispers into the ear of a short, effete young man. He is laughing softly. They are completely engrossed in each other. The woman turns, and her glittering, made-up eyes meet those of Milagros. It is Patsy Lozano. Patsy gives a little wave with her fan, then pantomimes making a phone call to Milagros later. With a faint smile, Milagros nods in agreement, noting how Patsy's surgically tightened features are frozen into a sleek mask belonging to a woman of thirty. Milagros wonders if Patsy recognizes Fely beside her.

Patsy's attention drifts back to the man next to her, and their conversation resumes. The judge enters the room. "All rise," someone orders in a loud voice. A hush falls over the courtroom.

The judge makes a motion for them to sit back down. From the press section, Basilio Cruz clears his throat so noisily that Milagros Rivera is terrified he'll forget himself and spit. Basilio adjusts the collar of his shiny shirt and brushes imaginary lint off the pointed lapels of his jacket. Milagros frowns. For a man with absolutely no taste, Basilio Cruz is incredibly fussy.

The chief prosecutor is speaking. An earnest man in a rumpled suit, he's a dead ringer for Al Pacino—but not very impressive when Bas compares him to Imelda's cowboy. Basilio Cruz tunes the prosecutor out and studies Imelda, memorizing every detail so he can go on about it later to his girlfriend. Imelda's helmet of blacker than black hair, which never moves. The subtle, black pearl button earrings. Her gray eye shadow and pale lips. A surprising woman, Bas admits to himself, one who should never be underestimated.

Over there sits Adnan Khashoggi, utterly relaxed and almost pretty. Is that rouge on his cheeks? Mascara on his curly lashes? Maybe he's *bakla*, Bas thinks. They all are, probably, including that macho cowboy lawyer of Imelda's.

A wave of pleasure washes over Basilio Cruz. He makes plans to come back to the trial for the rest of the week. After all, he is free to do as he pleases. Maybe he'll write about it for one of those local Pinoy papers, like the *Phil-Am Herald* or the *Daly City Messenger*. He could be their New York correspondent. Their national correspondent. Aren't they always looking for new talent? Money isn't the issue.

Like he often says to Fely, "Money isn't everything." Bas understands when it comes to community and the news media. He's a community man, a proud Filipino, eager to work for a modest fee. His wife says he has a way with words. So does that *chuplada* sister of hers, Miss Big-Time Milagros Rivera. It must be true. And now that he's chummy with the reporter sitting next to him ... what's his name? Bert. That's right. Bert Avedilla. Bert has connections.

The first witness is called. Not George Hamilton, but some FBI agent. Bert Avedilla scribbles on a yellow legal pad. Basilio steals a glance at what the reporter is writing. Today's date, the name of the FBI man, the chief prosecutor's first question. Such logic! Such detail! Basilio is inspired and copies down Avedilla's notes.

What an exciting day. This trip to New York had been worth all the expense. Bas looks back to wink at his nearsighted wife, who is nodding off into sleep. Fely falls asleep wherever they go. It's been going on since the day they were married. No matter how noisy it is or what they are doing, Fely nods off without warning. Her physician has diagnosed it as some mild, harmless form of narcolepsy and claims there is nothing one can do. There are brief periods when Fely's condition doesn't manifest itself—at her job, for example. Fely never falls asleep while she is working at the hospital.

What if Fely starts snoring?

Bas signals Milagros discreetly. In response, she nudges Fely gently with her elbow. No reaction. Milagros shrugs and turns her attention back to the FBI man on the stand. Fely's heavy body slumps against her. The agent drones on about secret Swiss bank accounts and the incomprehensible "trail of deceit" left by Imelda and her cronies. The agent gets off the stand and points to a chart. Figures are quoted, and the district attorney asks more tedious questions. Along with Fely, two members of the jury have also fallen asleep. Fely's breathing slows down as she begins to wheeze and snore, softly at first. Then the snoring becomes more audible. Basilio coughs. Milagros can feel Basilio's eyes boring holes into her, begging her to do something about Fely, but Milagros pointedly ignores him. Son of a bitch. Let him squirm. Let her sweet, tired, hardworking sister sleep.

During recess, Milagros and the now awake Fely go to the women's rest room one floor down. Fely starts to bring her shopping bags with her. "Leave them on the seat," Milagros suggests irritably, taking the bags from Fely.

"But—"

"Fely, please, nobody's going to steal them."

Bas has disappeared with the reporter. Patsy Lozano is in the hallway outside the courtroom, waiting for an elevator with her companion. She spots Milagros and signals her to join them. Milagros points to the staircase in the opposite direction and waves goodbye to her. Patsy Lozano looks annoyed by Milagros Rivera's elusive behavior and whispers something into her companion's ear.

The women's rest room consists of one toilet stall with a broken door. Someone is inside the stall, attempting to urinate and hold the broken door shut at the same time. Two Pinay women wait by the sink for their turn. As she enters, Fely trips and bumps into the younger woman, who glares at her. The first, heavyset woman is retouching her eyebrows with a dark pencil and assessing herself in the mirror. "How boring, *naman*!" She complains to her friend, finishing with her eyebrows. After a moment, she leans forward to draw a mole on her cheek. "Too many details, *dios ko*!" She mimics the chief prosecutor's voice. "If you say you took a taxi, what was the license number? Who was the driver? What time of day was it? The exact date and location where you caught the cab? Boring *talaga*! Ay." The woman gives an exaggerated sigh. Her friend joins her in a chorus of sighs. "Boring *talaga*!" she echoes.

From the stall, an older white woman maneuvers her way to the sink to rinse her hands. Milagros remembers her from the courtroom. Why is she at Imelda's trial? Milagros tries to work up the nerve to ask her, but the white woman leaves before she has a chance.

The heavyset woman keeps up her chatter. "Let's go home na! We have such a long subway ride."

"But what about George Hamilton?" her friend asks plaintively.

"*Ay naku*! I don't think he's worth it! Too many questions about nothing!" The heavyset woman flushes the toilet.

Suddenly Fely speaks. "Excuse me lang, ladies, but a case like this is really complicated. We have to be patient. *Di ba*, Mila? This is history. So many ins and outs. Slowly they are building a case. They have to ask many questions because …" She pauses to think. "Because they are grooving in the dark!"

"You mean groping," Milagros says dryly.

"Groping, that's it," Fely says.

Milagros pays her sister a rare compliment. "That's right. You're absolutely right." Fely is delighted.

The other two women exchange astonished glances and exit hastily.

"I could've sworn you slept through the trial," Milagros says, amused.

Behind her thick glasses, Fely's magnified gaze is open and innocent. "I did."

The End of Awkwardness

Edgar Poma

His computer apparatus was basically quiet, except for occasional *whooshes* and *plink plinks*, so the other priests couldn't complain about him generating noise as he wrote and filed stories electronically from his private quarters. Michael fulfilled his share of pastoral duties, so the other priests couldn't complain, either, about the time he was devoting to *Chimetro*, which was an amalgamation of Chicago and Metropolitan. It was a weekly news tabloid that had grown considerably from the time Michael had first begun writing for them, when he received his Masters in Sacred Music from a small northwestern university, and they needed a critic that could sit through classical concerts. When he entered seminary afterward, they coaxed him from the arts to write more turgid pieces: profiles with minor celebrities, reports like the one he did about the razing of an amusement park. He wrote that the bank that had taken over the land and all the park accouterments was in such a rush that they didn't bother to rescue panels from the House of Mirrors before demolition. He wrote that surely the Bank of so-and-so could have found a buyer for the mirrors in "a city as vain as ours." He was brave only because the paper allowed him to use a pseudonym: M. Capitor instead of Michael Capitora. They even allowed it now, since they liked his writing so much, even though it would have been a novelty to publicize that one of their staffers was a relatively young Father, newly-minted. They gave him assignments, about one story per quarter, sometimes two. The cardinal's office approved the arrangement on the condition that Michael's work for his parish came first; that he did not wear his collar when he conducted interviews; and that a portion of his earnings went to the parish school. (He donated all.) They made it clear that they wouldn't have given him clearance if the church wasn't so strapped. It still seemed foreign to them that priests could no longer rely exclusively on the collection baskets and bequests, and therefore had to be encouraged to generate revenue in every creative way conceivable. "Times have changed," they told him, rather bittersweetly. Recently they had to reprint a "Manual for Altar Boys" to reflect new language, "Altar Server," throughout. They had successfully fought off an external drive to include a paragraph in the manual on "How to Know If You Are Being Touched in the Wrong Way..." Their position was, "These things are non-occurring, rare or isolated—we will not treat the situation as if it is commonplace." And one of the prelates thought, besides, they did not want their priests to be more stoic and paranoid than they already were, because the changing times had somehow required them to be.

• • •

One morning, in late April, Michael was brushing his teeth in the priest's communal bathroom when he heard one of the visiting priests singing in the shower. He had often wanted to sing in the shower himself — he had a superb, trained voice — but a priest who taught at seminary since the Mesozoic era once said that it was improper for priests to warble with joy while touching their bodies. He said, "This is not to say that you are singing because you are doing anything self-injurious, but someone walking down the street who passes by and hears you might very well misperceive the situation at, uh, hand. While a case could be made that in the shower a bar of soap is actually touching your bodies and that when you do touch your bodies you are ostensibly scrubbing the dirt off, it is possible that you can inadvertently cross the line between a scrub and a caress with the same innocence that you play with a dog innocuously and it gets extraordinarily excited with your leg." Michael and his classmates had a look on their faces that said, "*Hunh?*" Then one of them said, "Well, is it proper, then, to sing sad songs in the shower?"

Since there was no one using the other sinks, Michael thought it would be all right to laugh briefly, even roar, at the recollection. But he decided just to smile wanly instead.

In the mail that day, Michael received from his editor the tearsheets of an article that the paper had published a year ago. A note was attached: "Tell me what you think." The article concerned the decade-old case of the Tracys, a lower middle-class white family forced by a federal judge to sell their suburban Chicago home within six months and vacate the neighborhood permanently. Rudy and Irene Tracy, their children Trent and Trisha, harassed any minority family who moved into their block. Inevitably they began to focus all their hatred on a young black family, the Safflers, who moved next door to them. They hurled racial epithets at the Safflers, often with Mr. Microphones — each family member had one or traded off; gathered their bathroom wastes and placed them all over the Saffler property; tampered with the Safflers' automobiles; stole their mail; wrecked their shrubs and landscaping; shattered their windows; threw trash in their yard; shot out their Christmas lights with a bb gun; threatened bodily harm with baseball bats and electric drills; made crank orders to their house, at all hours of the day, for takeout food and taxicabs, ambulances and groceries, strippers and big appliances; made obscene phone calls; picked fights; filed made-up complaints with the police, drive cars, trucks and motorcycles onto their lawn; turned their garden hose on to run all day; hooked up amplifiers to a stereo that was already cranked up high. The Safflers lived in terror and dread and anguish for nearly ten years before they filed a federal civil-rights suit demanding millions of dollars in damages. The Tracys claimed that they had no animosity against any minority group, including the Safflers, and filed their own lawsuit. The judge resolved the entire matter by issuing a temporary restraining order and making the Tracys sell their house. Although it was a fairy tale ending for the Safflers and the neighborhood, the staffer who wrote the piece expressed sympathy for the next victim family that happened to live next door to the house in which the Tracys resettled: "Pity them if they're not white, or if they're white and have non-white friends."

She concluded, "It'll just start all over again, let's be real. Serial bigotry can be banished for a while, but it always festers and comes back like The Weed That Will Not Die. You know what they say about these weeds that revive, that they come back stronger."

Michael couldn't contact his editor right away, because he was needed to sub for a home economics class. He reported to the classroom reluctantly and made the eighth graders, mostly girls, go about their sewing assignments on their own while he sat behind the front desk and read a book on music theory. He pled ignorance when one of the girls had a question, though his mother worked as a seamstress for years and had taught her son how to sew things like potholders with loops, first with needle and thread, then showed him how to use a sewing machine and how to make his own clothes by laying out and cutting patterns. To this day, he mended his own clothes and vestments and darned his own socks, but in the privacy of his room. He certainly didn't want to give any indication in the classroom that he knew how to do all this stuff, since the kids might gossip, and the whole school and the parents association and every Catholic in the Archdiocese would think him effete.

He looked up from his book and saw a group of kids flubbing up some hem work. He wanted desperately to tell them that they should simply use identically cut facings with two rows of edge topstitching to hold the hems secure instead of folding them up, but he went back to his book instead.

He tried to transmit the sewing hints telepathically, but he didn't break any ground in that department.

At the end of the day, he went to his room and fired up his computer to contact his editor. He preferred communicating on-line whenever possible, since it somehow did not make him feel as constrained as he normally would be in person or on the phone. Somehow it gave him enough cover to be a little indelicate, as if God were computer illiterate.

M: Read piece. Carrie did great job. Too bad the dailies snagged her. I suppose you want me to do a follow-up. Sigh. A Trace-the-Tracys. The family waging war against itself but don't know it. The Hatfields vs. the Hatfields.

E: Frankly, I don't like to think about these people. I don't think any other publication is thinking about 'em. The public interest has waned below sea level. I think we all hope that if no one thinks about 'em, the hate won't happen. That they've moved to an atoll in the Pacific with no neighbors at all, that they have no one to mind-fuck with except the coral. But this is not reality. The reality is, they are in the U.S. in another populated neighborhood, and if they're pulling the same crap, which they probably are, they should be exposed.

M: Where did they wind up?

E: Our contact at the Courts says they moved to Sacramento, California. I have their new address and phone number. I don't know anything more. Except that they are apparently living next door to a Filipino family.

M: So you want me to do this story because I'm Filipino.

E: Yeah, but also because I don't have anyone else to assign right now. Plus I seem to recall you telling me months ago that you have some vacation days you haven't used yet. Plus you're a damned good writer. What else do you want to know?

M: Okay. I guess. The timing isn't bad — Holy Week's over with. I have recovered from all the Masses during which I had to wash parishioners' feet. And compliments will get me anywhere, especially on a jetplane. I assume you're buying ticket. I'll save Chimetro motel expense — I have friends from college who live in Sacto. and I'm sure I can crash at their place.

E: I knew you were the right choice. Let's do lunch tomorrow to work out details. I'll give you the hate crimes legislation file and the Tracy file — both are voluminous — and maybe you can check out their old neighborhood. You know: talk to the people who are living in their old house, talk to all the neighbors who have canceled their nervous breakdowns by now. And whazthis about a plane? I was gonna put you on Greyhound.

M: Like hell. So I assume this won't take more than a week.

E: With Greyhound it'll take you a week to get there. Okay, seriously, if it goes longer than a week, all you need to tell your monsignor is that the project has turned out to be a little more involved, like an exorcism.

M: Why do I get the uneasy feeling that the exorcism might be my own?

E: If you're worried about getting in some type of crossfire.

M: I'm not.

E: Don't be. This is not the story of the century, although when I see the faltering race relations in this country, it should be. Anyway you're not G.I. Joe or the F.B.I. You know, Efrem Zimbalist Jr. and all that stuff. So if there's more trouble than it's worth, bail. You're just reporting on whatever's happening. I don't expect you to fix anything. In fact, you are not to fight someone else's battle. Stay detached and uninvolved and you'll live to tell your grandkids — well so to speak, Father. So later dude.

M: Who the hell is Efrem Zimbalist Jr.?

After dinner that night, there was a birthday celebration for one of the priests, with cake and balloons and a very tasteful, very clean singing telegram ensemble called The Von Won't-Shut-Their-Trapps (which Michael did find distasteful), but he skipped it all because his mind was elsewhere, on the Tracy story. He went to his room and sat on his bed and began to think about one of the first confessions he heard, a Central American kid who was seven or eight years old and who attended the parish school. Michael had recognized the voice. The boy's middle-aged immigrant parents worked for a hotel: his father was a janitor, his mother worked in the laundry. They rented a small walk-up in a quiet neighborhood. The boy's confession was that he was crazy.

"What do you mean, you're crazy?" Michael said.

The boy explained that signs had been posted all over the neighborhood one day: "Small 5-inch parrot, green and orange colored, finders fee: $25.00" About a week later, on a Sunday, he was in his room getting ready for church when he saw the parrot on his window sill. He got all excited, not only because he had found the missing bird but because he could use the reward money to help his mother buy a coat she had placed on the layaway. So he carefully captured the parrot and brought it to the neighbor who had lost it, but the lady said, "You little wetback, you probably stole him," and took the parrot and slammed the door in the boy's face. He was shocked and started to cry. Then he felt angry and cheated and rang the doorbell and confronted the lady again and asked for the finders fee. And the lady slammed the door in his face again. So he ran home and told his parents about it, but they thought it over and told him that maybe the lady...was right! In the end, it was much easier for him to believe that his parents ultimately lacked the courage to back him up, and that they were too wound up in propriety and not making waves to fight for him and with him.

• • •

The day before Michael left for his West Coast assignment, he had a wedding to officiate, and the pomp reminded him of his own wedding, sort of, his ordination. He had thought that his entry into the priesthood would be marked by the end of all inhibition, but it didn't happen. When, on that day, he shook hands and posed for pictures outside the church where he had been installed just hours before, he was characteristically bland and dull; it was as if he wore a sign around his neck that said, "Do Not Hug Me, Do Not Climb All Over Me, If You're a Kid Do Not Attempt to High-Five Me, Remember that I'm Allergic to Certain Scents, Keep the Line Moving." He had tried to make his body language looser than it was, throughout the day, but the whole effort was like trying to cut paper dolls from stiff, triple-thick cardboard. He tried, but failed, to have a sincere patter that went beyond "Thank you for coming" — he had planned to look people in the eye and ask them how they were and what he could do for them. He had wanted very much to convey that if God had bestowed on him some kind of introductory, one-day only powers of healing as a gift for entering the fold, he would make sure that the blessings went around as far as they could reach. But at the last minute he decided that he didn't want anyone to think that he was being invasive.

At his reception, when his cousin read a speech that ended with, "We know that Auntie and Uncle are looking down at their Mike from heaven and are, excuse the expression, as proud as hell," Michael was the only person in the entire room who didn't crack up. Even a prelate in attendance could be seen chortling and slapping his knee. But Michael was embarrassed, and to forget about it, he thought about his parents: he considered his mom a saint, though every Filipino-American man in his thirties and perhaps every man in the world, thought of their mothers that way; his father he did not think of as a saint because his father had never been much for churchgoing, but Michael admired the fact that his old man had at least worked hard for his family all his life.

When his father immigrated to the States in the 1930s, he harvested fruit, vegetables and nuts from fields, orchards and vines up and down Southern California and Northern Arizona. He was one of the luckier ones, who eventually made enough money to return to the Philippines to marry while he was still relatively young and able to bring his wife back to the States with him, while some of his compatriots, unfortunately, never made quite enough money, or only made enough after too much time had passed and they no longer felt a burning in their hearts to be close with anyone except each other.

He and his wife moved to Chicago, where he was hired on as a driver for a fleet of moving vans. His wife sewed for a small dress shop. On weekends, she joined him on runs and helped him pack up and tape up scores of boxes. He learned to service machinery, worked as an auto mechanic for nearly fifteen years, then bought a small gas station in the suburbs, where he worked until his retirement. He was well-known for fixing kids' bikes on the side and not charging them. Nowadays. kids hardly rode at all because of street crime, like bikejacking. When Michael heard on the news recently about the building of an asphalted rink in his old neighborhood where kids had to walk through metal detectors, then hop on their stored or rented bikes and ride around in an enclosed environment with constant surveillance and the pumped-in scent of crushed leaves, he felt rather grateful that his parents had departed before the world had come to this.

During the ordination dinner, the conversation at his table was monopolized by a business owner in the local Filipino community, who got carried away by one too many cranberry vodkas. Over the VIP's voice and the droning of others around him, Michael overheard two women, who were seated at a nearby table and had their backs turned to him, talking about him in his parents' Ilocano dialect. Very roughly translated, one said, "I don't think he has the warmth or the spontaneity to be a priest. He thinks too much and he's afraid to make mistakes." The other said, "He was always so lonely when he was little, but that happens to an only child. Siblings, with all that affection as well as all that fighting, give you backbone. Maybe becoming a priest will give him the backbone to be more caring."

Goshdarnit, he thought, *I care about people. What are we all doing here if I didn't care about people enough to become a priest?*

Then she added a Filipino expression that basically meant, " He should quit waiting for the band and just roll up the carpet and dance."

Dinner was followed by dancing, and Michael observed at one point, everyone at his table and all the other tables left to go off to the dance floor except for him and two others: an elderly Filipino man who knew his father and who Michael called uncle though he wasn't one, and a hairdresser cousin who was openly gay. It was like the Table of the Bachelors. The Bachelors who wouldn't even be eligible for the garter belt toss, if there was such a thing at ordinations. Men whose lives were without women. Michael and the cousin for obvious reasons. The uncle because he had worked in the fields all his life and never married because it wasn't convenient; he had had to get adjusted to the awkwardness of loneliness, and it would be with him until he died. Michael thought about this and it embarrassed and depressed him. He was certain that he felt the collective pain of his father's peers; it seemed to have somehow been passed on to the first generation Filipinos, like himself, who were American-born. The sons and daughters didn't have to work in the fields and packing sheds and canneries and fisheries, but they were made to feel, like the victims of some vague curse, the same isolation, the same exhaustion.

He noticed the cousin eyeballing him, which made him uncomfortable, and he said, "So are you with anyone now? I mean on a committed basis."

"I'm seeing someone who should be committed, but I'm not seeing him on a committed basis."

"You should have invited him to this." Michael only partially meant this.

"You should be happy I didn't. He's very attracted to Asian guys and gets aggressive. He would snap you up in a second. I still think you look like a Filipino Paul Newman in *Hud* and he would think so too."

Michael said that he had never seen *Hud*.

"You've probably seen it, but don't remember. You know, it's in black-and-white. Patricia Neal was in it, remember? This was pre-stroke." Kirk did an imitation of Patricia Neal as Hud's father's world-weary housekeeper, Alma: "Yer no goood, Huu-uuuud."

Michael found it extremely funny and wanted to laugh out loud, but he held it all back. A very long minute later, he said, "I *have* seen Paul Newman in *The Silver Chalice*."

"But you don't look like Paul Newman in *The Silver Chalice*. You look like Paul Newman in *Hud*. If Hud had brown skin and jet black hair and brown eyes."

Michael shrugged. "I don't feel handsome like Paul Newman. I've never felt handsome."

"That's obvious," Kirk said. "Look what you just did to yourself. You went to God when you shoulda went into modeling."

They talked rather enthusiastically about movies, at least the ones Michael had seen, until Michael worried that people were seeing him talking freely to Kirk with no compunction, as if church doctrine against homosexual acts or abortion or contraception did not exist. He felt in the end that he had to make it perfectly clear to Kirk that he was straight: "So I saw that particular movie when it was playing at a cineplex in Evanston, where I took my first date years ago. A girl." He paused. "A girl."

"Right. A girl. As opposed to boy."

"I like to compare that first relationship with a *girl*, one of many by the way, to a porch swing: old-fashioned, with a creaky future. Her family lived in an old house around the block from us. The swing that they had in front of their house, a couch-like number with a tartan covering, mostly grays and greens, gave me a hint of our mismatch during the time we made out, when it broke down, the swing I mean— "

"Right. As opposed to you."

"—and when it stopped its gentle rock and tipped to one side, then pushed my girlfriend and me off to one end. We didn't go hurtling down, it kind of poured us affectionately like cake batter."

Kirk was silent for a while, deep in thought, then said, "I can actually relate to cake batter."

And Michael said, "Hunh?"

"I mean, I like that metaphor. The cake batter. And it isn't even about being gay, that is in my case and I'm sure with others, it's about being a man and being Filipino. The average American doesn't see us as sexual creatures, they see us as dark-skinned migrant workers who aren't Mexicans, and as people who like to slaughter and eat goat and who aren't Satanists. I grew up feeling like cake batter in a pan. I always wanted to be baked, but the oven of America seemed to always be on the blink. When do Filipinos get to join the rest of America? Why aren't we invited to the party?"

Michael had absolutely no idea what to say. The question was much too complicated for him, even after years piled onto years of theological training. Then he noticed the elderly tablemate snoozing away, which inspired him to almost say, "I really can't answer that question—whey don't we just sleep on it?" But then he worried that someone nearby or passing might hear the tail end of what he was saying and think that he had sexual interest in Kirk, so he said, "Well, you know, it's not such a great party."

The wedding Michael officiated seemed to last the entire day. He got home, with an upset stomach because he had packed in too much food and punch. He got out his suitcase. The last thing he packed was a carefully-wrapped framed photograph of his parents. He couldn't sleep very well that night, so he slept on the plane to San Francisco the next day, in spite of feeling vacuum-packed, in spite of feeling that the close quarters were forcing fifty elbows to poke into his ribs the entire flight. The airline had offered him an upgrade to business class when he checked in, but he turned it down since he didn't want anyone on the plane recognizing him, even without his collar, and possibly thinking that priests made enough money to travel above coach and were in any way avaricious.

In San Francisco, he rented a car and drove eighty miles or so inland to Sacramento. He imagined arriving in the neighborhood, seeing elaborate cata-

pult set-ups of vats of hot burning oil slinging back and forth between the war-
ring houses. Flaming arrows flying everywhere. People from either house hauling out their garbage can or recycle box or picking up the paper or mowing their
lawns while suited up in armor. He pictured himself parking between both
houses and keeping score: Tracys, 9; Filipinos, 8. He could not, however, even in
his wildest fantasy, picture himself abandoning all journalistic and ethical neu-
trality and entering the fracas on the side of "his people," no matter how much
he despised all Tracys and their intolerance.

He stopped at a gas station along the way, in a town called Dixon, to use the
restroom. He was bewildered by the fact that the key, for security reasons, was
attached to an enormous wooden cross, almost three feet high. He thought about
Calvary. He thought about a spelling bee in the sixth grade when he spelled cav-
alry Calvary and how he heard his teacher, a nun, in the audience say,
"Dagnabbit!" He thought about his father, who kept the men's and ladies' rooms
of his service station open at all times. They were immaculate and well-stocked.
They were periodically and with industrial scents called, respectively, "Wet
Fisherman's Net" and "Swirl of Girl." The recollection comforted him, not the
smells but the names they went by.

Then he abruptly thought, though he tried to squelch it, about the times his
father would reiterate that as close as three blocks away from his business in
almost every direction, the conditions were different. There were no wet fisherman's nets and swirls of girls. "We're in a good district," he would say in Ilocano,
which Michael understood but couldn't speak, "but if it were just a little north
by rotten luck, we'd be held-up like crazy because that area's crawling with nig-
gers..." If his father had lived to read about the Tracys, he probably would have
said privately, to his family, that the Safflers should have been terrorized like
they were, that they got the treatment they deserved, and that they should have
left the neighborhood, not the people who tried to crush all the joy out of their
day-to-day life.

. . .

Three days later he was in his friends' downtown Sacramento condo, borrowing their home computer to contact his editor. He basically had the run of

the place, since his friends, Lois and Nick, were both white and had a small drafting business, had an important deadline to meet and were working eighteen hours a day.

In college, Michael remembered them as intense, but about each other and not their studies. For two years, he shared a dorm room with Nick, and put up with all the times Nick and Lois came over or she came over hungrily on her own, and between them he felt like he was living in Hormoneland. Michael didn't really ly mind going to the dorm lounge or the library during Nick's flings with Lois — they'd always hint by looking at Michael crosseyed. Michael liked to think that he would be studly like Nick if he were ever tested. It was an unusually good feeling, this vicariousness, while it lasted. He did not, of course, feel that now. Before seminary, he tossed the one porn novel he had ever bought and read in his life, "The Secret Life of Betsy Ross," along with all erotic thoughts, into a sack and onto a high shelf in his closet, and over time it seemed to elevate itself out of reach.

Michael transmitted to his editor:

I have a few photos and enough notes for a story. Good news: Tracys have kept a low profile here and are keeping to themselves. They've been here close to six months and so far they've behaved. This is in spite of the fact that their new neighbor is eerily like the one they left behind, except there are lemon trees here and the lots are bigger and the houses are spaced farther apart from one another.

The Tracys live in mid-block. There's a white family with a disabled kid on one side of them. And on the other side are two retired Filipino couples who are sharing a house after having worked in the fields together all their lives. Their children are grown and preoccupied with their own expenses, so the only way these couples could leave the camps and afford a place of their own was to pool their savings together.

Across the street is a Latin family. Chatted to them a little bit and they haven't experienced any problems in the neighborhood and haven't heard of anyone being hassled. They haven't seen any Molotov cocktails thrown in the middle of the night, anything like that.

I didn't tell them about the Tracys. I just told them I was doing one of those violence-in-America things. It does raise an ethical question: should they and their neighbors have been informed of the racist history of these newcomers to the neighborhood or should the racists be given a fresh start?

I've spent most of my time with "my people." I am going there again today and I will probably wind up the whole day with them. Part of me stays, on the chance that the Tracys are going to do something. A larger part of me stays because I kind of like their company: the trivial chatter, the sometimes long stretches of silence. I like being toured through their photo albums. I even like being around them while they nap. Does this sound nuts? Actually, I nap myself. It isn't because I am so tired, but that I feel so relaxed.

Yesterday, I helped them install a device that makes one of the lamps go on and off when the phone rings. It was such a simple thing, but it felt so satisfying. I liked helping out with dinner. Some things we eat are picked from their garden out back. I think about how my mom and dad would have loved to be here with me, with them. I have this urge to bring the photo of them from my nightstand where I'm staying and mix it in with all the family photos in the oldtimers' house.

They were cautious at first about talking with me, but then they've opened up a lot. We became friends much faster than I ever expected. I think it's simple intuition on their part, probably. I dunno. I think they trust me because I'm a Filipino and have a lot of their physical features, which I guess is sort of racist, in a way. I told them why I was doing my story, without revealing who the "problem" family was. They didn't want to know, anyway, because they're too polite to ask for specifics, and they kind of understand the situation and kind of don't. All four are really pushing the age envelope (mid and late eighties I'd say) and there are times when their hearing's bad or they're not so alert.

One couple, Romeo and Carmen, is healthier than the other. They move around a little faster, though all four of them move around fairly slowly. Romeo has the best hearing, so he's like the spokesperson. They all speak English, but Romeo has the, well, thinnest accent, so when he says something, I don't have to ask him to repeat himself. Romeo's the only one of the four who can still drive. The other couple is Sicoy and Dominga. He is weak and has to lie down most of the time and medication won't help. You know he has to be dying when his doctor more or less lifts food restrictions: you know, like, okay, Romeo, Carmen and Dominga, there's no need to hide that cinnamon roll from Sicoy, he can eat it now if he wants.

Anyway, he's already been administered the Sacrament of the Sick by their priest. He doesn't seem afraid of moving on to the better world.

Even if the Tracys were acting up, I think "my people" would be a formidable army in themselves. There's only the four and they're all very gentle and even shy, but they have the heart of four hundred. It's a schmaltzy thing to say, but it's true. You have the feeling when you're with them that they have been through so much throughout their lives — working in the fields, having to battle prejudice, being looked down on as dirty and stupid — that they can by now handle anything that the Tracys could dish out.

I was thinking of flying home tomorrow, but I might as well keep my ticket as is. My friends from college are busy on a project, but when they finish tomorrow, they want to show me around town.

One more thing. I'm struggling with this. I haven't told "my people" that I'm a priest. I don't want them to think of me as a kind of miracle emissary or something. Though I suppose that is my job. It's not, though, like I can lay my hands on Sicoy and stave off death. I feel I have an out: the head office forbids me to wear my collar when I'm on assignment. Which means not to reveal my identity. But maybe I should. But maybe I shouldn't. These people are devout Catholics — there are rosary beads wound around the tubes of Ben Gay. Why should a stranger who is in the faith come by to shake up their faith?

Oh the heck with it. Them not knowing doesn't affect the strength of my prayers that the Tracys haven't and will not harm anyone here, and that the present state of serenity in this neighborhood will last.

P.S. I'm going over to the Tracys later today. No big deal. Really.

• • •

Michael's friends' idea of showing their houseguest Sacramento was to take him to Reno.

On the drive up, Nick asked about the Tracys. He and his wife had read about them in clips Michael had sent before his arrival. "Are they, like, obese and have hair growing out of their lips, and they own broken down Lay-Z-boy recliners — you know, stuck in one position because of wear — and they've got pitbulls in the backyard?"

Michael said, "No, they're not like that at all. They're not monsters, outwardly. They're neat in appearance. They're fit for being in the sixties. Well, sort of fit. It's sad that there are no books or newspapers in the house. The TV's probably on all day, but it's that way in a lot of homes."

He described his trepidation about going up their walk and ringing the doorbell, then telling them he was a writer from Chicago who was doing a story and wanted to see what their new life was like. "I didn't say, though, I came to see whether or not they were up to no good. I doubt I would have made it inside the door if they felt that I had prejudged them."

Lois shook her head. "I'd have phoned them if I were you. Weren't you afraid they'd slam the door in your face because you're a minority, never mind a reporter?"

"I talked to people in the neighborhood — minorities or not — and no one was having any trouble with the Tracys. The Filipino couples next door have seen the Tracys and the Tracys have seen them. But no fireworks on the Tracys' part. So I figured they wouldn't go ballistic if I came by."

"Maybe it's only African American families that they hate so much," Nick said.

"No. In Chicago, they went after everyone close by that wasn't white. so anyway, when they invited me inside, I didn't feel like I was in any danger. We sat and talked in their family room, about five, ten minutes. Their two kids got jobs — they had been unemployed in Illinois — and now they were living on their own, one in Bakersfield, one in Oregon. They told me about that and — "

"Now what about them?" Lois said. "Are you tracking them down too?"

"The court documents show that the two kids did what their parents told them to do. I think they're probably okay without their parents playing their puppeteers. So anyway, they just talked at me, this old couple. They said they were still in shock over having lost their home in Chicago. They said that they felt misunderstood, that they never attacked anyone, that they weren't sorry for what they did because they didn't do most of what they were accused of, and if they did, it was only because they were provoked into it. And they want to go back someday, even if the Court says they can't.

"It was an astute judgment, the forced eviction, in one way. Having lost their roots shook up their lives like nothing else. They are the kind of people who feel even more at a loss because they don't have the imagination to take their roots with them. The Court understood this.

"So, anyway, I thanked them for their time and left. And I came out in one piece."

In Reno, Nick and Lois insisted on staying an extra day. They weren't having too much luck with the slot machines, but they seemed to like the mindlessness of it all. And when they got tired of the casinos, they gave Michael crosseyed little signals before they walked back to their motel room and left him with their plastic tubs of nickels. Michael was anxious to get back to Sacramento. He missed the company of the elderly couples. He felt that he had to stay overnight at their house at least once. It was a Filipino thing: he was raised with the concept that one hasn't really visited unless one has stayed the night. As a boy, he remembered visits he would make with his parents, even across town, and older Filipino women getting all excited making up the guest beds and fluffing up pillows and planning elaborate breakfasts the next morning. His mother had been the same way with visitors, especially kin.

The next day, he bought things like caps and stuffed animals from a casino gift shop for the Filipino couples. He regretted it later, as they drove down from the mountains, since he didn't want them to think that he thought of them as children. The fact is, he decided, they were just material for a story. He decided that the time he had spent with them was nice, but it was kind of cloying, too, like when he napped on a couch at their house one gloomy and rainy afternoon earlier in the week and Carmen placed a light blanket on him from his shoulders to his feet. He was leaving shortly and he was never going to see them again. They would simply take their places in the part of his brain reserved for Pleasant Small Memories, behind or next to the nets and swirls of his past.

• • •

The day before he left Sacramento, he thought about getting a photo of the Tracys and the two Filipino couples together. A part of him wanted to do it. Another part of him told him to cut his losses and forget it, *don't elicit more than you have to*. He wound up going to the Tracys and proposing it, and they looked at him open-mouthed. There was a definite raw edge in Irene Tracy's voice when she said, "Where do you think you are? In Mister Rogers' Neighborhood? No, we are not going to take any pictures with people we don't know. And we are definitely not going to take pictures with people not of our own race. Why would we do that? Can you believe this guy asking us this?"

Rudy Tracy had a sour look on his face. "Yeah, you've gone too far," he told Michael. "We've talked to you for your story. What's in it for us? You'll probably write nasty things about us anyway. I never liked the press. Reeny, I'm taking a nap."

"Okay, hon." Irene Tracy watched him protectively as he walked down the hall to the master bedroom, and then with a scowl on her face she escorted Michael to the door.

"Do you really think these things just go away?" she said.

"Things?"

"Somewhere out there, there's a family who is doing exactly what we did to the Safflers. Mind you, we didn't do all the things that the Court said we did, but, yes, we did some of those things. But somewhere out there, some family is getting the same shit from someone else, except they are doing things far worse than my husband and me ever did or could ever do. And no one is doing a thing about it."

"I don't know. I think God gets around to all of these miserable situations in one way or another, and He cleans house."

"When God cleans house, what does he do about fencesitters like you?"

"I think," Michael said, because he did not want her to get the last word in, "He gradually breaks down all their fears."

She had the last word anyway. She said it so softly that Michael thought she was probably talking to herself rather than directing it at him: "Do you really think we've changed?" she said with a cackle. "Honey, we're like a car idling."

• • •

On Michael's last day, he told the two Filipino couples that he wanted to see the Sacramento Delta and asked them to be his guides. It was merely a ruse, since he knew Sicoy wanted to make the trip, which was thirty miles give or take, but Romeo's old car, which could hardly get to the nearby Safeway and back, wasn't all that reliable on the winding levee roads. So the five of them piled into Michael's rental and traveled to the river, along the narrow roads, past small towns and drawbridges, huge orchards and small corn and sugar beet fields. Romeo gave Michael directions. Dominga told Michael where to stop. They parked on a safe, grassy spot on the side of the road, near some fig and walnut trees, overlooking the Sacramento River on one side and an orchard of pear trees in full blossom on the other. A soft breeze blew. Birds flew past. Sicoy's eyes were closed, but he seemed to breathe in the familiar scents that enveloped him. He stretched his body on the cool grass as if he were feeling the pull of the same soil and sky and river which he had been with nearly all of his American life. Dominga, Carmen and Romeo sat or knelt at his side and began to say the rosary very quietly. Michael began to join them, but Romeo stopped and said, "There is enough people praying, Mike. Can you sing a song?" "Can I do what?" His mind remained on the irony that he didn't seem to be needed for prayer. "How do you know I sing?" "I don't know if you sing or not. But Sicoy—he likes music."

"Well, what do I sing?"

Romeo shrugged. "Maybe something about the river?"

Michael couldn't think of any song having to do specifically with the Sacramento River, so he began to sing the first river-type song that came to mind. He had heard a Jo Stafford recording of it when he was a lonely, bookish kid who hid out, during lunch hour, like a frightened animal, in the record listening booth of the school library of his boyhood:

Oh Shenandoah, I long to see you
Roll on, you rollin' river
Oh Shenandoah, I long to see you
Away, my heart's away, 'cross the wide Missouri

Oh Meadows warm that Spring embraces
Roll on, you rollin' river
Though I have seen a hundred places
Away, my heart's away, 'cross the wide Missouri

Oh Valley Green I am your daughter
Roll on, you rollin' river
Forever more, your faithful daughter
Away, my heart's away, 'cross the wide Missouri

It did not escape Michael that he had not changed the pronouns and didn't care what anyone was thinking while he sang. He felt an exhilaration, as if he realized for the first time that God was not with His shepherds whose heads were pointed rigidly to some awkward, emotionless horizon of perfection, but with His priests who rolled up the carpet and danced. Michael's exhilaration intensified when he saw that Sicoy was holding on. And he grasped the old man's hand. And the old man opened his eyes. And their eyes locked. And Michael knew in his soul that he would fight next to him or in his place if his friends ever needed to defend their quiet life, and that even in Chicago, many hundreds of miles away, even in the clatter of the world, he would hear the dog whistle pitch of their need.

Home

Peter Bacho

Vietnam hunted Rico over time, leaving marks of its pursuit—a piece of flesh here, a hole in his soul there. It started in 1968, just after the generals dropped acid, entered a trance, and spoke of lights shining at the ends of tunnels—a hallucination quickly snuffed by the fury of Tet. Rico was there, running for cover in the rubble of a city called Hue. Somehow he survived the carnage, the bodies piled upon bodies piled upon lies.

He even survived the rest of his tour, and resurfaced in Seattle, our hometown. He called, and one dreary morning, we sat over coffee in an old, smoky cafe near the University of Washington.

He was tired— thick, dark stubble and bloodshot eyes— but that was nothing new. I'd seen him in worse shape during the day, and wearing the same clothes he'd worn two midnights before. "Partied too hearty," he'd mumble. "Too good, too sweet, too hard to quit. So I didn't." As I studied him, I figured that back in his old haunts, he'd reverted to form.

Despite his haggard appearance, he sounded fine. He just wanted to talk. At the start we tried to pick up where we'd last left it: girls, music, cars, the old neighborhood (still poor, still rowdy). He smiled. Topics raised, discussed—loud easy teenage laughs from a big trunk of memories—and quickly discarded, pushing us too soon from our common past.

As kids we were best friends, inseparable compadres, promising to be there whenever and forever—from weddings to funerals and all points in between. "Say in your life you fuck up," Rico told me when I was thirteen. "You know, everyone hates you and you die, I'll bring you home, man, dig your hole, say a prayer and burn some incense, you know, purify your butt. Then stick you in the ground." He paused. "You can do the same for me."

I nodded. It was an odd thought for someone so young, but strangely comforting. Vietnam changed it all.

I was in first year, I said, here at the UW.

He shrugged. "I know, Buddy, maybe I'll join you."Sure. The truth was Rico hated school, and the teachers hated him. He was a hard dude, project raised by his Indian mother, his Filipino father having left for an evening stroll to Chinatown without bothering to return. At Franklin High, the teachers dogged him— too much pomade, too much attitude— and counted the days until graduation or expulsion, whichever came first. For guys like Rico, college was out of the question; their counselors kept telling them so. Two choices, they said, the military or jail.

I knew he still hated school, whatever the level. He was just talking to make me feel at ease, like we still had something in common. His hope, mine too, but neither of us was sure.

"Maybe I'll join you." Each word a piece of cork, to plug gaps between his first day in Vietnam and now. For a guy not yet twenty, he'd already seen and suffered too much.

I wasn't sure if he'd talk about the war, wasn't sure if I wanted him to. For now, Rico just stared at his coffee mug, lost in a distant, foreign zone I was happy not to know.

"Damn, Buddy," he finally said. "This is what kept me goin'." He stared at the large mug that he was squeezing with both hands. "Just sittin' here, you know, drinkin' coffee, kickin' back'n bullshittin'. Just when I'd lose it, or think I would, I'd come back here. And now I'm here, and I don't know how to act."

He paused. "Hated it, man," he finally said. "Bullshit. Figured that out quick, the whole fuckin' war. Used to think maybe somethin' good'd come outa this. That's what I used to tell m'self. But that's bullshit, too. Maybe someday LBJ come check out the crib and say, 'Sorry for the bullshit, Corporal Divina.' And I say, 'What took you so long, you pasty, big-eared cowboy motherfucker.'"

He then started to laugh, softly at first, but the sound soon rose swiftly to its apex—a loud, table-pounding, bug-eyed crescendo, full of rage and unseen wounds. I glanced at the floor, unsure of what to say.

But I had to say something. "Rico," I said softly. "Remember me? I ain't the enemy."

That seemed to calm him; he stared at me for a moment—blinking like he was trying to identify my face— then slumped in his chair like an old fighter, badly overmatched and beaten beyond sport. "Sorry, man," he mumbled. "Shit was way outa line. Sorry."

"Cool," I said as I grabbed both cups, now empty. A diversion; I needed one, we both did. What could I say next? I rose quickly and headed toward the self-serve refill stand, making sure I took my time.

"Sugar?" I asked loudly, knowing full well the recipe: two lumps well stirred, no cream.

He held up two fingers.

I could only stir so long and started to walk back, unsure what to say, but hoping for the best.

Rico let me slide. "It was hard," he said evenly as I settled in my chair. I recognized the somber tone, and knew he saved it only for serious matters. But almost two years had passed, and I wasn't so sure anymore. I looked at him, studying the lines and contours of a face I knew as well as my own. Looking for hints—a twitch, some giveaway. He was clean, no trace of that wild, unforgiving look that struck fear in childhood enemies. I figured it was gone, not likely to reappear, at least not today. I relaxed.

"The hardest part was comin' down here," he said evenly as he rolled his eyes toward tables full of young folks with long hair. A few were sneaking hostile glances at this young man who didn't fit.

"Shoulda seen the looks when I strolled in," he said.

"You ain't been back long enough," I said. "That, plus your fatigues, your haircut, and that damn Marine bulldog you got painted on your arm. Man, you hard to miss."

I started to chuckle, but stopped when I looked at Rico. He didn't hear me. "I did some foul shit," he said in a monotone, "stuff I ain't proud of. Like one time, we got hit hard, lotsa guys down. Lost friends, ace buddies. Then we found 'im, this one VC." He paused, his breath labored, his face flushed. A thin film of perspiration started to form on his upper lip and forehead. I didn't want to hear this; it rode him too hard.

"Rico."

He ignored me and continued in his monotone. "Three of us dogged 'im, man. Dude was wounded— a big hole in his shoulder—and we hurt 'im some more. By the time we was done, he was beggin' to die. Didn't understand a word but I know the look."

"Rico," I said, this time more forcefully. I gestured wildly with my hands. He ignored me.

"Took parts, man. Stripped'm like a Chevy, startin' with the ears..."

I slumped in my chair and massaged my temples, trying hard to make the grisly image disappear. If he noticed my reaction, he sure didn't show it. There was no emotion, not the slightest trace of pain or remorse.

"But they can't judge me," he continued, "'cause they ain't got no right. I was there for them—with their safe, smug-assed lives and their daddies' accounts—doin' fucked up things. Livin' like some hunted animal. And they had the nerve to give me these looks, like I was a criminal. But no one said nothin', least not yet, least not to my face..."

I wondered as I listened—each bitter word corroding our bond—do I still know him? Do I stay or leave? For a moment I wasn't sure as I tried to reconcile the present and the past. Recollection brought resolve as I remembered childhood scenes and lessons learned. In our world, friendship meant loyalty, simple as that. Whatever happened in Vietnam, Rico was still my friend.

"Rico," I said sharply and grabbed his sleeve. The move surprised him.

"Huh?" he said, as he yanked his arm back.

"You out now, man," I whispered. "Outta the jungle."

He stared at me and blinked. For a moment, his eyes showed no sign of recognition. Finally, he sighed. "Maybe not, man," he said softly. "Been thinkin' and I figured it out. Growin' up like we did, we was screwed. 'Ceptin' I took it one step further and screwed myself. Now I'm bringin' it home."

I nodded. He sipped his coffee.

"Coulda died there," he said with a shrug. "Maybe shoulda, but so what? Wouldn't a mattered no damn way." He took another sip. He said that by coming home he'd come to grasp a disturbing truth: in this, his hometown, none of it would've mattered. He felt that no one— except his family, me, and a few other friends— would have cared, or cried, or even known his name.

"Just like before," he shrugged. "Ain't nothing changed."

"But you can change it," I said. "Man, with GI, you got college."

"You got college," he said bitterly. His tone surprised me. "Killers don't go to college," he said as he drifted back to the zone.

"Greg, John, Henry..." He was speaking softly now, reverently, almost whispering this litany of names that I knew by heart. They were young Filipinos like

Rico and me, draftees from a poor neighborhood that the war hit hard. Most made it back from Vietnam, a few didn't. Like Rico, they went to public high schools. Voc class, their counselors said, *since you got no future anyway*. For those who didn't go to college, voc class was a holding pen on the road to the draft.

Me? I was lucky. My mom had a dream. She was a recent immigrant from the Philippines and didn't know any better. College, she said, to avoid your father's blood-money life of cannery and field. That meant Catholic schools, but she was willing to pay the price. Scrub floors, cut hair, whatever.

So she did, and in high school I found myself learning from the feared Christian Brothers, big rough Irishmen whose vow of celibacy soured further their bad dispositions. Still, it was a minor flaw, because in the end I had choices, something Rico never did.

"... Teddy, Norman, Vic, Eddie," he droned. "Shit," he said. "Eddie didn't make it."

"I know," I said solemnly.

"Check it out, man," he said. "Saw Teddy there in Saigon. Eddie, too. Remember Eddie? Big lipped, fat head, can't walk without trippin' Eddie?"

I nodded as Rico recalled the memory of our homely, awkward friend. "Teddy says he gonna help 'im out, throw down some coin if he got to. Eddie's first taste."

Rico smiled then stared at me. "Then a week later, Eddie's gone. Boy never had no kinda luck. Probably messed up in Saigon, too'n died a virgin."

"Damn," he sighed and sipped from his coffee. "A fuckin' virgin, man," he whispered. "Died a teenage fuckin' virgin."

As Rico slowly shook his head, I sat silent, edgy, without a reply. He'd have to finish, and I'd just have to ride it wherever it was going.

"Man, seeing 'em in Saigon, what's the chances? Just like home. Everyone's there..." He chuckled— hollow and joyless—then looked at me, his gaze burning through the present to recall too soon each detail of the past.

"'Ceptin' you, Buddy," he said quietly. "'Ceptin' you."

I shivered. His accusation demanded my response. He was testing me—like he'd tested others—and in the process, had crossed a line we both knew from childhood. Friend or not, I had to come back. Hard.

"Rico," I said calmly, "we'll talk about it, but not here. You got shit to say,

say it there." I nodded toward the door.

I rose quickly and turned to walk away. Rico just stared. He said nothing and made no move to follow.

Once outside I waited, a bit nervous, hoping he wouldn't show. There was a gulf between us, that much was clear. But old friendships die hard, and he was still my friend.

After a few minutes I glanced at my watch. Ten minutes till class. I started walking toward campus, knowing that if I hustled, I could still make it.

This was my first year of college. Mom's dream, mine too. I didn't want to be late.

• • •

It was easy to get lost at the UW, with its spacious and beautiful evergreen campus—prettier than the picture on its brochure— its crowded classes and arrogant, impersonal professors. It was easy to forget a troubled friendship, to ignore the devils that chased Rico while I chased a dream. But even then, buried as I was in books and papers, I'd surface to pause and think, and mourn a wounded bond. I promised myself I'd call, make the first move to reconcile, but later, after this mid-term, this report, this final. I never made that call, didn't have to.

One evening near the end of spring term, Rico just showed up at my dorm. He was clean shaven and neatly dressed, a long-sleeve shirt hid the bulldog on his arm. "Thought I'd visit," was all he said with a sheepish what-can-I-say grin. It was all he needed. I dropped my books and we talked through the night.

Rico claimed he was better now, that each new day meant another one away from hell. He figured it was progress. To help speed the process, he'd done the unthinkable by enrolling in school, a jc, where, for the first time, he was taking his studies seriously. He had no idea where he was going, but wasn't in a rush. His GI bill covered tuition plus provided a stipend, not much, but enough to buy more time away from hell. At the end we parted friends, not like before, but better than the recent past. At least it was a start.

Over the next few weeks, we saw each other a couple more times, more in passing—a quick cup of coffee, lunch on the run— than anything else. We were both buried in finals, but agreed to meet when they ended and hang out just like the old days.

When exams ended, Rico was gone. I called his mom's house. No luck. He left two weeks earlier. No warning, or word to anyone of his destination, if there was one. She said she'd call me if she heard. I sighed when I hung up the phone. Vietnam was still too close; the devils, I figured, were closing in.

I didn't hear from Rico until September, when I received a card postmarked Boston. "Had to leave, Buddy," Rico wrote. "Explain later."

He never did explain. The best I got were postcards with no return address, care of my mom's house. Ours was a cryptic one-way correspondence, a few scrawled lines proving he was still alive.

The next card was from Missoula. Urban/rural, I figured, he's comparing the two, looking where to settle. Then came several from big cities—from LA, New York, and Chicago—followed by two from postmarked dots on the map like Dickinson, North Dakota and Marysville, California. I'd kept all his cards in a shoebox, all arranged in chronological order.

On my wall, hung a map of the US on which I'd marked and dated each city and burg, straight red lines joining one to another. At the start, I wondered: Did he have a geographic preference? Was there a pattern? The jumble of lines said no; Rico was running. I wondered when he'd stop?

Maybe he already had.

After Marysville, the cards suddenly stopped coming. As months of silence turned into one then two years, I didn't know if Rico was well, or even alive. I called his house. "Gone," his mother said. "Just like his dad. Your guess's good as mine."

Even Kitty, his favorite sister, couldn't help. No word, she shrugged.

There was nothing to do but wait and hope that somehow he was still on the move, that the devils hadn't won. They hadn't, at least as of September 1973, when I finally received a card. Judging from the postmark, Rico was in Santa Fe. Unlike his previous brief messages, this one was expansive—three full paragraphs. He apologized for his silence, but explained he'd found a woman. He was thinking of bringing her home, having her meet family and friends. Marriage was next, he said, and would I be his best man? Of course, I thought, but had no way to convey my acceptance. Just like the other cards, this one had no return address.

As always, I'd just have to wait. Still, this was good news, the best in years, but with a shelf life of one month. In October, Rico wrote again, this time from

Miami. "Messed up," he said. "Keep trying 'til I get it right."

Miami was the last one, not just for 1973, but for several more years. It was a period during which I'd managed to graduate from law school, married and divorced, and entered and left law and other professions. Throughout this time, there was no word from Rico and frankly, I'd stopped thinking about him, except for those rare occasions when I'd see Kitty or another family member.

When asked about her brother, Kitty would just shrug. Same with the others. No word, same as before. I sensed Kitty was getting tired of the question; the last time I saw her, I didn't even ask.

Even if he was still alive, Rico had died to those he'd left behind. I'd moved on, my memory of him slipping to the point that I was starting to forget details of the events we'd shared. These I used to recall with precision and fondness. Now, each time I replayed the tape, they changed. I knew that over time they'd change again. And again. I 'd forget words, actions, emotions that once made our friendship strong.

Rico stayed dead until a drizzly September afternoon in 1988, more than nineteen years after he left town. I was sitting alone in my apartment, listening to the rain and the drone of a baritone radio voice. I'd been thinking about him, maybe because I was nearing a mid-point of sorts, my thirty-eighth year, a melancholy mark on the line somewhere between hope and the grave. As kids, we used to celebrate birthdays, his and mine, with great abandon, trying to squeeze in every second of those magic twenty-four hours. And now, between marriages, and near the end of another unsatisfactory career (I swore I'd quit teaching math to ninth grade assholes), I suddenly wished Rico was here, just hanging out.

Two days later, on the day of my birth, I dropped by my parents. Mom always treated my birthday much more seriously than I. She hugged me and gave me the rundown on the invitees, which included immediate family (father, brother, and sister), plus a list of shirttail relations that grew with each passing year. After parading me in front of these new and vaguely remembered faces, she whispered in my ear. "You got a card on the kitchen table," she said. "It's from Rico, but I thought he was dead."At first I was silent, too stunned to reply. "He was," I finally said.

I rushed to the kitchen to see an oversize postcard featuring the garish lights of Reno at night. Quickly I flipped it over, skipped the message, and started at the end. Rico's initials, no doubt.

Then the beginning. He said he was wishing me happy birthday, seeing as how he'd overlooked a few. It was almost twenty years since he'd left; he needed to come home. He was missing friends and family plus more— the mountain skyline, clear rivers and lakes. The beauty of the place— I knew what he meant. And because of it, folks from here tolerate the rain, an eight-month squall. They don't wander much, and if they do, the direction's circular.

It was Rico's time to come home.

The card lifted the pall on this, the first day of my thirty-eighth year. I managed to even enjoy the party despite the crush of strangers and the personal inquiries Filipinos so dearly love. Sample Question: "Where's your wife?" Sample Answer: "She left me."

At the end, I took the card with me back to my apartment. Somewhere in my closet was an old shoebox. Tonight it would house a new tenant. I hoped it would be the last.

• • •

The rest of 1988 passed without a word; by year's end, I'd given up hope. Then in January Kitty called. Rico was dead, killed in a flophouse fire in Stockton, California. (Stockton? Our immigrant fathers were there in the thirties and forties, bent low over asparagus rows, some drooping from the heat. Slave wages, slave lives. They got smart and left, but Rico returned.)

Kitty wasn't sure of the details, just what the coroner told her. He was almost a John Doe, a body burned so bad it took awhile to find out who he was. His family was planning to ship what was left home, to Seattle, for burial. She wanted to know if I'd be there for the funeral, nothing fancy, she said, just family and a few friends.

I said I would.

Rico would be burieed in a cemetery atop Capitol Hill. It was an especially beautiful spot, quiet and still, from which could be seen mountains on two sides, and closer, deep blue lakes that almost touched the base of the hill. On the morning of the burial, I walked with Kitty to the grave. There, an old priest, possibly bothered by the cold, rushed through the prayers. It seemed we'd just arrived, and suddenly, the ceremony was over. It was an odd, indifferent end. I looked at Kitty, who pulled me toward her.

"Rico left you something," she whispered. "Before he died, he'd given a lady friend a box of stuff for each of us. She called and said that he'd given it to her the week before the fire. Made her promise she'd send it if anything happened. Got it yesterday." Kitty handed me a small box wrapped in newspaper, no larger than a fist. My first name was in the right-hand corner.

"Damn," I said softly, and put it in my coat pocket.

Kitty and I walked toward the gate, where we parked. She joined her family, while I headed toward my car. As I drove away, I wondered about the box. What did it contain? What message from the dead? Did I even want to find out? I sighed. Decisions could wait on a cup of coffee, which on this morning had to be strong and black, no cream or sugar. I drove toward the UW and the nearby coffee shop where, on a cold, cloudy morning much like this, Rico and I once sat.

• • •

Between sips of black coffee and puffs of smoke, I stared at the packet that lay on the table before me. I couldn't imagine its contents, not even after a third cup and the near exhaustion of my pack of Marlboros. Apprehension had checked curiosity to create gridlock. After several hours, the packet was still sealed. This couldn't go on. Whatever it was, it was also my friend's last word. I owed it to Rico to open it, but at the cemetery, not here.

• • •

As I walked slowly toward Rico's grave, I started to shake, but not from the cold. I slowed but didn't stop, because I knew if I did, I wouldn't continue. "Damnit," I screamed from some black psychic hole; I hoped that a noise so fierce and focused would purge my fear, or at least suppress it enough to keep me moving. It must have worked. I soon found myself ten feet from Rico's freshly filled grave.

On the headstone, I gently lay the box and opened it quickly, before I could change my mind. On top was a note and a medal, a Silver Star resting on a tiny cardboard bed. I paused to stare at the medal; he'd never mentioned courage. I then grabbed the note and walked to the base of a nearby pine.

Since you're reading this, guess I didn't make it home. Least some stuff did, part of which I'm proud of. Take care of it.

I exhaled. Not too bad, nothing too eerie. Just two items. I'd fold up the note and put it in the shoebox, maybe the same for the Silver Star. Simple. I returned to the grave to pick up the medal.

As my fingers nudged the cardboard, it gave way. There was more at the bottom of the box. I removed the cardboard and a flat, tiny bundle, about the size of a dime, wrapped in gauze, which I quickly peeled back. I gasped as my fingers touched a black piece of something shriveled, drained, and pressed. It might have been flesh, maybe part of an earlobe.

I dropped the bundle and stepped away from the grave, curses trumpeting my retreat. I stopped, lit up a smoke, and nervously started to circle the bundle, first left to right then reverse. I had no idea what Rico wanted, or what I should do next.

I might be circling still, but for a loose piece of sod on a fresh grave adjacent to Rico's. My right foot rode it as it quickly gave way. I first tried to steady myself, but I realized it was too late. My unplanned momentum was too fast. So I relaxed to prevent injury, and just accepted the fall. When I landed, I was eye level with the hated bundle, maybe two feet away.

As I lay there, I started to laugh—it was hard not to—and fished for a smoke. I slowly sat up and lit my last cigarette. The slapstick tumble, which had ruined my slacks and removed my dignity, had also stolen my fear. I just sat there, trying to focus through tiny swirls of smoke on what Rico wanted.

Bring him home, I thought. But how? I scanned the years of our friendship, especially our time as kids. I started to recall with unusual clarity a conversation in which he'd promised to bury me. It was an odd thought then, less so now. I'd promised the same.

I rose and walked to Rico's grave where I picked up the medal and placed it gently on the headstone. It belonged here and nowhere else; he'd earned it. Next, I put the bundle and the letter inside the box, which I then lay on his grave.

"Fire to purify," I said, and lit the four corners before stepping back to watch the small flame flare toward a darkening, afternoon sky. The fire rose then fell, leaving embers then ashes— then nothing more.

It was dusk when I started to walk slowly toward the entrance. Outside the gate, a streetlight's glare and the sound of cars signaled that life moved on. I would join it soon, and gladly, but not before turning one last time in the direction of Rico's grave. In the distance, the running lights of small boats shimmered on the lake and beyond, the jagged white tips of the Cascade silhouette lingered against the onset of night. A gift for the senses, a gift to my friend. Reason enough to come home.

Elvis of Manila

Eric Gamalinda

He looked at himself in the bathroom mirror and felt a twinge of remorse. The lightbulb over his head hissed like a heckler, casting a pale, jaundiced sheen over his unshaven face.

"I'm not going out on that stage tonight," he called out to someone in the bedroom.

"Of course you are," a woman answered him. "Everyone will be disappointed if you don't show up. You're the star of the show." Her last—encouraging—statement was immediately drowned out by the whir of a hair dryer.

"Let Mario Lanza be the star this time," he said, rubbing his chin. "He deserves a break."

"Honey, Mario Lanza died two years ago. Don't you remember? Choked on a piece of steak. Champagne brunch at the Odyssey. We were *there*."

He stared at his face, remembering. Then, without taking his eyes off the mirror, he stripped his shirt off and pinched his love handles. "The Everly Brothers then," he said. "They're still around, aren't they?"

"Honey, the Everly Brothers were never as big as you."

"Or that new girl, Barbra Streisand."

The hum of the dryer stopped. "She *is* good," the woman in the bedroom said. "Sounds so much like Barbra. I swear, I can't tell sometimes if she's actually singing or just lip-synching, you know?"

"There you go," he said, and began to shave. "Let her steal the show."

In the mirror he saw the woman walking into the bathroom. Her hair had been teased to a kind of pouf. Her face was pale and pasty; she was holding a matte pressed powder case in her hand. She walked behind him and ran the other hand against his bare back. "Honey," she said. "*Nobody* steals the show from Elvis."

For close to a decade he was the Elvis Presley of Manila. Not just an Elvis— for there were hundreds of Elvises all over the archipelago, including a novelty act from Baguio who once sang *Blue Suede Shoes* dressed in feathered headgear and loincloth. He was *the* Elvis. Patsy and Pugo, the hosts of the talent search program *Tawag ng Tanghalan*, proclaimed him no less after he beat a succession of pretenders for eight consecutive weeks. Immediately after winning the grand prize, Sampaguita Pictures signed him up, and he swivelled his hips and snarled seductively for a good number of box office hits.

He was going to be immortal. He knew it, watching the *colegialas* squeal and faint in the studios of Channel 9. He could feel it in his bones when they went on tour, out in barrios light years away from Manila where farm maidens swooned as he gyrated on *entablados* festooned with buntings and balloons. He went stumping on the campaign trail with a succession of politicians, and no shift in political power ever faded his star. He told Manila to vote for Lacson, and they did. Then he told them to vote for Villegas, and Lacson was out. He sang , for Marcos, and Marcos returned the favor by giving him top billing at his inaugural ball, where Imelda, despite a butterfly-sleeved *terno* that seemed to make all movement impossible, danced the twist with him for a couple of minutes. And when Marcos declared martial law in 1972, he was still on centerstage, urging people to support the New Society.

Soon after that, however, for reasons he could never fathom, Elvis—the *real* Elvis—went out of style. No, worse: he became *baduy*. Disco edged him out of the clubs, the restaurants, the cocktail bars along Roxas Boulevard, the dance floors of swanky hotels. His records disappeared from the shops, only to resurface in bargain bins along Calle Raon, where they sold two for the price of one. Kids cringed and giggled whenever *Love Me Tender* crooned over the radio. They thought it was too sentimental; they thought Elvis was too *smooth*. And the real Elvis had turned ugly and bloated like a stuffed turkey in Memphis, where nothing was happening.

He, however, remained Elvis of Manila. He could never shake that image, just as Elvis could never stop being Elvis. Once he got invited to perform at the noontime television extravaganza, *Student Canteen*. To his horror he was presented in a series of novelty acts, all of them clones. There was James Taylor of the Philippines, all nasal twang and hair. And then a sorry copy of the Village People who sang the Village People's songs—in Tagalog. And then two sets of the Eagles, both of them rendering *Hotel California* as faultlessly as the original.

111

Sometime after that, he met his future wife, a lab technician from Malabon, and he decided to give up being Elvis. It all happened naturally, not unlike molting, and with very little ceremony—he woke up one morning and decided, with little forethought, to shave off his sideburns. When he saw Lally later that afternoon, she merely remarked, "You shaved."

"Yes," he said.

"It looks good," she said.

Not that she wasn't interested in his career, or his history. She was young then, and she wanted a life, which meant a life beyond his being Elvis. She kept an album of his interviews and press shots and sometimes they looked at it and he told her stories about the crowds, the politicians, the midnight trips to nowhere. She liked it when hairdressers at Minda's Beauty Shoppe gasped, "You're married to Elvis of Manila?" But she felt relieved when that phase was over. She kept the album on a shelf, like a relic.

And Elvis of Manila felt he was transforming, but the transformation was gradual and painful. He welcomed it nonetheless, because when the crowds lost interest in him, he lost interest in the business. It was like that, he kept telling himself. You can't love with a one-way mirror. He wanted to get a job, but people kept telling him Elvis shouldn't be working as a sales clerk or an insurance agent. Finally, his wife got a post in a food lab in Encino, California, and they packed their bags and left the country one rainy day in August. He accompanied her on a tourist visa, but it was easy to stay on in those days, and lawyers were more than willing to take his case. He found a job as a filing clerk in a travel agent's office right next to Lally's lab. People in the Filipino grocery stores in Los Angeles still recognized him, but as the months wore on they got tired of yelling, "Hoy, Elvis!" and let him shop in peace. Soon he became not Elvis, but his real self, and he no longer felt uneasy writing his own name: Eddie Valdez. One evening he sat alone in their apartment in Encino and wrote his name over and over, saying it under his breath like a mantra, or a mike test.

He was happy being Eddie Valdez until the Filipino community, or the ragtag, nebulous diaspora that represented it, decided to stage Nostalgia Night at the Civic Center in Pasadena and called for a meeting three months before the concert. The show was for the benefit of the victims of the eruption of Mount

Pinatubo. Nobody knew where Mount Pinatubo was except that it was making summer ten degrees hotter in Southern California, but they all pitched in: the Tribung Iloko, the Bisaya Confederation, the Veterans' Association and the Filipino Christian Renewal Association, among others.

The benefit was being coordinated by Sweetheart Pantig, who had immigrated to California around the time that Eddie Valdez and his wife did. They had known her from way back when they played marathon mah-jong sessions in her duplex in the Valley. Sweetheart was a mean mah-jong player and had wiped out many a Manila celebrity's savings.

"Where are you getting the money to put up the show this time, ha?" someone was asking Sweetheart when Eddy Valdez and his wife walked into the conference room of the Civic Center.

"Oy, I sued the nursing home that was taking care of my mother, they were treating her like garbage, *puta*, "Sweetheart replied. "Oy, here comes Elvis."

"You look as gorgeous as ever," Eddie Valdez said, bussing her on both cheeks. "You don't look a day older." Sweetheart must have gained fifty pounds since her recent hysterectomy.

"Oy, Lally," Sweetheart said. "You watch your husband. He hasn't lost his touch. All the matronas will be running after him."

"Let them find their own Elvis," Lally said, walking towards a service tray burdened with rice cakes. There was little she could do to hide her annoyance every time Sweetheart, or anybody, teased them like that. "Is this *puto* real?" she asked, to change the subject.

"*Loka*, nobody makes real *puto* in America," Sweetheart said. "They're flour cakes. Very good, though. Shirley made them." The woman she referred to, a tiny, elderly lady sitting in an armchair, waved a tiny, ring-encrusted hand at Lally.

"Shirley *Temple?*" Lally gasped.

The elderly lady smiled and nodded her head. She primped her hair more out of reflex than vanity—her once much-envied peroxide ringlets which she flaunted in the heyday of Sampaguita Pictures were now clipped shore. Beside her, sitting in another armchair and vigorously waving a fan across her face, was Carmen Miranda, once the rage of Philippine television, but now, thanks to plastic surgery performed during a visit to Manila, a raspy matron with her face pulled back to a look of perpetual surprise. Next to her were the Everly Brothers, Juanito and Alberto, who still had enough hair to sculpt into teddy boy waves with megahold gel, but who had both gained considerably around the girth. (Rumor had it, Sweetheart later confided to Lally, that they could only perform with their guitars tilted upwards, against their beer bellies, like a koto.) Then there was John Travolta, who had won the title in *Student Canteen* and even danced for Denny Terio during the semifinals of *Dance Fever* in Manila. And there was a younger performer whose name was Anna Marie Lepanto. She could sing any song, even Tagalog *kundiman*, like Barbra Streisand, and for the show she would-n't mind being called Barbra of the Philippines, even if she had lived in California since she was seven.

They discussed the line-up of performers—including Filipino versions of Matt Monroe, Simon and Garfunkel, the Four Tops and Bob Dylan ("Ay," Sweetheart exclaimed, "he's better than Bob Dylan—he can *sing*!"). But when they began discussing the sequence of performances, they reached an impasse, because Carmen Miranda wanted to be the finale.

"No," Shirley Temple insisted, "Elvis should be the finale. Rock 'n' roll is a hard act to follow."

"We're not talking about acts," Carmen Miranda protested. "We're talking about who the people want to see most. I've been in more than two dozen films, many of them with Leopoldo Salcedo. I am not *just* Carmen Miranda."

"I've been in movies myself," Shirley Temple said.

"When you were a little *girl*, Shirley," Carmen Miranda said. "That's how they *remember* you."

"But if I hadn't come to the States—"

"Coming here had nothing to do with it," Carmen Miranda said. "You either last or you don't—"

"I was just trying to be helpful," Shirley Temple said. Tears were beginning to well in her eyes, not unlike the way they did when she made audiences cry in movie theaters.

"All right," Sweetheart cut in. "We'll draw lots."

"You're kidding," protested Carmen Miranda.

"It's the only way," said Sweetheart. "I don't want any hard feelings here. We're doing this for a *cause*."

They threw their names in a Tupperware bowl, including those of the absent performers, and finally drew a list. The Everly Brothers were to open the show, followed by Shirley Temple, then Simon and Garfunkel, Matt Monroe, the Four Tops, Barbra Streisand, Bob Dylan, and John Travolta. Carmen Miranda would follow, and the show would close with Elvis. The line-up seemed satisfactory for most, though predictably Carmen Miranda stormed out of the meeting and threatened to convince her fellow Ilocanos to boycott the show.

As they filed out of the room, Anna Marie Lepanto walked beside Eddie Valdez and said, "I'm so glad you get to close the show. I mean, Carmen Miranda's probably OK, but she seems a bit, like, *dated*."

Lally slipped her arm around Eddie's and said, "Honey, you chose the perfect word."

"Have you ever been to Graceland?" Anna Marie wanted to know. "I mean, for research or whatever. You being Elvis and all."

"No," Eddie Valdez said. "I wanted to, but it just seemed so—well, distant—"

"We wanted to go there for our second honeymoon," Lally interrupted him. "But we went to Las Vegas instead. We won six hundred dollars on the slot machine."

"Oh, how wonderful," Anna Marie said.

"Beginner's luck," Lally said.

Later that evening, as though she were merely continuing the thread of the conversation some hours ago, Lally told Eddie, "That was some honeymoon, wasn't it?"

"What?" Eddie Valdez said. He was trying on a pair of leather jeans and was struggling to zip the fly.

"Las Vegas," said Lally. "I still can't believe we won all that money."

"Sent by God," Eddie said.

"She's a nice girl, that Anna Marie," Lally said.

"Who?"

"The Barbra Streisand girl."

"Goddamn!" Eddie Valdez gave up pulling at the zipper.

"You've got two months to lose weight," Lally said. "You can do it."

"I wonder how Elvis did it," Eddie said, slipping the leather jacket on. He faced the mirror and looked at himself critically. "Do you think we should have gone to Graceland instead?"

"If we did, we would have ended up dirt poor," Lally said.

"We would have found a way to make ends meet," Eddie Valdez said. "We knew how to make money." But she was right. They used their winnings in Las Vegas to pay for two months' rent, because most of Lally's salary went to Eddie's immigration lawyers. How grateful he was to her back then, and—although he seldom acknowledged it—how disconcertingly dependent. But that didn't really matter. When they first arrived in America he not only stopped being a public figure. He became a shadow. He lived in the buffer zone of total anonymity, and could be anything he wanted to be.

That was long ago. *That was long ago* was something you said when things were beginning to change in your life, he thought. But he was in those moments before that, before things changed. He wanted change, and the thought filled him with trepidation, because he didn't know what he wanted to change into. "You know, I could really be Elvis all over again," he said to himself, and looked back to see if Lally had heard. But she was already in the bedroom, asleep before the TV, which had been left talking to itself.

On the night of the show he felt he was going to die. When was the last time he stood before a crowd? At Plaza Miranda, during one of the martial law anniversaries. No—at the Catholic Church in Encino, one Sunday, when the parish priest requested them to introduce themselves to the community of Filipino and Latino faithful. But that was different. He felt like he had walked into a party where he knew nobody, but the effusive camaraderie, superficial as a Sunday bazaar, soon engulfed him in the suffocating comfort of belonging. Tonight's performance, in comparison, was going to be hell. Why? Because Nostalgia Night was drawing bedroom communities from as far south as San Diego and as far north as Daly City. Because he had to show that once upon a time, in the Manila that everybody had forgotten, Elvis was alive and immortal as a pulsar....

But by the time Simon and Garfunkel were strumming away onstage, his trepidation turned to panic. It didn't let up even as each number was boisterously applauded. People threw roses at Anna Marie Lepanto. Some sang along with Bob Dylan. And someone—a distant, disembodied voice from the balconies—shrieked shamelessly when John Travolta wiggled onstage.

"Good crowd, ha?" Carmen Miranda said to him as they stood by the wings. Even she seemed to be in high spirits, and conceding the finale to him—deftly negotiated by Sweetheart Pantig just a few days before the concert—seemed totally bygone. "People miss us, that's why," she said.

That was what he heard in his head the moment he went onstage. *People miss us.* But surely there was something else. When I swing my hips, he thought, the women in the orchestra seats scream and swoon, as though that gesture turned some automatic switch on. When I snarl, the faces in the front rows, all bathed in the garish stage lights, melt to sighs. Nobody can sing *Jailhouse Rock* like me. That's why I was Elvis of Manila. That's why everybody got lost in the bog of obscurity. That's why I'm here and they're some place I don't want to be: nowhere.

That feeling kept mounting to a crescendo even after the rousing curtain calls, even as they gathered backstage after the show and embraced one another with both elation and relief. He felt he was swirling in a daze, drunk and young and carefree. He looked around for Lally, but she was still in the orchestra rows, accepting kudos from friends. Anna Marie Lepanto, holding a bouquet of roses, walked to him and said, "You were the best." She planted a kiss, firm and confident, on his lips, her body pressed so close he could feel her warmth rising to him like a strong perfume. "I hope we see each other again," she said, as she placed a rose in his trembling hand. He stared at the rose and it seemed to enclose him in a cocoon of stillness while everything whirled around him: in that single flower was encapsulated the change that he knew was happening, now, in the eyes of the whole world, but only he could see it unfolding. He looked up and saw Anna Marie walking away, and wondered why he was filled with so much longing.

Then he saw Lally and started walking in her direction. But before he could reach her, a swarm of youngsters crowded around him, asking for his autograph. They were teenagers from one of the local high schools, and they were all dressed identically, with homeboy buzz cuts and oversized jeans.

"Man, that was *awesome*," one of the kids told him. "How long have you been doing that act?"

"A long time," he said. "Long before you were born."

"It's *great*, man," the boy continued. "Like, me and my friends, we were rolling down the aisles, you know? Like, it was *wild*."

"Glad you liked it," Eddie said.

"Hey," the boy continued, "I don't mean to put anybody down. I mean, I thought everyone was funny and shit, but you were the funniest of them all, man. Like, you were hysterical, man. You got real talent."

Later that evening, after all the wine, the food, and the interminable good-byes, Eddie Valdez and his wife trudged up to their apartment in Encino. They walked straight to the bedroom, as was their habit. With their backs to each other, they changed into loose, frumpy, comfortable clothes—a cotton duster with lace hemming for her, boxer shorts and a loose undershirt for him. It was this transformation of apparel that delineated the borderzone between their life and the rest of the world, and it was a ritual that never failed to give them some sense of relief. Lally turned the coffeemaker on—only out of habit, because she wanted to slip right into bed but saw him sitting under the lamp in the living room.

"Best show you ever had," she said.

"Yes, it was," he said.

She turned the Panasonic player on and slipped in a tape of Elvis Presley standards. He smiled and tapped his feet to the music, but when she went into the kitchen to get the coffee, he pulled the tape out and was still looking for another when she came back.

"Didn't you like that one?" she asked him.

"I want to listen to something else," he said. But he didn't know what he wanted to listen to. Nothing. Silence. But it was never silent in Encino, at least not where they had lived since they first came here. There was always something that precluded even the idea of silence: the rumbling of traffic, the wailing of sirens, the chopping of helicopters beaming lights on runaway cars. When they first came here, he sat up all night listening to all the noises, still unable to believe that they had moved to another world.

Two Deaths

Marianne Villanueva

In September my mother came again, this time bringing my sister's three children back to New York for the start of school. It was different this time. This time I didn't look forward to her coming, I don't know why. It seemed to me during this visit that my mother talked endlessly. Once she shocked me by carrying around the picture of my dead sister that I had framed and put on the mantelpiece. Then she looked at it for long moments, sometimes rubbing a forefinger over the dusty glass.

In the picture, which is black and white, my sister looks slender and charming. It was a way she sometimes used to look, though not often. In her last years, she was gaining weight and tended to look puffy. But in the picture she looks very nice. I have one just like it on my desk at work.

When the time came for my mother to go, I didn't ask her extend her stay. I suppose I should have; I guessed this was what she might have been waiting to hear. And as the days dragged on and my mouth remained stopped up, my mother's face began to acquire a disappointed look. We said nothing to each other, however. When I took her to the airport, I didn't even park the car. Just dropped her off at the curb, gave her a quick hug, and hopped back on the freeway. I remember looking behind me once in the rear view mirror, but the view of my mother was obscured by other people and moving vehicles.

Then I heard from time to time about her doings in New York. Sometimes I called. Once I called on a Sunday afternoon. It must have been early evening in New York. I could hear the voices of my sister's children in the background. Arguing about something. I imagined the twilight creeping down the avenues, the muffled noise of traffic. She said, "Oh, where were you, where were you?" She'd been trying to reach me all afternoon, she said.

"I was at the office," I said. "I have so much work."

"Oh," she said. "I called and called, but no one answered the phone."

"Why? What's wrong?" I said.

"Well," she said, "They went to the park, and I said it's better that *sila na lang*, you know what I mean, three is a crowd, I didn't want to be *asungot*."

"What are you talking about?" I asked. "Who is 'they'?"

"Oh, you know," my mother said. "Richard and Carmen. Oh, but it hurts, it hurts."

Carmen is my brother-in-law's new girlfriend. She manages an art gallery in mid-town Manhattan. They had been seriously dating only a few weeks, just since August. She has brown hair and a deep golden tan. She looks nothing like my sister.

I imagined my mother alone in the apartment, surrounded by my dead sister's things. I wondered if her needlework were still in the drawer. Soon, I thought, my mother will start having to put them away. I thought of my sisters pretty silk dresses hanging in the closet, her shoes lined up neatly on the wooden shoe racks. While some of her shoes were very badly scuffed, others seemed barely worn. I remembered my mother telling me how once, borrowing one of my sister's coats, she'd reached into the pockets and found an old tube of lipstick, worn down almost to the stump, and wads of used kleenex. This of course made my mother cry. I remembered my reaction when my younger brother wanted to cash a Traveler's Check with my sister's signature on it. "No, no!" I cried. "Here's a hundred dollars of my own. Take it, take it!" I was beside myself.

Once, when I was visiting my brother-in-law, we wound up talking about my sister's shoes, I don't know why. Perhaps it was my first visit to the apartment after her death, and my first look at her closet. It was strange that I had never actually seen the inside of her bedroom when she was alive.

I had been amazed by the sheer quantity of her things, and especially by the neatly arrayed rows of shoes, rising along one wall from floor to ceiling. "Yes," my brother-in-law, Richard, said to me, "she hardly even used most of them, poor thing."

And it was actually hard for me to think of my sister in that way—as a "poor thing." Because actually she had never been what the nuns at our convent school might have called "good." In fact, she was rather mean. Even when we were teenagers, I can read in my old diaries about times she dragged me off my bed and kicked me or pulled my hair. But thinking of these episodes now does not fill me with bitterness. On the contrary, I am glad I have such memories, because I can say to myself that at one time I did have a sister.

It isn't true, what my mother-in-law said. She was visiting from Manila and we were talking, and the talk suddenly turned toward my sister. We were in the kitchen, and suddenly my mother said in a vehement way, "A sister like that who pulled your hair and dragged you off the bed—is that what you miss?" At first I thought: She's right. I thought no more of my sister for a few weeks. But now I think she wasn't right at all. Because in fact it is those hard slaps my sister used to deliver to my face, my arms, that makes me remember her and brings tears to my eyes. Those hard slaps and scratches—one scar still visible on the back of my left hand, after all these years.

It isn't sentimental. I don't like to sentimentalize. It isn't the same thing as my mother walking around with my sister's photo all day. It's just remembering her the way she was. She slapped me, so that's all there is to it. She also pulled my hair and, during blackouts, used to pretend she was a witch and cackle and put strong hands around my throat until I screamed. All those things she did.

And in fact, in a perverse way, I do remember her more because of those bad things. Those things I thought were purely evil. Like the time she slammed the closet door over my fingers as she saw me climbing to open the top drawer. I must have been —what?—five years old and she six. Already in her mind that obscure hatred of that Other, that Other of flesh so dissimilar from her own. Because I was bouncing and jolly and plump and easily given to smiles and laughter, my sister was a skinny little thing, with hard knees always covered in scrapes and bruises, and a small mouth my mother had to pry open with a spoon sometimes to get her to eat her vegetables. Once I'd come home from somewhere and seen my best doll, the one with the cornflower blue eyes and the curly brown hair, thrust upside down into the toilet. I howled then as if someone had actually killed me, as if a knife had actually been plunged right into my chest. There, there, there. But it was only my sister. Only the pain and confusion over having such a sister.

Now, I tell myself, it isn't wrong to slip on her pantyhose or to wear her shoes. They were the first things my mother brought over from New York. I didn't question my mother then, though I am sure I could have. I do not question her now.

The pantyhose was sheer and fragile-looking, mostly in shades of gray and blue. At first I kept them tucked away in a corner of my closet. Out of sight.

The shoes we spread out in the garage. They were in all colors: blue, green, black, red. Some were misshapen, and reminded me of my sister's feet, with their bunions and their plump toes.

The first ones I wore were brown, with straps and pointy toes. I looked in the mirror at myself wearing them. My legs suddenly looked very long and slim. "I like these," I said aloud. My mother didn't seem to take any notice.

The other shoes she gave away—to my cousin Montserrat, to our impoverished aunt whose travel agency had just gone bust. I did not like to think of my mother giving my sister's things away, but she never asked me. I saw my aunt and my cousin leaving the house, their arms bulging with paper bags.

My sister had a black sweater with a green rosette pattern. That one I wore in Vermont one weekend, and everyone exclaimed how good I looked, how "young." I felt like telling them," This is my sister's sweater. She's dead, you know. She died last year." But I thought it would be too strange. No one I know says things like that. Though saying things about my sister makes me feel good, perhaps because I did it so rarely when she was alive.

Now there are times when I find myself telling perfect strangers: "My sister died last year. Streptococcal pneumonia. It was quite a shock." Sometimes the stranger will frown and say nothing. Other times he or she will shake their heads and look concerned. Most often, they will look solicitous and say, "I'm sorry!" It's the ones who look silently mournful that I despise. Because I know it's a pretense. How could someone else possibly understand what it is like? "There, there," I feel tempted to say. "It's not your fault. I'll survive."

During my mother-in-law's last visit, she complained that I keep too many lights on in the house. She said that in Manila, everyone is trained to turn the lights off whenever they leave the room. But then, she said, "I know why you do it. It's on account of the little boy." She is referring to my son, who is six years old, and not particularly afraid of anything, not even of the dark.

I remain silent, knowing I cannot answer her, wishing to preserve some peace. But in bed at night, strange thoughts creep into my head, and one time I imagine myself saying to someone, not necessarily my mother-in-law, "Someday, someday, all the lights will be off, and then I'll be dead."

My sister, it is important to tell you, died in a Manhattan city hospital six days before Christmas 1991. The cause of death was officially listed as "sepsis" related to bacterial pneumonia.

. . .

And then, it is one year later.

I am in the Philippines, for another death. This death, somehow, in this warm climate, seeming more benign than the other one of my sister in New York, in that cold time of year.

Yet the two, each occurring thousands of miles from each other and a year apart, are somehow connected.

My father loved my sister best. This I knew only later, much later. this was confirmed when he quietly slumped over in the hospital, only a year after my sister.

In the year in between, he came to spend a few months with me in San Francisco, in the summer. He was there for an operation on his foot.

My father was a diabetic. He'd lost parts of his limbs over the years. Now what worried my mother was the right foot, where he'd already lost a big toe. Now there had been a cut that refused to heal, even after my mother diligently poured saline solution and covered it with a fresh bandage each morning and night. When he came to stay with us, parts of the foot were completely black. I marveled at my mother's nonchalance. "Perhaps," she said, "the doctor will only need to cut away a little of the flesh."

A little of the flesh? She cleaned his foot with disdain for my wild imaginings. My dreams were filled with the sight of my father's blackened foot on her lap. When she first removed the bandages and revealed it to me, I had to press my fist tight against my mouth to stop from crying out. Yet, my mother said, "This is nothing. The doctor will take care of it."

But the doctor was not available for a month. It seemed to me the foot was getting blacker. Unbeknownst to my mother, I would call the doctor's office and plead with the nurse. "Please," I would say. "This is an emergency. You should see his foot. My mother doesn't realize...it's almost completely black. But because my father doesn't complain, my mother thinks it's all right. But he doesn't feel any pain; he's a diabetic, his nerve endings may have been damaged."

The doctor finally agrees to see my father, and, yes, they have to amputate. This news almost destroys my mother. And I think: it's just his foot, no one is blaming you, you were a good nurse. But he really needs to have this done.

In the hospital in San Francisco, nightmare upon nightmare: they give my father a faulty bed, one with a side guard that will not rise. And in the middle of the night, after his operation, my father falls off. He lands on the floor with a thud which awakens his roommate, a Mr. Schmidt who is retired and lives in Marin County somewhere. Mr. Schmidt asks my father, "Are you all right? Shall I call a nurse?"

And my father says, yes, I am all right, and by who knows what test of will manages to pull himself up and back on to the bed.

The next morning, he says nothing to the nurses. He waits until my mother arrives and then tells her. She is angry, but in talking to the nurses finds no relief. The nurses are defensive. They begin to criticize her for talking to my father in Tagalog in front of them. My mother is upset, she is always upset. My parents go home. My father lives for six more months, and then he dies. A few months after Christmas. I had a letter I had started the previous September, still stuck inside my stationery pad: "Dearest Dad," it began, and then, the blank page. My father died in February.

I flew home. There was a nine-day wake and a funeral.

My father's death was a culmination. It was not tragic or shocking, in the way my sister's was. Although he was only 63 years old, we didn't expect him to live very long. We had eyes; we could see how stiffly he moved down the long corridors, groping along the walls. How his legs looked, stick-thin and pale, the color of fish bellies, as his robe dangled open. My sister's death was a further blow. How would he take it, we all wondered. I remembered him sitting by her hospital bed, his face serene—the phrase "like a Buddha" comes to mind, because of my father's girth, his inscrutable features, never marred by emotion of any kind, whether pleasure or anger. And even afterwards, when my mother told me they would need tranquilizers to get to sleep, he never talked about my sister. Even when he could hear my mother crying on her side of the bed, he never talked about my sister. He would merely shift his body slightly, so that my mother knew he was turning away from her, and that was the only sign he gave my mother that he heard her and was affected by her weeping.

And yet, I feel sure he felt her death more than my mother. My mother now carries the picture of my dead sister wherever she goes. Her wallet is stuffed with pictures of my sister. I looked in there once, and they were all the same: twenty black-and-white pictures of the same smiling face. Yet her talking doesn't shake my conviction that it was my father who loved my sister more. And that she was the one my father loved best.

• • •

Last year I received a letter from Mr. Schmidt. The letter said: "How are you? How is your father? I see your book in bookstores here. It is very nice."

I kept the letter in my handbag for weeks, waiting for the right time. Then, one afternoon, when it was bright and sunny out, when my son was at school, I took out pen and paper and began to write:

"Dear Mr. Schmidt, my father died six months after amputation of his foot. He died in Manila. His death was quick and painless and I am sure he did not suffer. My mother is a strong woman. She busies herself with piano concerts, in Manila and elsewhere. I wish you all the best. I hope you are recovering nicely."

For weeks after posting the letter, I kept expecting to hear from Mr. Schmidt. I remembered him well: a nice man, who reminded me a little of that fatherly actor on "Saint Elsewhere." But there was no more news from him.

Later, my husband told me, "It must have been a shock, your writing to him that your father died." And, yes, I think now that it must have been. And I regret the letter, and its tone. What kind of tone was that? How does one really know how to write about death?

Her Wild American Self

M. Evelina Galang

It's like my family's stuck somewhere on the Philippine Islands. My grandmother, Lola Mona, says that I'm wild as Tita Augustina. That I have that same look in my eye. A stubborness. And if I'm not careful I will be more trouble than she ever was. She says her daughter was a hard-headed Americana who never learned how to obey, never listened. Like me, she says. My family believes that telling her story will act as some kind of warning, that I might learn from her mistakes.

When she was young, Augustina wanted to be chosen. Maybe it was all those movies about Teresa and Bernadette, flying off to heaven, but she imagined she would be a modern-day saint from Chicago's north side. Sitting at her window before bedtime, she'd divided the night into decades and mysteries. The moon was a candle offering and she surrendered prayers to Mary by that light.

When she was eleven, Augustina wanted to be an altar girl. In a red robe and white gown, she dreamed of carrying the Crucifix down the aisle. Her mother wouldn't hear of it. "God loves your devotion, *hija*," she'd say. "He loves you whether or not you carry Him down the aisle at church."

To rebel, Augustina stopped going to Mass with the family. "God loves me," she'd tell her mom. "Whether or not I show up on Sundays."

Augustina's dad, Ricardo, clenched his jaw tight, spitting words through the space of his gold-capped teeth. "How can you do this to your mother?" he demanded. He gestured a bony brown finger at his wife who was collapsed on the living room sofa sobbing.

"How will this look?" her mother cried, "My own daughter missing Sunday Mass. People will talk."

Augustina tried bargaining with them. "Let me be an altar girl, let me keep playing baseball with the neighborhood kids and I'll keep going."

Mona let out a little scream. "Even worse!" she said. "Your reputation, *anak*!"

Mona dramatically curled her palm into a tight little fist, and pounded her chest, keeping time with the painful beat of her heart.

Ricardo placed Augustina into the back seat of the car, threatening to send her to the Philippines for lessons in obedience. The threats meant nothing to her. She sat in the car all during Mass, making faces at the people who'd stare into the windshield. Next Sunday, her parents let her stay home alone.

This did not sit well with the family. When Mona and Ricardo moved to America, they brought with them a trunk full of ideas—land of opportunity, home of democracy, and equality—but God forbid we should ever be like those Americans—loose, loud-mouth, disrespectful children. Augustina was already acting wild, and stubborn, opinionated too. To tame her, they sent Augustina to all-girl Catholic schools.

On her first day at Holy Angels, she walked into the cafeteria with her cold lunch—a Tupperware of leftover rice and fish. There was a long table of girls sitting near the window. Recognizing some of them from class that morning. Augustina walked over to a space at the end of the table and as she got nearer, their voices grew silent. She greeted the girls and they smiled at her. They nodded. "Mind if I sit here?" she asked. They stare at her as if Mary Mother of God had swiped their voices. They just stared. Augustina sat with them anyway. Then Colleen Donahue said, "This school's getting cramped." She was talking to the girl across from her.

"Yeah," the girl answered. "What is that smell?"

Augustina scanned the table—the girls were eating oranges and apples. Some say with nothing in front of them. She was the only one with a Tupperware of food. Then she said to the girl sitting next to her, "What kind of lipstick is that? It's wild." But the girl turned her back on Augustina as if Our Lady had plagued her.

"I think it's coming from her," said the girl as she held her nose.

Augustina looked down the row of milk-white faces, faces so pure and fresh, it was hard to tell if they were born that way, or if they'd simply scrubbed the color out of them. She looked down at her hands, at the red nail polish peeling, at her fingers stretched out stiff in front of her. She would never have a single girlfriend among them. In fact, they say, that Augustina's only real friend was her cousin Gabriel.

When Augustina got home that first day, she begged her mother to let her transfer to the neighborhood school, but her mother wouldn't listen. Instead she sat Augustina down on her bed, brushing the hair from out of her face and told her, "Your father and I work very hard to keep you in that school. It's the best, *hija*," she told her. "You'll see."

So she started hanging out with her cousin Gabriel in places they'd find disturbing. We have pictures that Gabriel took of Augustina dancing among tombs and statues of beautiful women saints at Grace Cemetery. In many of the photos, her image is like a ghost's. There's the snow-covered hills and Augustina's shock of black hair, her elephant-leg hip-huggers, moccasin-fringed vests and mid-riff tops, the scarves that sailed from the top of her head, the loose beads and bangle earrings flipping in the wind. They say her cousin Gabriel was in love with her, that he was what made her wild.

Mona used to complain to her husband, "Why does she always have to go to that place? Play among those dead people? Maybe we should have sent her to public school after all, Ricardo, or maybe we should have encouraged her friendships with those children, those boys next door." Her father, a hardworking surgeon, denied there was anything wrong. "Nonsense," he'd say, "She's a girl and she should act like one."

One night, when Augustina was sixteen, she locked the door to her bedroom, hid away from everyone. Her room was a sanctuary where Gabriel's photos plastered the walls, a row of votive candles lined her window ledge, and postcards of Lourdes and Fatima decorated her bedpost. She had built an altar of rocks from the beach up on Montrose, a tiny indoor grotto where she burned incense. She put on an old forty-five. Years later, Augustina would sing that song about Mother Mary and troubled times and letting it go, or was that be? Whatever—at parties and weddings and funerals and any event where she could bring her twelve-string guitar. Lighting a cigarette, Augustina waved a match into the air. Then she slipped a hand underneath her pillow, pulling out a fine silver chain. At the end of the chain was a small medallion, oval like a misshapen moon and blue like the sky. From the center of the pendant rose a statue of the Virgin Mary, intricate and smooth like an ivory cameo. Augustina had taken the necklace out of her mother's jewelry box and kept it for herself. She believed it was her lucky charm.

She held the necklace between her fingers, rubbing its coolness into her skin, begging the Virgin to hear her. You were young, she whispered. You know what it's like to love a boy. She imagined her mother's swollen heart bursting and water spilling out, cascading down her tired body, mourning as though her daughter were dead. She'd never forgive her. After all the trouble her parents went through to keep her away from the bad crowd, the boys and lust in general, Augustina still managed to fall in love.

Her mom stood at the door, knocking loudly, but Augustina pretended not to hear. She took another drag of her cigarette, then snuffed it out in the cradle of a votive candle. Reaching to the side of the table, she lit a stick of incense, disguised the smoke with the scent of roses. She slipped the pendant under her pillow and held a picture of her sitting on the rocks at Montrose Harbor. She was wrapped in the cave of Gabriel's chest, curling her body tightly into his. The waves were high and one could see a spray of water falling onto them. Her mother would die if she saw that picture. "Augustina," her mother said, "Open up, *hija*, I want to know what's bothering you."

"Nothing, Mama," she answered. "I'm just tired."

Her mother jiggled the door. "Open up. Let me look at you, you were pale at dinner." She waited another moment and then asked, "Why don't you talk to me, Ina? Let me know what's wrong."

Talking to her mother was like talking to the house plants. With good intentions, she would sit, gladly nodding, smiling, but she wouldn't hear. Like the time Augustina tried to tell her mother about the nuns, how they pointed her out in class, saying things like, "Thanks be to God, Augustina, the Church risked life and limb to save your people, civilize them. Thank God, there were the Spanish and later the Americans." All her mother said was, "She meant well, *hija*. Try to be more patient."

The next morning Sister Nora gave her annual lecture to the sophmore class. Standing against a screen, a giant projection of the world splattered across her face and the gym at large, she waved a long pointer in the air, gestured at the map. "There are cultures," she said, "that go to great lengths to keep their daughters chaste." Augustina envisioned a large needle and thread stitching its way around the world, gathering young girls' innocence into the caves of their bodies, holding it there like the stuffing in a Thanksgiving turkey. She had to excuse herself.

The heat in the building was too much, too suffocating. Every time she closed her eyes she saw her mother's image on the screen before her or she'd picture the girls in South Africa, their stitches bursting wide open. Augustina ran out. She sat on the curb, cupping her hands against the wind, her thin legs sprawled out in front of her. She slipped a cigarette between her lips and listened to the girls' voices wafting out of the building. She hated everyone at that school.

A low-riding vehicle, brown and rusted, snaked its way along Holy Angel's driveway. Augustina took another drag from her cigarette. As she moved away from them, she could hear the girls howling.

"It's her sexy cousin," yelled one girl, "the Filipino houseboy."

"You'll get caught," Colleen said plainly.

As she climbed into Gabriel's Mustang, Augustina swore under her breath, asked, "Yeah, so what's it to you?"

He drove uptown, taking side streets, weaving the car about pedestrains. His camera, a thirty-five millimeter he had inherited from his grandfather, was carefully placed next to him on the seat. It was his lolo's first possession in the States. Reaching for it, Augustina played with the zoom, slipping it back and forth, in and out like a toy.

"Don't break that," Gabriel warned.

The light from outside framed his profile. She could see the angle of his cheekbones, how they jut from his face, the slope of his nose and the dimples that were set in his half-smile. She snapped a picture of him, click, rewind, click. Snapped another. She pointed the camera out the window and watched the streets through an orange filter. They rode most of the way in silence and then he finally said, "So did you think about it?"

"Yep," she sighed, "it's all I can think about."

"Me too," he said.

"Maybe we should stop hanging out so much," she said. "Maybe that would help."

But Gabriel shook his head. "That's not right either."

The window was splattered with slush from the streets. Through the view finder, she caught a girl carrying a baby. The infant, dressed in a light blue snow-suit, draped its body across the girl, curled its head into the crook of her neck, slept comfortably amid the winter traffic. Click, she snapped another picture.

Augustina thought the girl carrying the child looked like Emmy Nolando. Apparently, Dr. Nolando refused to give his daughter birth control and when she came home pregnant, the Nolandos sent her to a foster home in town. Disowned her. Augustina's parents milked the story for almost an entire year.

"Can you imagine," her mother whispered as she leaned over her bowl of soup. "The shame of it."

When Augustina asked why Emmy was sent away, her father shook his head, and muttered, "Disgraceful."

Ricardo leapt into a long lecture concerning those loose American girls and their immorality. "She's lucky she's not in the Philippines," he said. "There she'd have that baby and her parents would raise that child as their own."

"That's stupid," Augustina said.

"Oh yes," Mona said. "That baby would never know who his real mommy was. That's how it's done back home. That's how they save the family's reputation."

Even though Emmy had spent her pregnancy in a foster home, and even though she gave her baby up for adoption, Augustina was still not allowed to speak to Emmy. No one did. The Filipino community ignored her. "Better not be wild, better not embarrass the family like that girl. Better not, better not, better not."

Of all their hangouts, Grace Cemetery was their favorite. At Grace, the sun shattered into a thousand bright icicles, splintering brances into shadows, casting intricate patterens on hills of white. New fallen snow draped the statues of saints and beautiful ladies like white linen robes. They stood at the doors of these tombs and they prayed for souls. They stood guard no matter what—storms or drought. Once a twister ripped across Grace Cemetery and trees broke in half— a couple of tombstones even uprooted. But these women stood strong.

She sat at the foot of St. Bernadette's statue, gathering snow into little heaps. When Bernadette was visited by the blessed Virgin back in Lourdes, they thought she was crazy. They didn't believe her. But Bernadette didn't give a fuck what they thought. She just kept going up that hill, praying, talking to Holy Mary like it was nobody's business. Augustina ran her hands along the statue's feet, tracing the finely etched toes with the edge of her finger. She listened to the wind winding its voice through the trees like a cool blue ribbon.

Gabriel fiddled with his camera, flipping through filters and lenses. She watched him sitting on a hill, his long body bent over the camera, his hair falling to either side of his face, shining midnight under the hot winter sun. Augustina believed Gabriel was an angel in another life. She could tell by his pictures, black and white photos of the city and its people. He once told her that the truth cannot possibly hide in black and white the way it does in color. Colors distort truth, make the ugly something beautiful. She considered him brilliant.

"Bless Gabriel," she told the statue. Augustina looked up at the saint's full cheeks which were round and smooth like the sun. Her eyes were carved into perfectly shaped hazelnuts— so lifelike that from here Augustina could see the definition of her eyelashes.

"Augustina!" Gabriel yelled. "Look up." He jumped up onto someone's tombstone. The light behind him glared at Augustina, forming a haze of white around his black mane. "This light's great," he said. "Your eyes are magnificent."

"I'm squinting," she said. He leapt from the side of the tomb, and leaning over her, he tugged at the ends of her hair.

Augustina placed a cold hand on the side of his face and he shivered. "What would your parents say?" she asked. "What would we do?"

He stared at the graves. The sun slipped behind a crowd of clouds and suddenly it was cold out. Augustina lit a cigarette and offered him a drag. He buried his face in his hands as he pushed her away.

Getting up, she walked underneath the rocks that formed an archway where Mary stood serenely veiled in paint—sky blue and gold. Tossing her cigarette to the ground, Augustina walked past the bench, pushed up against the iron rail, leaned her pelvis into the gate and pulled at one of the rods. She stared at the thick wooden rosary that draped Mary's white hands. Augustina told the Lady, "It feels natural. Why not?"

She had not meant for any of it to happen. A few weeks before, *The Chicago Tribune* awarded ten prizes to the best high school photographers. A manila envelope came to Gabriel's house thick with a piece of cardboard, his prize-winning photo of the Rastafari woman on Maxwell Street, and a check for two hundred dollars. Second prize. The letter that came with the announcement talked about Gabriel's use of light, texture and composition. The judge said Gabriel's intuitive eye was not only a gift but a way to see the world. Gabriel should develop his potential.

When Gabriel showed his father the letter and winning photo, Uncle Hector blew up. Told Gabriel he was wasting his time again, taking risks with his life, traveling into dangerous neighborhoods and for what? A picture? "Don't be stupid," Hector told him. What if something would have happened there on the Southside? He could have been mugged or knifed or beaten. He could have been shot. Was he crazy, Hector wanted to know. Grabbing Gabriel's camera, Hector shook it over his head like a preacher with a Bible, its strap casting shadows on his face. "Enough of this," he said. "Stop wasting your time." As he threw the camera across the kitchen, the lens popped open, came crashing on Tita Belina's marble floors and shattered.

That night, Augustina had sat on the rocks at Montrose Harbor, holding Gabriel's head on her lap, brushing the hair from his face, wiping the tears as they rolled from the corners of his eyes. "Count the stars," Augustina whispered. "Forget him." Augustina felt so bad for him, so angry at her uncle. And when Gabriel glanced up at her, she leaned down to meet him and kissed. She let her lips rest there, held onto him, and something in her stirred, some feeling she was not accustomed to. She let go a long sigh, let go that little bit of loneliness.

Augustina thought she saw the Lady smiling at her, looking right through her. Okay, she whispered, I can't stop thinking about him. Am I bad? At night she imagined the weight of his body pushing down on her, covering her like a giant quilt. She saw his eyes slipping into her, his beautiful face washing over her in the dark. She tried to remember the feel of his hair, how the strands came together, locked around each other. Sometimes she thought she could smell the scent of him, there at the lake, a fragrance of sandalwood, a breeze from Lake Michigan. I'm crazy, okay, she thought. A tramp, if you will. But he loves me, Mary, doesn't that count?

She thought of Sister Nora and the girls whose parents made sure of their virginity. How they'd mutilate them in the name of chastity. And does that operation keep those girls from love, she wondered. Does it keep them from wanting him? Sister Nora would find out and tell everyone. Use her for an example. No, she'd rather die. She imagined her body floating, swelling in the depth of the lake. She imagined herself swimming eternally. Augustina closed her eyes, putting her face to the sky. The sun came out every few seconds, ducking out of the clouds so that Mary appeared hazy and kind of aglow—but only for seconds at a time. "Hail Mary," she said. "Hail Mary full of grace, the Lord is with thee, so please, please, please, put in a word for me, Hail Mary." She was so deep in prayer, she didn't even hear Gabriel sneak up behind her.

"Are you worried?" Gabriel asked.

"A little." she said. He put his arm around her and they embraced. Kissed. Slowly fell into that long black funnel, slipping across borders they had never crossed till now. They spent the rest of the day lying under the branches of the grotto, watching the changing sky and waiting for the sun to sleep. Neither one of them wanted to go home.

The house was locked when she got there, so Augustina fumbled for the key she wore around her neck. When she opened the door, the symphony from her father's speakers rushed out to her like waves on Montrose Beach. Music filled the house so that when she called out to her mother, her voice was lost and small.

Mona stood at the stove, her feet planted firmly apart, one hand on her hip and the other stirring vegetables. Augustina snuck up behind her and kissed her softly on the cheek. "Hi, Mommy," she whispered. Mona continued to mix the stir fry, beating the sides of the frying pan with quick movements. Beads of sweat formed at her temples as she worked. "Do you want me to set the table?" Augustina asked. Turning, she saw the table was already set. Four large plates, a spoon and fork at each setting, a napkin, a water glass. "Okay," Augustina sang, "Well maybe I'll wash up and I'll help you put the food out."

The music was blasting in her father's room. She popped her head in and waved at him. "Hi Dad!" she called. He was reading the paper and when he didn't look up she tapped him on the knee. Leaning over, she kissed him.

"Sweetheart," he said. "Is dinner almost ready?"

"Yeah, Dad. In a minute."

She felt as though she had been up all night. Her body ached, was covered with dirt from the cemetery. Gabriel's cologne had seeped into her skin, and she was afraid that her mother had sensed it. So instead of simply washing her hands, she bathed.

The cool water, rushing down her body, washed away the cigarette smoke, the cologne, the dirt. She could almost feel the water coursing through her, washing over her mind, cleaning out her tummy, circling about her heart.

When she got back to the kitchen, she found she was too late. Her mother had placed a huge bowl of rice on the table, a plate of beef and vegetables and a turin of soup. "Sorry, Ma," she said, as she grabbed a cold pitcher of water. "I just needed a shower."

"Is that all, Augustina?" her mother asked as she looked up from the sink. "What did you do today? Ha? Where were you?"

She felt her face burning bright red. "At school," she answered. "Where else? Then Gabriel and I went to the mall."

"School?" she whispered. "They were looking for you at school." Augustina stared at the table, ran her fingers around the edge of the water pitcher. It was cold and moisture shivered from the pitcher's mouth and ran down its sides. Her mother's voice was low and angry. "How many times do we have to go through this, *hija*? Why can't you just stay in school?"

"But I was feeling sick," Augustina said.

"So you had Gabriel pick you up and the both of you were absent?" Her mother threw a dish rag on the counter. "You were at the cemetery again?" She pulled Augustina close to her. "Do you want your father to send you to the Philippines? Maybe that would teach you how to behave." Her parents often threatened to send her there, to all-girl convent schools, where nuns pretended to be mothers. "If you think the rules are strict here, wait till you have to live there."

"Sorry, Mom," Augustina whispered. "But the truth is that Gabriel had another fight with Uncle Hector and he was upset. He came to get me so we could talk."

"Still, *hija*, that's no reason to be absent from school." As Mona brushed the hair out of her face, and kissed the top of her forehead, Augustina's father stepped into the kitchen.

"*Ano ba*," he asked. "What's going on?"

Mona tucked her hair behind her ears and told him, "Nothing, nothing, Ricardo. Dinner is ready. Come sit. Ina, call your brother."

Augustina spent the next two days locked up in her room, blasting her record. The needle slipped over that old forty-five, bumped along the grooves and scratches, whispering a mantra. "Mother Mary," she sang along. "Comes to me." An old church organ cranked a sacrilegious funk, a honky tonk, that seemed to fade into the slow rise of the electric guitar's bridge. She played around with Gabriel's photos. She mounted them on cardboard and painted borders around them—daisies and rainbows and splotches of love and peace and kiss drawn in giant bubble letters. Her mother stood at the door, knocking, forever knocking, but she pretended to not hear. "I'm not feeling well," she had told her mother. "I don't want to go to school." Bile rose up in her throat, churned in her stomach, swamped up against the cavern in her chest.

Her family came to the door one by one. First her mother, then Dad. Even Auntie Belina, her cousin Ofelia and Uncle Hector came knocking, but the door was locked and there was no opening it. When Gabriel stood at the door, she whispered through a crack, "I'm sorry, I can't let you in. They can't know."

When she finally went to school, Sister Nora stood in front of the classroom, whacking her giant pointer stick across the blackboard. "There has been disgraceful conduct. Sin, sin, sin. Apparently, the story of the young girls and their experience with genital mutilation has not taught you anything. You girls must be punished."

Augustina thought the nun knew, was about to expose her when Sister ordered the girls who attended Kat O'Donel's slumber party to step forward. Apparently the sisters found a video tape of "Marlin the Magnificent" dancing in his elephant mask—and that was all he wore—a mask. The tape was found lying in the cathedral—second to the last pew, across from the confessional. Fran Guncheon, class librarian, and Augustina were the only ones not in attendance, so they were given permission to leave. Augustina took this opportunity to run to Grace Cemetery.

The clouds drifted north, slipped by fast like the second hand in her grandmother's wristwatch. Her body was numb, frozen like the Ladies in the court. She thought they had grown sad. Her constellation of saints, like everyone else in her life had stopped listening to her. Snow melted around St. Bernadette; the sun burning holes in the ice underneath her. Augustina smelled the earth, seeping through the slush. It was sweet and fertile. A trickle, a tear, maybe the melting snow, slipped down Bernadette's face. Inside Augustina, something grumbled, roared. She had stopped praying weeks ago. God confused her.

Augustina looked up from the statue and saw her mother climbing over the hill. The sun shrouded her in light. She wore her off-white cashmere coat, the one that fell to her ankles because she was so short. She wrapped her black hair in a white chiffon scarf that trailed past her shoulders, followed the wind. There was a cloud of white smoke trailing from her breath, rising up and floating away from her. When she came near, her mother said, "She's beautiful."

"She's strong," Augustina answered.

"So this is where you go." She tugged at Augustina's braids, examined her face, kissed the top of her forehead. Then, pulling the chain from Augustina's neck, she said. "Where did you get this, *hija*?"

"Isn't it my baby necklace? I found it in your jewelry box."

Her mother shook her head. "I got this from my godmother. You shouldn't have taken it without asking."

Slipping her head onto her mother's shoulder, Augustina felt her body soften, the energy draining from her. She considered telling her mom about Gabriel. Would she understand? She closed her eyes and fell in time to her mother's breathing. Maybe, she thought. Her mother embraced her, told her, "Whatever is troubling you, *hija*, don't worry. Family is family."

Of course, *Lola* Mona never tells me that part of it. The story goes, that *Tita* Augustina went to the Philippines six months later. Some of the relatives say it was to have a baby, others say it was to discipline her wild American self. Still stuck back on the islands, they tell me, "You're next. Watch out." Even my mother thinks her older sister was a bad girl.

"How do you know," I ask her. "You weren't even born when she left. You hardly knew her." My mother always shrugs her shoulders, says she just knows.

Last time I went to see Tita Ina, she held out her tiny fist, wrinkled and lined with blue veins, and slipped me the Blessed Virgin dangling from the end of a fine silver chain. "Here, *hija*," she said, "take this." I placed the necklace up to the light. The paint was fading and chipping from its skyblue center, but still there was something about Her. The way her skirts seemed to flow, the way her body was sculpted into miniature curves, the way the tiny rosary was etched onto the metal plate.

Fredo Avila

Gina Apostol

Fredo Avila's dream was to travel to Beverly Hills, California, in the U.S.A., to be a contestant in "The Price is Right."

"Have you ever seen a group of happier people?" he said to me. "Everyone is so happy: look at how they all cheer wildly when the camera falls on them—and they're just the audience, not even contestants. It's just like heaven."

He acknowledged that winning a prize was mere luck, yes; it required only a talent at guessing. He'd once seen a Chinese man on the show who could hardly speak English—"dollar" and "car" were all he could sputter—but he knew his numbers, and he could point. He won a grand piano and a bath tub.

What would he, Fredo Avila, do if he won a bathtub? He'd plant it in his backyard, he would, near the bougainvilleas on the street. No more pumping on the *bomba*, slaving on the jetmatic pump for him, Fredo Avila. He'd hire someone to fetch water in pails and line them by his bath tub, while he, Fredo Avila, "The Price is Right" champion, would sit in splendor for all his neighborhood to see. He'd be in his jockeys, of course, new nylon swimming trunks, as he lay in his free, glistening bathtub in the open, Filipino air.

All of us in Barugo knew what Fredo's dream was. We all knew Fredo: in real life, he was our town's boxer. Stocky and squat, with a mean right jab and always steady on his feet, Fredo Avila won fights in towns as far south as Ormoc. He whipped to shreds and pathos lesser men right next door in Calingcaguing, all on the strength of his feet's stubborn steadiness and his "good conditioning," the hours he spent sparring in the space below my uncle's sala, on the dirt floor where the pigs were also kept for slaughtering on fiesta days.

He fought during fiesta bouts, when the gambling mood was contagious, and my uncle, the mayor, had a decent excuse for getting drunk and singing *Please Release Me* and *Besame Mucho*. There was always a smell of jubilation, hectic mindless happiness, and the plaster odor of Salonpas around Fredo when I saw him. But that's because I always remember him amid intensities, in the middle of fiesta fever when all men are friends until the next round of beer.

Fredo didn't drink, and whenever he fought a fiesta march, scheduled always before the Angelus so that the concerns of the body never interfered with the silence of the soul, he would return promptly to my uncle's house, win or lose, jawbone bloodied or intact, to watch "The Price is Right" at six o'clock.

"Heretic and blasphemer!" my aunt would say, crossing herself as the Angelus bells tolled. She was sick of having Fredo at the house at the Angelus hour, turning on the TV as if he owned it. But my uncle, the mayor, allowed him free reign of the house. And then, after a raced rendition of her prayers, my aunt would settle next to Fredo, to watch with sainted exclamations, "Susmariosep!" the genius of generosity in Bob Barker's parade. With loud awe, she'd comment on washers, dryers, steel machines of all shapes, gadgets imagined beyond delirium: lawn mowers for her stretch of crabgrass, answering machines for the municipal office, which had the sole telephone in the entire town, and electronic flea collars for her doomed pigs.

Shows were beamed via satellite from Manila, way up north, a twenty-four-hour bus ride away (including the three-hour dawn wait for a ferry from Allen, Samar). In Manila, we imagined, the show was beamed in miraculous simulcast from Beverly Hills. We got the show a month after, as was our due—when sophisticates in Manila were tired of hoarding it from losers in the province. I remember Fredo once punched a pomaded visitor from Manila, when the man told him who would win the trip to Venice, Italy, in the jackpot portion of the show. That's what he got for showing off.

We all had our dreams. Mine was merely to study in Manila, maybe take commerce or philosophy in Letran or San Beda, like my uncle, the mayor, who had flunked both schools. Spinoza "Chong" Botictic, my good high school friend, wanted to meet Jaworski, the basketball player. But he wished for a specific type of meeting: after a game in overtime, when Jaworski broke a tie in the last four seconds, hitting a three-point shot from the exact, requisite distance. Jaworski always did that in Chong's dreams, and he'd hit Fernandez, the enemy's center, right on the jaw, too, secretly, in that suave way of his. Chong wanted Jaworski to blind Fernandez forever. But that last was only extra. In his dream, Chong would then jump onto the court while the Ginebra team raised their sweaty arms in victory, embracing everyone, including Chong. At that opportune moment, he would meet Jaworski, shaking his hand with all due respect and coming up with something like: "Sic transit gloria mundi" or "Ad maiorem dei gloriam,"something witty like that. That's so Jaworski would know he had smart fans, even the ones from the provinces.

"Hope you take a bath after you meet him," we heckled Chong when he told us his dream. "Those guys smell like pigshit after they play."

"Shit," Tio Sequiel, my uncle's cousin, said, slapping my shoulder. "You won't find me crapping in my pants to dream of Jaworski's smelly armpits, let me tell you."

Chong was ready to leave the room. He was fifteen, and he hardly had any hair on his face, although he was still fertilizing a mustache he had started months ago: he cried easily, in sniffles.

"Get off his back, Exequiel," someone said from the back of the room. Then we heard a snort and a hand banging on the table.

It was Fredo. He'd been playing solitaire while a variety show from Manila was on.

"He's entitled to his ambition," Fredo said more quietly, laying still more cards on the table without skipping a hand. "That's what he has. And besides, you smell like a cow in sweat everyday: you're just a champion of the chamberpots."

Everyone knew about Tio Sequiel's historic diuretic trouble, handed down to males in his branch of the family for three verifiable generations. We all agreed it was this that made Tio Sequiel chronically red-faced and excitable—and simple-minded in the bargain.

"Oh yeah," he said, flustered and blushing. "So what kind of champion are you? Champion of elbow boxing?"

We couldn't believe Tio Sequiel's guts. We stood up, scraping chairs and shaking heads. I held on to Tio Sequiel's steamy arm, and some of us rose as if casually but really to block Fredo's view of Tio Sequiel, crazy red man. We didn't dare touch Fredo.

The truth was, I don't remember anyone referring even once to the baffling time a few months before when Fredo in his last known fight knocked a man out by elbowing him in the face, gashing cheek and jaw. He won in points but lost by this foul. He returned from Ormoc to Barugo with no comment, our compassionate curiosity unrewarded.

Since then, Fredo had refused to fight, fiesta or not.

Fredo merely looked in contempt at our timid shuffling about the room and then swept cards cleanly off the table.

"Another dead end," he muttered to the cards then left the house. He'd lost his game of solitaire.

I thought of this scene some months later when I heard the news about Fredo. Eusebia the midwife and tolerated quack doctor told me all about it: Fredo was going to America.

Secretly, Fredo had been sending letters to America, addressed to California, for three years. He sent his letters through the next town's post, so that not even Claudia, postwoman and bigbreasted notary public, would know about it. One day inexplicably he got a letter back. "Congratulations!" it said in red, block letters visible from outside the envelope. Claudia expertly peered through it and memorized the return address: "The Price is Right," Beverly Hills, California, U.S.A.

Fredo received the letter without immediately opening it. But news spread that afternoon that Fredo had called upon the intsik Go Long Tiu and had borrowed a sum rumors judged to be three thousand to maybe half a hundred mil— the wealth of a sugarman or the prized futurity of a pedigreed cock; big bucks he'd pay off with his winnings from "The Price is Right."

It was all over Barugo: Fredo had won the solitaire stakes, hit the jackpot, caught the secret of the royal flush. He was going to America.

"Dreams are wounds," said Eusebia, snapping wisdom from the air as was her duty as a quack. "But with Fredo, who knows? God smiles slantwise on simple men."

Fredo soon left for Manila to arrange his booking for abroad: this at least he imparted to us, but before we could arrange the farewell drinking feast and happy-tearful backslapping and stabbing. And still the town glowed with the pure miracle of his departure. Flagrant hopes and undeclared dreams took shape and vigor in its wake. Chong talked with simple certainty about his meeting with Jaworski. Men filled cockpits with avid knowledge of how their luck would change. Tio Sequiel dreamed on his chamberpot of blonde women, chrome cars, white Christmas and other metallurgical treasures of Beverly Hills, saying "Sonamagun" and "Damn" as if he were Fredo Avila in California. And my aunt prayed the Angelus with more fervor and speed than usual and, without any surprise, played bingo as if with a mad streak of clairvoyance, winning the salad casseroles and paired candlesticks with all the ease of the indecently charmed.

As for me, I did go to Manila that June, studying philosophy, accounting and many other wisdoms; in those first months, many of the books I read seemed to refer directly or casually to Fredo Avila's imminent appearance on "The Price is Right": for his destiny was now a constant puzzle to me: how do dreams come true?

There was the stodgy plodding over ledgers, balancing credits and debits with optic and cumulative anxiety: in accounting, there was no triumph but stability, no virtue apart from diligence and care. In my classes in religion, we were shown images of Saint Anthony in the desert, Saint Jerome before his skull and pen, men of abstinence and learning whose holiness was directly proportional to what flesh they had on their chins. And in the stories of philosophers, most clearly I would see Fredo Avila: Thales with the vision that led him to the hole in the well, Pythagoras of the singular solitude and madness over beans. In my twisted, one-track state of mind, I saw how Fredo Avila was one with mystics, philosophers and accountants: he stuck to one cause with the purity of a historical ascetic, stubborn and faithful to his dream, against odds, against distance, time, fate, and against reason.

In December of that year, Fredo was to appear on "The Price is Right." Claudia the postwoman knew about it before Amanda, Fredo's wife, did: she had a talent with penknives on sealed envelopes. Amanda and her two children were invited as guests of honor at my uncle's house when the day arrived. It must be explained that my uncle, the mayor, had one of two television sets in the town of Barugo. Go Long Tiu owned the other, but no one but flies and a cat had ever entered the Chinese man's house; he lived alone with his cat, sacks of flour and rice his millers sent him, and tins of money and creditor's bills that he stashed under his mattress like a good man of Guangdong.

My aunt made pudding with pig's intestines, leche flan, rice cakes in pastel colors, pancit and pork jumba. Amanda entered bearing vegetables; it was said that Fredo had taken her savings from her earnings as a vegetable vendor, along with the money from Go Long Tiu, and left her only with the garden plot and two pudgy-cheeked kids who looked eerily like the Santo Nino. We pinched the kids when they came in, their cheeks lumpy like the unpigmented, flour-faced Christ's; as the Angelus bells tolled, we did our quick stumbled prayers; then we turned the tv on.

It was a gathering of the town's worthies: drunks, gossips, the compassionate and the wise. Chong's father, Enoch Botictic de Enage, held center position, being the town's most learned man: he was a constantly crocked former teacher of philosophy and defrocked Jesuit whose last nod to his youthful learning was the naming of his children, Archimedes, Heraclitus, Baruch and Spinoza—more commonly known to us, respectively, as Boy, Bigboy, Bulldog and Chong. Chong's brother Heraclitus, aka Bigboy, despised "The Price is Right" because he favored "Jeopardy"— "you have to think to play it," he said, "unlike that stupid game, where even if all you did was fart, you'd win." But even he was present that night.

"Heraclitus, give me the odds on Fredo's name being called," his father said to him.

"What's infinitesimal?" Bigboy said. He spoke often in stupid riddles we forgave him for because his father was, after all, made crazy by intelligence.

None of us had any doubts that Fredo would be chosen from the audience right from the start. When the names were called and three exultant white ladies and a longhaired man came forward, we were puzzled.

"There's Fredo!" someone yelled as the camera panned on a group of wildly clapping people. But no one could tell for sure.

The first prizes were two sets of billiard balls.

"What's the use of billiard balls without a pool table. What a stupid game," said Chong's father, already red from tuba, incendiary coconut wine I was still not allowed to drink, except in secret.

Then the pool table was shown, a richly green board: you could tell from its harsh color how new it was.

"See, see," Tio Sequiel sneered at Mr. Botictic, elbowing him.

The professor merely shrugged, drinking.

"Ssh!" my aunt said.

A blonde woman won the round. She looked like a version of Claudia, chest pendulous and torso abridged, except that she was from Texas.

"Where the best chickens are raised," Tio Sequiel said; with chickens, he was a man of learning.

She was to bid on—suspense and gasp, in Beverly and Barugo—a trip to Honolulu!

"Pearl Harbor!" Chong said.

"Waikiki, aloha oe," we answered.

The woman squealed as the fake view of Hawaii was displayed.

She played a game called Circus Gong. She pounded on a board that then rose up a vertical range of prices. When the board stopped under what she believed to be the cost of the trip, she hit the board with an oversized hammer.

"Twenty thousand dollars?" my uncle guessed.

"No, in American money, maybe five hundred dollars," Tio Sequiel said. "Big difference between dollars and pesos, you know."

The woman pressed the button at five thousand. The trip cost four.

"Poor woman," my aunt said. "But she still gets prizes after the show. No one loses in America. Unlike in that game with Jeanne Young, where you can win corniks."

Her scorn for all Filipino goods increased phenomenally when she watched "The Price is Right"; you could measure her disgust.

"There's Fredo," someone yelled again.

But the camera was too quick, although the blackhaired man at the end of the row looked blurredly like Fredo in California, pensive and robust in light-tremored sunglasses.

A woman won a xylophone complete with sticks and pedal. Another narrowly guessed the price of Funai 5-Setting Whirlpool Bath.

I liked best the models, Diane and Janis, who lay on the beds or played the musical prizes with delicate, otherworldly gestures.

The four original contestants had either won or been disqualified except for the young man with long hair. I can tell you the sequence of play in "The Price is Right" even in my sleep. The announcer calls four players; the winner of the first round of price-guessing gets to play a game. After the games, one player is added to the three remaining slots, to make a constant four, and each player tries to win a spot in the game-playing segments. You could remain in contention until the end of the show, until you get lucky. This was the case now with the longhaired guy. A crowd of people cheered crazily whenever he made his wrong bid. And it was becoming clear to me that Fredo Avila's dream was going to end in obscurity, without even the witless consolation of bidding too high or too low on a barbecue from Amata.

The second to the last number was called, and the spotlights raised hope again among the crowd of Californians, Omahans, Nashvilleans, Mormons, Yosemiteans, Cherokees and Presbyterians, all the great gamut of Americans on the set of "The Price is Right."

Looking at them, I'd wonder why people never looked like that on "Charlie's Angels," with their necks seemingly attached directly to their earlobes, or with bare, splotched, broad faces that made one think momentarily of the dangers of frontal nudity. I'd feel bad for them; it was like they were America's secret people, these people forever barred from primetime.

"There's Fredo!" someone yelled again.

And sure enough, a name was called out.

The camera panned above a cheering mop of heads. Someone stood up: a t-shirted man in shining boat-heeled boots, boxer-shouldered and sunglasses-less—Fredo Avila in California took the long steps down, "Come on down!" to his place in the spotlight as a self-made man.

We were stunned in Barugo.

Long afterwards, we would replay the moment when Fredo took his place before the stage, and Bob Barker asked him, a propos of everything, "Where are you from?"

"Barugo, Leyte, in the Philippines, Sir!"

But that didn't happen until Fredo won the round's bid, edging out the long-haired man by a hair of a dollar or two, winning for himself a high-tech, mirrored, 4-speed bubblegum machine.

History was made on "The Price is Right" when Fredo ascended and stood next to Bob Barker, he of Miss Universe fame.

"What diction!" my aunt would say of Bob when she heard him say "a neeeeew car!" I'd keep correcting her, saying diction meant choice of words, not enunciation; and anyway, Rod the announcer said those things, not Bob. But I myself coveted Bob Barker's smoothness and charm and practiced in a mirror the way he smiled and waved his hands, his charm stuck permanently to him like a gun in a gangster's hand.

The man with the best diction in America and Fredo, the best-conditioned man in Barugo, stood side by side. Fredo's head didn't reach quite as high as the knot in Bob Barker's tie, and he looked strangely like a stunted cowboy in his tall, gleaming boots.

"And what do you do, Fredo?"

"Boxer," Fredo said promptly. And he added: "Bej-etable vendor, too."

We hooted in Barugo and gave high fives.

And I remember every single second of Fredo Avila's appearance on "The Price is Right." He had the best prize of all, a Chevy Nova waiting in the wings as he picked out numbers from a jumble of oversized cards in Bob Barker's hands. I remember the luminous quality of each minute in which he guessed: wrong, wrong, wrong. I see the erect posture of Fredo Avila in the shining moment when the actual price of the Chevy Nova was revealed and Bob Barker shook Fredo's hand, waving good-bye, Fredo Avila waving to the crowd, almost saluting— good-bye, losing the Chevy Nova and the chance at the showcase that the long-haired man won, of course. The boy, for he was a student, we learned, from Clyde, Ohio ("Nowhere place," Heraclitus sneered, forgetting where he was in the excitement of the moment), won his bid finally in the next round and garnered, in all, a trampoline, a trailer and a trip to Tokyo, Japan: $18,000 in prizes! The crowd went wild because, it turned out, the longhaired boy's entire fraternity was with him on the show, perfect recipients of the trampoline's elastic high.

Then Rod, the man in the hat, announced the prizes every contestant would take home, win or lose, and they were shown on the screen in still photographs without the happy complicity of the models' hands: Geritol Extend Vitamin Capsules, Seminole Flea Collars that glow in the dark, and Vita Bikini Underwear for men and women at home or on the beach— "Sexy as you wanna be!"

No one expected Fredo home after his appearance on "The Price is Right." We knew, for instance, that when a group of Leyte Girls Scouts left for the U.S. on a goodwill tour, they'd return with someone missing: in their case, the assistant scoutmistress who stopped over and vanished in Milwaukee. We hear that now she has a successful thousand-dollar business buying groceries for rich, old people who've "lost their qualities of mind," she wrote. Then there's Claudia's fabled, filthy-rich cousin who paid thirty thousand pesos to buy a nurse's certificate, and there she is in Passaic, New Jersey, sending pictures home of her pink Mitsubishi Eclipse and herself in Washington, D.C., shaking the large-as-life hands of Ronald Reagan: my aunt swears it was him—as if you couldn't tell him apart from cardboard.

I imagined Fredo staying behind in California, outstaying his visa to become, perhaps, a flyweight contender in fights in Fayetteville, Nevada, or a strong-armed burger flapper in MacDonald, New York. He had achieved his dream: he was a self-made man in America.

I returned to Barugo in the summer. Instead of a boxing match, my uncle had arranged a marathon for the fiesta of Saint Jude; streamers lined the paved parts of the town's streets, and coconut wine and lemonade stands stood ready at the corners as the bus drove into town. I had arrived on the day of the fiesta, wishing almost that I hadn't returned. I didn't know what my sickness was all about—the nausea I felt as I saw the familiar turns and tin roofs of my hometown, the usual layabouts gathered about the corner near my uncle's house drinking *tuba* and wasting their lives as if they were immortal. Bums, of all the people I know, seemed most fixedly to have some hold on the notion of eternity.

I hung around on the street with my bags stickered "Letran" and a guilt in my lack of affection as people surged around my uncle's house, where it seemed the marathon was to begin.

"Danilo!" my aunt cried from the window. "That's my nephew, the future accountant!" she said excitedly to her cronies in the house.

"Manila boy," the Botictic brothers passed by— Boy, Bigboy, Bulldog, and Chong.

"Letran, ha." Heraclitus swiped at the sticker on my bag. "Big deal."

I thought of why I must be more sophisticated even than Heraclitus, because I had spent a year in Manila, a city boy studying philosophy. But I couldn't remember, in this dust, what I had become, what I had done in the city, the books that had wrought what changes, what made me superior, a man with significant dreams. It seemed that the suddenly stable ground of arrival had left me sick, reeling.

"Watching the race?" I asked. I pulled a lone, crushed cigarette from my pocket, the one I had had since the beginning of my trip. "Who's the main contender?""Fredo, of course."

"New guy? From Barugo or no?"

"You joking? Fredo Avila, I mean."

"The boxer? He's home?"

"Yeah. No one knows what happened," Chong volunteered seriously. He had always been my favorite among the brothers. His mustache now vied with his Adam's apple in temerity, in serious growth. He was still as skinny as a lizard. "Immigration got him maybe. Bad luck."

"Stupidity," Heraclitus corrected.

Chong was quiet. Heraclitus continued:

"Yeah, formerly of Beverly Hills, back to Barugo. He didn't even have talent for hiding."

"Works for Go Long Tiu now. Him and his kids. Hauls flour and stuff. You should see him," Chong said.

"But still," said Bulldog knowledgeably, "he's the best-conditioned man in Leyte. He'll win this race. No one can touch Fredo."

I smoked my limp, pocket-shredded Camel as I digested the news.

"But he's not really Fredo anymore," Chong said suddenly.

"What?" I asked.

"So he's a disguise now? He's really Gary Cooper?" Heraclitus laughed.

"I don't know," said Chong. "He doesn't box. He doesn't even talk."

A makeshift stage fronted my uncle's house. The vice-mayor made his speech, then my uncle, the mayor, made a longer one. Finally, the runners were called to their places, and I looked for Fredo Avila. He was in the middle, a runner with a number like the rest of them. I looked for a momentous change in the way he looked, in his stance before the crowd. he looked as sturdy as before: but he was so small as the TV screen had made him out to be. But I was taller now, a veteran of the city, Manila boy and future accountant: disoriented by arrival and queasy in the stomach. I coughed from the cigarette smoke and waved at Fredo.

"Hey, Fredo."

A visitor from Manila, a Barugo boy who became a judge in the big city, rose to the makeshift stage to speak. I walked over to Fredo.

"Hey, Fredo. What's up."

He nodded at me without really looking.

"When did you get back? How was America, ha, Fredo? The blonde chicks and all?"

Fredo still stood like a brick man with big shoulders. I did notice the bulk in his stomach, a bulge unthinkable in the boxing champion of old.

I poked him in the stomach.

"So what was America like, ha? Eating all those steaks and ham?"

Fredo wiped his brow. It's quite true: the summer sun blazed almost painfully.

"What did you find in America, Fredo?" He looked at me, and I thought—I had gone too far: one didn't mess with Fredo.

"Danielboy," he said finally. He held my arm: his touch was firm, and I remember his expression of seriousness, like a teacher. It was the Fredo of old, the Fredo who lounged on the dirt floor of my uncle's house, stacking up cards. "Danny, did you know there is dust in America?"

The race started early with a boy from Calingcaguing in the lead, Fredo following close behind. "Go, Fredo, go!" Tio Sequiel and other drunkards waved him on. Barugo's dust flew in Barugo's sun. Young kids in slippers, bearing ice candy, brought up the rear, laughing and shouting. I rode in my uncle's jeep to get to the finishing line, leisurely following the runners' route. Dust was dense, adding to my discomfort; the paved road was pocked with pork-barrel providence; my uncle waved benignly as we passed the crowds. We were about to turn into a dirt road, a shortcut to the end of the line, when the fiesta crowd turned into a commotion, and someone ran after my uncle's jeep.

"Mayor, mayor, stop!"

I turned around, kneeling on my seat to look.

It seemed that the race had halted.

"He collapsed, right in the middle of the road, mayor."

"Who is it?"

"The boxer."

"Fredo Avila."

We rushed him to the nearest hospital, which was three towns away. In his delirium he kept saying, with spirit and old feistiness: "Come on down!"

The opinion in the town was—Fredo's body was well-conditioned, but his heart was foolish: should boxers run marathons? But still, they shook their heads, saying: "The best-conditioned man—how could that be?"

He died on the day of his heart attack, an end that astounded even rumor.

"From Beverly Hills to Barugo—only to die," Tio Sequiel shook his head and spat. "Foolish!"How could that be?

He left his wife the high-tech, 4-speed, mirrored bubblegum machine. To his mother, a bottle of Geritol Extend. He lost the Seminole Flea collar on the trip home, pilfered from his bag by someone possibly deranged. On his deathbed, in the last throes of glory as he raved in delirium: "Boxer, sir! From the Philippines, sir!" he wore the sum of his dream's progress, Vita bikini briefs, coral pink, for men and women at home or on the beach. Sexy as You Wanna Be.

How could it be? I vomited on the jeep on the way to the hospital, vomited days after at home and at the funeral; my aunt forced me to bed before the lines formed to walk to Fredo Avila's grave. I had the most serious case of intestinal flu Eusebia the quack had ever seen.

"You vomiting your life out, man? Coughing up even your dreams?" she said, pasting leaves and hot wild forest roots against my chest.

I rested my head against her arm, my cheeks hot.

"It's the spirit of absence," she said to my aunt. "He needs to rest, to see his world again as if he had never left."

Night Sweats

joel b. tan

for Jose Rivera, my first great love

Even now, I remember the sweat between us. I can smell our love-making, a mixture of cologne, lube, saliva and sweat. I can feel him, heavy on my chest. I look up, and I can still see him rubbing, beating his hard throbbing cock on my face. I can taste the lubricant, his kisses, our perspiration... and the *sharp* taste of his semen. I can see all this. Manolo was my first love.

Watching Manolo move was like watching soft-core porn — the mother-fucker was fine. Manolo made me proud to be with him. Women and men alike were drawn to his raw sexiness. He had dark curly hair and slanted eyes. His goatee framed his pretty but masculine face. He was 5'11 with a stocky, boxer's build. We were the same *cafe con leche* brown. From the get go, I knew fucking was inevitable. It was something about the way we danced together. I've always believed that you can tell how a person fucks by the way they dance. We attributed our rhythm to our tropical ancestry. We were both island men. Manolo was Puerto Rican. I am Pilipino. Given all the Roman Catholic, Spanish-colonized baggage we both carried, we were doomed. Nevertheless, we fell in love.

We were extreme opposites. I was openly being gay. Manolo was into the straight-acting, straight appearing macho posturing. I was a book fiend. Manolo was a TV junkie. He was a troubled but practicing Catholic. I preferred to meditate. I was the talker. Manolo was often quiet and moody. Our union was riddled with our differences. Our differences added to desire.

Manolo and I fucked a lot. Although we shared very little common ground, we learned to find our affinity in each other's flesh. We never really learned how to talk to one another. We never found a common vernacular. Instead, we articulated feelings with our kisses. We probed with our tongues. We expressed joy with our fingers. We responded with our cocks. It got to be so that we could express grief, sorrow, anger, fraternity, empathy, sympathy, any and every feeling in our love-making. At the end of our heavy breathing, we were always silent. In the dark, we would lie on our sweat-soaked sheets, satiated, oddly, understanding the other's thoughts and feelings. We developed a language of our own.

Our bodies fit together perfectly. A brush of the hand would lead to a soft caress. The soft caress would turn quickly into fingers pinching nipples. Twisted nipples would turn into wide canyon kisses. Zippers would fly open, shirts flung. Waistbands of boxers yanked down, knife-like tongue on adam's apple, teeth gnashing delicate corners, ring fingers probing, cocks hard, ready and drooling.

We weren't much for slow, gentle exchanges. In fact, we fucked with the ferocity of a brutal joust. Manolo cursed in Spanish when we fucked and I would egg him on. We would grunt, yell, scream, kick, bite, taunt and push. Our mating habits invoked notions of pre-science. If anybody would have heard us they would have probably thought we were trying to kill each other. Sometimes fighting and fucking became the same thing but on the verge of his orgasms, he would yell, I love you, or Te Amo (as if surrendering). When we milked our last drop, he would engulf my body with kisses. I too would surrender and confess, Mahal kita, I love you, Manolo. Mahal kita.

I believed him when he told me he loved me. It wasn't easy establishing trust with him. See, Manolo had a problem with lying. His sister confided that his lying started when he was young. Apparently, Manolo's father had a severe drinking problem. They said that he died with a bottle in his right hand and a gun in the left. Manolo's father left his mother and his sisters a legacy of violence, disappointment and brutality, nothing more. Shortly after his death, Manolo's mother buried herself under extravagant mounds of cocaine. What was left of their family soon disintegrated. Manolo never could accept reality as it was, so he fabricated his own.

Our beginning was magical. We were both young and handsome. We needed to be needed. We moved hastily and before you knew it we were living together in a three-bedroom apartment (we couldn't really afford) after only a few months of dating.

We created a beautiful home on credit and silences. We littered the house with tasteful antiques, paintings by contemporary Puerto Rican artists, native Pilipino art and small talk. We created the perfect environment. We fucked in every corner of our large apartment. We christened three bedrooms, two and a half baths, an outdoor patio, a fully-equipped kitchen, a formal dining room and

FLIPPIN': FILIPINOS ON AMERICA

a sunken den with our sweat and semen. We played house knowing that we couldn't possibly pay back the debt we'd incurred. We created a perfect environment knowing that we were quickly falling apart. When the last stick of furniture was bought, we knew it was over.

In retrospect, I realize that my leaving Manolo was inevitable. Nevertheless, the pain of walking away from us was excruciating. He was the first man ever that made me feel needed or loved. Young love like that was never meant to last that long.

His absence became a void I desperately tried to fill with drunken Friday nights. I became an indiscriminating receptacle for anyone's attention or affection. I searched for men who resembled him, no matter how slight. I sought refuge from one bedroom to another. I was barely breathing.

Through mutual friends, I tracked his moves. He tried to replace me as well. He made his reality happier and higher with his crystal, booze and whatever else he could snort, shoot, swallow or smoke. He blamed me for abandoning him. He tried to convince everyone around him that he didn't need me. He said that he couldn't understand why I left. He thought we were perfect.

Ironically, the vices he once rebuked became his salvation. The addicted parents he once disowned came back to haunt him through his own reflection. Manolo's habit altered his lifestyle to the point where he couldn't keep a job. So, he got involved in credit scams, petty theft and other types of bullshit. His amateurish criminal activity increased to meet the needs of his quickly growing appetite. Crystal and everything else he was dropping slowly devoured him. His once heavily-muscled frame caved in, giving way to a thin, jackal-like shadow with sharp teeth and sad eyes. When he had nothing left to sell, he gladly traded his mouth, his cock, his ass for another line, another hit.

I saw him once at a burger shack on Santa Monica and Virgil. He was facing the street, smoking, hunting for prey. He looked into the intersection and recognized me. We made eye contact. I was tempted to pull over. He quickly turned away. The light turned green, I sped off fighting the temptation to look back.

After that incident, I didn't hear from him for another six years. One day, I received a call at work. It was Manolo. He was inviting me to his graduation from a drug rehabilitation program. Proudly, he told me that he finally completed six months of abstinence and sobriety from crystal and alcohol. This was his fourth attempt in this particular program. His counselors were placing him in a transitional house in Oceanside with other recovering addicts so he could gradually make his way back into society.

In great detail, he told me his story. He recounted the past six years — needles, fat lines on slick mirrors, dollar wine, more lies, hooking, loan sharks, the old men, jail, rape, the police, suicide attempts, the program, back to selling drugs, doing drugs, five dollar tricks, robbing, being robbed, the program again, back out, the habit again, hotels, a drug bust, conviction, sentencing, the pen, parole, rehab and finally, graduation.

I accepted his invitation. I was his only guest. Six years of rough living definitely took their toll. He looked older, weathered. He put on about thirty pounds of muscle around his shoulders, chest and arms. He had a slight belly that only complemented the menacing bulk of his muscles. His trim beard and shaved head brought out the delicate slant of his eyes and the stubbornness of his jaw. The back of his neck, his forearms revealed tattoos in Olde English script that weren't there in our youth. He looked sinister, menacing. He was even more alluring than I remembered.

To my surprise, he broke from his fellow graduates to hug me. Unabashedly, he planted a wet kiss on my lips. I froze, shocked by both his spontaneous display of affection and my lips' quick return. He drew back, eyes down, apologizing. Before I could react, a group of his friends came over to introduce themselves.

"So you're the famous Lorenzo..." they said teasingly.

The graduation was packed with hugs, gratitudes and confession. Manolo delivered a painfully honest speech about his journey to recovery. I've never heard him articulate his feelings before. I've never heard him take responsibility for his actions. This excited me and made me nervous at the same time. Was this the same man I knew six years ago?

When the ceremonies were over, we quickly broke from the crowd, I offered Manolo a ride to his new home in Oceanside — a two-hour drive from Los Angeles.

We took the ocean view route along the Pacific. I skimmed over the dull events of the last four years and recounted one failed relationship after another. Keith, Fernando, Greg, Arnel, another Greg, Robert, Magno, Enrique, Keith again, and, now, single. Although I was apprehensive, I asked him if he had any current love interests.

Manolo flatly announced that he had recently tested HIV positive. He told me he tested a year ago after waking up from night sweats and other unexplained ailments. Since he had slightly under two hundred T-Cells, he had an official diagnosis of AIDS. He countered the severity of his news by explaining that he was currently on medication and treatments that have greatly diminished his AIDS-related symptoms. He suspected that he may have been infected for some time but he was glad that the program was there to help him deal with his situation. No one knew, not his family nor his friends. He confessed that although he saw his diagnosis as the wake-up call that finally brought him to sobriety, he often felt like a leper. He confessed that he hadn't been able to touch anybody since his diagnosis. He was afraid of potentially infecting anyone. After a millennium of silence, he placed his hand over mine and asked me if I was negative or positive.

I told him that I was negative and that I tested every six months. I tried to put him at ease by sharing that I was no stranger to HIV or AIDS. The past few years taught me how to accept the reality of AIDS in our lives — the lives of gay men, the lives of men of color. In fact, many of my friends, and a couple of my past lovers, have lived with, and some have died from AIDS. It's all such a crap shoot, isn't it? He said nothing and just held my hand tighter. A familiar heat seeped through his fingers into mine. Impulsively, I pulled off the freeway and drove into a roadside Econolodge.

I parked my car, headed toward the rental office and asked for a room with a large bed. Manolo seemed confused. I said nothing and simply led him to our designated room. In the dark motel room, I removed my clothes. He said nothing and just watched each article drop to the floor.

Naked, I headed toward him until I found his lips. His hungry tongue probed my mouth as I tugged at his shirt and yanked at his jeans. When he was completely disrobed, I pushed him away. I wanted to drink in the sight of Manolo's nakedness. He was slightly weaving, as if he were drunk. A thin film of sweat that covered his heaving body glistened silver-blue from the sunset's dying light. I got on my knees and met his half-hard cock. The dark, purple knob was beginning to protrude from its sheath. Without hesitation, I swallowed his quickly stiffening member in my mouth.

"Lorenzo, please! Don't," he begged.

I ignored his pleas and brought the fat monster to life. Surrendering, he gripped my bobbing head and started to fuck my mouth. I slid to the floor. He sat down, bringing his whole weight down on my chest. Hypnotically, he started to rub and tease his saliva-wet prick all over my face. His hairy thighs scraped roughly under my arms. His cock blocked my airways. His knuckles scraped rhythmically along my face. We were drenched with sweat, pre-cum and spit. The air was pungent with our union. Releasing myself from his grasp, I climbed aboard the creaky motel bed. I handed him a condom and ordered, "Manolo, you gonna slip that jimmy on and we're gonna fuck like we used to fuck."

Without hesitation, he rolled a latex sheath over his throbbing tool. I propped my legs over his shoulders. He then hurled a mouthful of spit into the tight recesses of my ass. In one confident stroke, he pushed his steely, throbbing prick into my waiting chasm, forcing my tight muscle ring to accommodate his fevered thrusts. Waves of pain washed across the length of my body. I was drowning in acid sweat and memories. Instinctively, I remembered our rhythm. I looked up to see Manolo intently studying my face. I remembered his fascination with my labored expressions. We were dancing again. At the end of our intense melee, I love you, Te Amo, Mahal kita and tender kisses were exchanged.

We called on our lost language of lovemaking to articulate what we weren't able to. It became clear to me then. When we were young, we were both unwilling and incapable of negotiating or working through any fears or anxieties we might have felt. Fate, distance, maturity, recovery, shared pain and the reality of our impending mortalities afforded us this opportunity to finally establish resolution. We did it in the best way we knew how.

He called room service to send up more sheets, the damage we created was irreparable. We took a shower together. The hot water, his odor mingled with mine, the gentle kisses, the aftermath of our ferocious melee brought back happy young memories of matrimony. Like children, we washed each other's backs and laughed. (pause)

That was the last time I saw Manolo healthy. He landed a job at a local rehab program in San Diego. My writing career demanded more time. He found his niche peer-counseling other HIV positive addicts. Life events were traded via letters and long distance calls. Months melted into years and Manolo evolved from childhood lover memory to an occasional hello on late nights, funny birthday cards, religious Christmas cards, and oddly enough, anniversary cards.

One Sunday, Pedro, one of Manolo's co-workers called. He asked me to come to San Diego as soon as possible. Manolo was dying.

Manolo never once hinted how serious his condition was. He downplayed all his symptoms over the phone. In fact, colds were really bouts of pneumocystis. He was also battling a variety of other opportunistic infections that his immune system was no longer able to resist. Manolo lied to me again. I was furious.

With great regret, Pedro informed me that Manolo slipped into a coma two weeks ago. I was speechless. When I arrived at the hospital his case worker had informed me that his condition was terminal. The case worker outlined the terms of his living will. According to his wishes, Manolo was to be taken off life-support systems at eight the next morning. He requested that no one was to be contacted but me. His savings covered his crematorial expenses. Finally, his case worker handed me an envelope. It was Manolo's handwriting. The contents read:

Mi Vida,

Please don't be mad. I know you are, but I didn't want to worry you. I guess you wouldn't be surprised if I told you I couldn't find the words to tell you about my condition. Forgive me for everything. Papa, I will always love you. I will always be with you. Until next time...

Te Amo,
Manolo Santo

That night, the nurses, the doctors, the case workers left me alone with Manolo. AIDS destroyed his Herculean body. There was nothing left of him but a bare skeletal frame. His breathing was labored, heavy, monitored. His hair clung in thin sorry patches. His unattended beard grew wildly around his hollow cheeks and jaw, still beautiful, still stubborn. His eyelids, paper-thin and veiny, sunk deep into his sockets as if his eyes had retreated or been removed.

His body was a highway of wires and thick plastic tubes. The air-conditioned cold room beeped and pulsed with the sounds of technology and its cruel miracles. A small dim light came under the crack of the room's closed door. It illuminated his chemotherapy-tanned face, now angelic and grotesque at the same time.

In the darkness of the hospital room, I removed my clothes and headed toward matrimony. I untied the gown that fell easily from my lover's body. He was curled in a fetal position. With great care, I maneuvered my body under the wires, under the tubes and laid spoon style with my dying Manolo. My arm slipped easily under his featherweight body as I placed my hand over his weakly beating heart. I protectively wrapped my fleshy legs around his bony, jutting hips, burying my face in the wispy patches of his hair. Painstakingly, I pushed his catheter aside and gripped his flaccid penis. In the dark, I rocked him.

His body gave off a cold night sweat, our final baptismal. This would be the last time. My erect penis moved bitterly along his sagging buttocks. That night, I spoke to him. Words were insufficient, so I spoke to him in our primary tongue. I held him tighter, making love to his hollow shell. That night, I buried prayers in his hair. I hid blessings in his mouth. I rubbed his lips with my tears. That night, with one final thrust, I bid Manolo farewell.

When it was over, I dressed him. I took my razor and shaved the scrape remains of his beard. Carefully, I washed his feet and hands and combed his hair. At 8 AM, the doctor and his case worker arrived with long, regretful faces. I insisted on hitting the last switch. I was barely breathing.

Even now, I remember the sweat between us. I can smell our lovemaking, a mixture of cologne, lube, saliva and sweat. I can feel the heavy weight of him on my chest. I can taste the lubricant, his kisses, our perspiration and the sweet taste of his semen. I can see this all today. Manolo was my first love.

States of Being

Bino A. Realuyo

In this city, the States fill people's faces, blink in everybody's eyes. When they get tired of brownouts, the heat, the mosquitoes, the States appear in every word they speak:

May tia ako sa California.

Ako? may sister ako, CPA *sa Nuyork*.

My son—*abogado in Ha-why*.

Look at my shoes. PX goods. Stateside *'yan*.

Kumusta to your father, huh? Tell him not to forget us here, huh? Say hello for me. But tell me how's Woodside, Nuyork?

When is he going to send me my Samsonite? Groovie promised me you know? When is he going to send me Yardley and Ivory? They're not too expensive in the States I hear?

Here in Manila. Here in Manila. Everything, everything too much.

. . .

An aerogram arrived at the doorstep. Handwritten in a backdrop of blue. Blue, the color of the States. Mommy looked at it then ripped the edge with her fingers, so slowly I could almost hear. Before unfolding, she released a very deep sigh then handed it over to me. Read this. Inside, lightly penciled lines. Daddy Groovie's handwriting, practiced to perfection. Over and over, on scratch paper. Then transcribed. I could tell by the way letters curved and angled, time must have slowed down when he wrote them. I couldn't see him doing that, taking his time.

It's been so many years since I saw Dolares last. She has changed a lot. Her kids are all so big now. This picture was taken recently. See how her kids are now, your cousins? See how healthy they are? Very busy here. More jobs than I thought. I have two jobs, day and night. Many jobs here for those who aren't picky, unlike there, not much to choose from to begin with. During the day, at a hospital. Evenings, at a restaurant nearby, washing plates. Dolares recommended me. She told me, take anything you can get, you need the experience. She knew the owner. She knows a lot of people.

His voice. My auntie's voice. Dolares, his only sister, who I had never seen except in pictures. On the back of one, he wrote her name, the same way he had been saying for years. Dolares. She was Daddy Groovie with a huge wig and nice Stateside clothes, The one who petitioned for us when I was three.

So many places here to go. So many things to buy. So much food here. Bacon, do you know what that is? I eat bacon in the morning. There is no Spam here. Dolares is a good cook.

Dolares this. Dolares that. Dolares. She spoke to me in pictures and the Christmas cards she sent to us regularly. She called me "little one," and never seemed to remember my name. Once, she wrote it: Gregorito. So glad I was that I showed it to all my playmates in our street. English-speaking Titay almost ripped the card because she hated to see anybody with anything from the States. Auntie Dolares. The goddess of Daddy Groovie's future that he's probably build an altar for her.

I finally got a schedule for a medical check-up at a local doctor. Remember my stones? It's not that bad after all. So you, you always take care. Eat well.

He used to complain about us getting sick, comparing us to my cousins. Auntie Dolares' children—*There, they don't get sick.* He took the picture out of his thick wallet, this wallet dangling with several keys—*you see, healthy, healthy children.* I saw the picture once. Once and never again. He always kept it in there. This brown, cow-skin wallet which, like our house, had a window, except he wasn't at the window but this picture, it wasn't me, Mommy, or Pipo. But Auntie Dolares and her two children, outside their house in Woodside, in the snow. They wore thick clothing around their heads and neck, all over themselves, as thick as the whiteness around them. I could tell by their dark faces that I was related to them.

Whenever I thought of her, I smelled the difference of another country, a story of coloring book houses I saw on TV at English- speaking Titay's house, its theme song repeatedly playing in my mind, and in my mouth, a taste of melting ice.

Eat well, he always wrote.

Hunger, the taste of it I would never forget. it also melted in my tongue when my stomach began to ask for something I could never get. Then I was conscious of the little things, leftover bread that the ants rushed to in a blink, or the roaches. I began to dry stale rice in the sun so I could make crunchy rice cakes afterwards. And fish, the taste of fried fish, became even more flavored because I'd wanted it to stay in my mouth longer.

• • •

I squat here again, on the concrete-block fence, imagining you.

I think about the States a lot more, wonder what is there. I think in circles—rain, flood, heat, sun, then back to rain again but where you are it's not like that. It's cold there, isn't it? Like sticking my hand in the Frigidaire? And not too much sun. There is snow, isn't there? Before the snow, I think of the States as a coloring book house, wider than our street, sometimes a green, sometimes so white, sometimes you can lie on there and sometimes my feet could sink into the snow. Not like houses here with peeling paint that nobody thinks about repainting. These brown boxes, all attached, one looking older than the other each day, like the faces of people here. You don't live in one like that. Yours must be newly painted. A Christmas card house with green trees sparkling with lights. I think about how you and Auntie Dolares walk together in the streets of Woodside Nuyork. D'merica, sorry, that's the way you write it now. Sometimes with my cousins too. You laugh. You forget all about the window, the one I'm looking at now. You forget all about the street that overlooked it. You forget about the room, the noise, your bamboo stick, how often it kissed Pipo's skin. You forget about many things. I know. I can see you now. You laugh with Aunt Dolares, with her children. You practice your English with them. She tells you to pronounce her name right, with an O not an A. Do-LO-res, she will tell you, just like what Mommy always told you, but you are so used to saying her name your way, you don't hear her. I'm so used to saying her name that way too. The way I got used to saying yours, but never really understood what it meant. Groovie, you just called yourself one day. Stateside name, you said. Groovie, I know you tell them about us. But you don't tell them what you did to us. Only the paperboat times, the hours before the hitting. The ones after. You tell them how Pipo takes after you, just like you. How you brought us up so well. You tell them, Daddy Groovie, they will see us soon.

• • •

States was the body of an imagined brother.

Born in Daddy Groovie's mouth, he grew up in the mouths of our house. He was the youngest, the boyish one. with an enormous power over Pipo and me. He occupied the empty space in Daddy Groovie's insides, one made especially for him. States would sit beside me, hands between his thighs, sitting like a street boy, smelling like a newspaper boy, not looking like me, not like anyone else, just like himself, a look all of his own, the face of a future that might not be there. He would stare at me, his eyes blue like English-speaking Titay's dolls, his skin light as the stomach of a dead toad in a flood. Lighter than Pipo's. He would speak English so well. "This Gregorio, so gooood in English," Miss Huffy used to say about me but now she would say States was ten or twenty times better, after all he's States, the only one that made Daddy Groovie's small eyes grow as big as a coin, so big you'd think he just had San Miguel again.

"What do you want?" States asked me, appearing beside Jesus with a glowing heart, looking much like him, a child's face of him. "Why you looking at me like that?'

I wouldn't think of him being there, if there was somebody here to talk to, if those newspaper clippings Daddy Groovie sent could talk back. There were questions I wanted to ask. And States, the only one who could answer.

"What is it really like there, where you come from?" I asked him.

"Where I come from?" He folded his arms, pushed his head back to stare at the ceiling. Pointed his lips.

"Where Daddy Groovie is now?"

"Woodside?" he said, not looking at me.

"D'merica."

Then he fell into silence as if he was climbing the ceiling with his eyes, searching for the answer there, something he does very well. He pulled his little body back up. "Why do you want to know?""I don't know. curious. I just wonder...is there a place for someone...like me there?"

• • •

Whenever I close my eyes before I fall into deep sleep at night, when the coils in the mattress begin to poke the small of my back and I slowly forget the lingering smell of fried salted fish in the air, that someday, somehow I will also leave. Some place where I won't be hearing noises at the tip of my ears. Where Daddy Groovie will become a father from the coloring book house. Where I won't talk to States because Pipo will be the brother from the coloring book house. And Mommy, the mother who will tell Daddy Groovie that we should all start acting like the family form the coloring book house.

Dear everybody...how is the family? Hope everything is well. It's winter now. The snow is falling outside and it's very chilly. Christmas is here. It's different here, Christmas. Children don't knock on doors to sing carols. Hardly any midnight masses. People don't take it seriously as much. But the snow, the snow, you can't imagine how beautiful it is. It seems that time is flying fast. We are okay. Dolares' kids are already off from school and shopping for gifts. I heard about the big typhoon. Hope everything is all right there...Here, we have no floods, just snow. It's wonderful...Thank God I left. Merry X'mas... All the love in the world, ho-ho-ho, Daddy Groovie.

A Stateside Christmas card wrinkles in my thought. Mommy left the card on the table. Pipo saw it first. I waited for him to leave then I took it, kept it, put it under my pillow, memorized what was inside. I have never forgotten it since. In my deep thought, it formed like a crumbled ball of paper. Slowly unraveling.

The Lowest Blue Flame
Before Nothing

Lara Stapleton

Lourdes and Luz would have a field day with the weight categories. Light-on-the-heavy-side-not-too-much-mayo-weight. Itsy-bitsy-teeny-weeny weight. Fly-in -the-buttermilk weight. Fly in-the-face-of-convention weight. Baton weight. Bataan weight. Needle-in-a-hay-stack weight. Not-at-all weight. Sneeze weight. Lourdes, whose sophomore algebra was fresh in her memory, observed that Light Heavyweight must be like $X+ -X$ and means you weigh zero and that must be the lightest category of all. They went on into equations, what is Junior Dust-Under-The-Couch-Weight minus Wet Towel weight? That's negative, clearly, Luz said. Okay, Lourdes said, Miss Know It All—Toe-Nail-Clipping-Weight by Passing Wind. Disgusting, Luz said, and then they stopped, grinning. They bordered on ruining it by going on too long.

And later again, Lourdes would say that that was the turning point. Lourdes would say that that was the day which destroyed Dulce. They had lost her once and for all. Luz, who was the eldest and held greater strength of conviction, would say that it was just a coincidence, that that day, the day Dulce met Zuke the boxer, was only a normal teenage act of rebellion. She would argue that she herself had done the same thing, at thirteen, the night she drank three beers at Maria Luna Saguid's house. Testing limits, Luz said. You, Lourdes, she said—for a week straight you skipped ballet and made out with the Impala. Where did he get that damn Impala? I never made out with him, Lourdes said, we only drove around and held hands and they had money because his father had been a diplomat.

Lourdes begged to differ. Lourdes, who knew deep down inside that she was right but had trouble arguing with her elder sister, said that the day they met Zuke was a foreshadowing. A clear sign of things to come and if they—the women, the two older and wiser sisters and their mother, if they had knocked some sense into Dulce back then the later tragedy would have never arisen.

No, Luz said, the first time was normal, later—it was crazy. Later, they had already lost her.

Beg-to-Differ Weight. Shadow-on-A-Cloudy-Day.

Dulce—she woke that morning into a stillness all her own. Before she even opened her eyes there was a mint flavor, and her breathing stung slightly, a good cold sting, balm. From the moment she woke she longed to be outside so her skin could drink the sun. She was euphoric. She was fifteen. She sat for a moment on the edge of the bed and blinked the sleep from her eyes. Lourdes lay in the twin bed across the room. They would be going to a fair that day. The three sisters would go to the International festival at the park.

For Lourdes, that day had been something else entirely. What she tasted was not something you're supposed to taste. Slightly poison. Like not getting the last bit of paint off your hands, or soap. She knew from the start that it would simply be a day to get through. She couldn't lay her finger on it but it was everything. She heard the morning noises of the house—the pipes with their refusal of rhythm, her father urinating in the bathroom—the obscene swallow of the toilet. Her scalp itched. Her white bras were all dingy and full of lint. There was certainly a pea in the mattress, boy.

Lourdes tried to keep it to herself, noticing that Dulce was ecstatic, that Dulce carried the expression of a child about to break into a run. Lourdes knew instinctively that Luz and Dulce would not tolerate her foul mood, would mock and further irritate her. And so she was silent. And so she didn't complain when Dulce turned the radio to a station that didn't come in clearly, that she let that static burn and sizzle through to ruin a beautiful song.

Dulce with her incomprehensible outburst of affection. She kissed her parents and sisters. She grabbed their hands and danced while the others were still staring with weariness.

Dulce pinched her shoulder blades back and put on her most womanly dress. A bright yellow thing that fell just over her knees. She looked curvier.

She was, indeed the curvy one. Dulce was thick and dark like her mother's side. Luz and Lourdes had the look of Chinese girls like their father, slender and yellow. Dulce was the dark one. Her hair was just a bit coarse. For this reason she was their mother's baby, the island child.

Seemed Baning spent all those young years braiding Dulce's hair at the kitchen table. Braiding and unbraiding, braiding and unbraiding towards an absurd perfection. The other two were jealous and watched huddled from the bottom of the stairs.

That day, Luz and Dulce couldn't stop touching each other and Lourdes walked briskly ahead. The two linked arms. They pressed their cheeks together. The three of them had been given two dollars a piece. They were to be home by nightfall.

Dulce imitated Lourdes' walk. She always walked like a dancer. Feet turned permanently out into second position. One arm squeezing a bulky bag against her side, one arm arranged with delicacy—that slightly extended pointer finger, that curve of the wrist. Luz whispered loudly enough to be overhead "You think that maybe one day she would leave the house without her hair in a bun."

Dulce did her own big clunky imitation of a pirouette. Luz's was closer, being that she was slight-framed like a ballerina, being that her body worked that way. They asked did Lourdes want to go back and get her tutu.

The sun was raging, interrogating, but there was a breeze strong enough to bring relief, goose pimples. The wind lifted Dulce's skirt slightly and she liked it. Lourdes' skirt was a narrow fit and Luz's defied gravity and stayed put. Dulce turned her face up and opened her mouth, as if there were a sweet rain. Lourdes looked for shade. She would walk swiftly ahead with her outturned feet and then pause to wait under an awning for the other two. And then she'd do it again.

Their mother had packed them a bag and Lourdes had it squeezed under an elbow. Baning had insisted on giving them six large pork buns, each wrapped in aluminum foil. There would be food at the fair, but Baning insisted. She gave them a thermos of Koolaid. She could hear it sloshing as she stepped. The bag was bulky enough that when Lourdes turned sideways she was not conscious of her girth. They stopped in a little deli for candy, and things behind Lourdes got knocked off the shelves and when she turned to eye the tumbling cans, boxes fell. Luz and Dulce snorted into their fists.

Lourdes reminded herself that sometimes you feel like this. That sometimes you have moods where little things mean more than they would on other days. Her headache was a barely perceptible hum, the lowest blue flame before nothing. She wanted to grab Luz by the hair, not Dulce but Luz. Luz could so easily gather Dulce against Lourdes, when for the most part she didn't care. It was Dulce and Lourdes who shared a room. Lourdes who spooned Dulce when she cried.

Lourdes was seventeen and Luz was one year older.

Lourdes grew increasingly resentful that she was burdened with the heavy bag while the other two skipped and fell over each other. "You take it," she said, holding it at arm's length to Luz. Luz said no way Jose, and then Lourdes looked to Dulce. She would have said please to Dulce, but Dulce looked to Luz.

Lourdes grumbled. There was the sloshing of the Kool-Aid and the embarrassing scent of the pork. She was a block ahead of the other two anyway when she paused to open the thermos. "Do you want any?" she asked with a seriousness that made the other two giggle. Luz shook her head with a choreographed stiffness. Lourdes poured the sugary purple slowly on the edge of the sidewalk as she walked. She tried to match the stream with the crack. When she was done, she threw the pork buns back at her sisters—the aluminum foil was hot by now, and they threw a couple back again and Lourdes didn't laugh but she sighed.

By the time they entered the park, the three were walking together. It was overwhelmingly crowded. Luz said it was a fire hazard. It was like registration— she told Lourdes who would be registering for the first time that Fall.

Lourdes wanted to go home immediately. It stunk in that gross human way. Dulce said they should go back and get the pork buns off the sidewalk and sell them for a dime a piece. Luz said it would be a nickel to lick the kool-aid off the cement. They bought lemonades and intricate clay dragons on sticks from a Chinese lady. Most of their money was gone. They ran into their mother's best friend's daughter and walked with her a while until she took off with her boyfriend. A white girl wasn't looking and almost dropped her ice cream on Dulce. Dulce cursed her with the dragon and then imitated. They stood next to a bench waiting for a mother to take her children and leave. Dulce called them brats and waved her monster on a stick when the woman wasn't looking. The lady finally got up and the girls collapsed against each other and fanned pamphlets over their faces.

There were boys on fences. There were boys on fences all over the park. In pairs and threesomes and ten at a time. Lourdes and Luz weren't particularly fond of these young men but Dulce, she couldn't help herself. Dulce had lingered a few steps behind whenever her sisters got distracted. Her spine curved up. She smiled back at the hissing, calling boys and then ran with her secret naughtiness back in step with the other two.

There were two particular boys not far from where the sisters fell into each other on the bench. They were facing them from the other side of the fountain. The fountain blocked half of the tall, skinny one but his friend was clearly in view. One was tall and skinny with glasses, clearly a sissy and the other was short and also thin but very muscular. The short one wore a t-shirt fit to burst and a loose pair of chinos. He had a lot of energy. He hopped up on the fence and then down, up on the fence and then down. He gesticulated to his friend and turned to watch girls pass this way and that. The tall one stayed on the fence. They were Mexicans. The short one had a buzz cut and a thick, vague face. The tall one's bangs rolled over in front and were greasy.

It was obvious that the short one would do the talking. They were the kind of friends, where one would do the talking while the other one stuffed his fists in his pockets, shrugged his shoulders, and hovered awkwardly. The tall one would stand back a bit and nod at what the other one said and blush when the short one embarrassed him.

Dulce liked the short one. He had big, rich, brown eyes, darker than his hair. His eyes were big enough that she could see them from her side of the fountain. She liked the way he made fists loosely at his side, how quickly he turned from one direction to another.

The short one said something that made three girls laugh. Three Mexican girls suddenly bent a bit and one with a ponytail looked back. The girls kept walking and the short boy turned to his friend on the fence and raised his hands for a little victory pose. Dulce kept watching until he glanced in her direction and then she looked quickly away.

He called to her in Spanish across. Dulce looked one way and then the other to make sure it was meant for her. "What?" she called back, scooching forward and upsetting the way her sisters were balanced against her. He called again and she yelled back that she didn't speak Spanish. Luz and Lourdes looked to each other. He called back in English, and asked her her name. Luz yelled "She does-n't speak English" and broke herself up, but Dulce yelled "Dulce" and grinned.

The new friend turned for a moment to conference with the tall one. Everything that short one did was exaggerated. When he nodded it was to be seen for blocks as when he shrugged or waved his hand in disagreement.

What the hell are you doing? Lourdes said through her teeth but Dulce sat where she was scooched, waiting, and ignored her.

The tall one got off the fence and arranged himself against it. He leaned where he had been sitting with his elbows slung back and one foot crossed over the other. The short one gestured to Dulce, come here, come here, with big arcs of his hand, and Dulce stood and smoothed her skirt over her ass.

What the hell are you doing? Lourdes said again, but Dulce sached away.

Luz looked to Lourdes "We shouldn't let her go by herself."

"We shouldn't let her go at all."

"So go grab her by the scruff of the neck."

"Go with her."

"You go talk to those hoodlums."

They watched for a moment as Dulce swayed back and forth like a four-year-old with her thumb in her mouth. Then went to slowly join them. As they got closer it became apparent that something was very wrong with the short one's face. It was thickened and leathery and his nose was on crooked. His eyes were fine, but just the eyes, not the lids. The lids were as puffy as an old man's. It was like a doe behind a mask.

"I was just telling Dulce here," the boy told the older sisters. "I used to know some Filipinos and they was good people."

Luz and Lourdes stood close enough together and far enough away to speak under their breath without being heard by the others.

"And then you killed them?" Luz whispered but she nodded appreciatively.

"He ate them like the jolly green giant." This was Lourdes.

"The jolly brown dwarf."

Zuke was indeed a very small person. Smaller than Dulce, certainly, who stood out in the middle, giggling an octave higher than her sisters had ever heard, with her butt up in the air. Dulce with her thick calves, her solid limbs.

The boy was just as short and downright skinny but with these muscles tacked on. His arms swelled out at the biceps, a snake with prey in its endless throat.

"My name is Zuke." He put his hand to the side of his mouth like he was calling across a canyon, mocking Lourdes and Luz for standing so far away. "This is my cousin, Rudy." He pointed to the tall one who rearranged himself against the fence.

Luz nodded like peace-be-with-you, a few pews away, as if hands were too far for grasping, an enforced friendliness. Lourdes smiled but her top lip inched up in the middle. They didn't return his gesture. They didn't mention their names.

"Those are my sisters," Dulce said, this too with bubbles. "Lourdes and Luz," and Zuke said he never would have guessed, no, for real, that the two looked alike but not Dulce.

There came a moment of silence. There came a moment of heat, no wind to break that unforgiving sun. Rudy pulled his shirt away from his arm pits and readjusted his glasses.

"Gee, it's hot," Dulce gushed, waving the bottom of her yellow dress around.

"Yeah," Zuke said "I have to be careful, with the heat, you know, I have to be careful with my health, cuz I'm a athlete. I'm a boxer, ya know."

Dulce visibly gasped. She bounced up on her heels. You would have sworn she'd clap her hands goodie.

"Yeah, I'm a bantamweight. Rudy here, he's a jr. welterweight but he don't fight so that's okay. What are you?" he asked Dulce.

Dulce: I don't know *gush, gush, giggle giggle.*

He: You look like a *he looks her up and down. The sisters lean forward first with their mouths open in disbelief and then quickly, they sneer* maybe a featherweight. No offense but that's more than me.

She: *puts her hands on her hips in mock anger and then runs the scales in laughter.*

He: Or, maybe a junior. Let's see *He walks towards her with his arms spread, as if he's going to grab her by the middle and lift.*

The sisters moved forward, the sisters, linked at the arm as one unit, took a step in and Zuke must have seen it out of the corner of his eye, because he did not pick up Dulce by the middle. Dulce swayed this way and that.

Lourdes wanted to mash that mashed face. "We should go home," she called to Dulce who ignored her.

"Look," Zuke said. "I'll teach you—heavyweight, cruiserweight, light

171

heavyweight, supermiddleweight..." Dulce repeated and uncurled a finger for each category.

The breeze disappeared again. The sun made them moist, made them all squint and shade their eyes at once. Luz took a handkerchief from Lourdes' bag and mopped her brow. Lourdes fell to dreaming, awake, in the heat. In the dream she was dancing. There was a recital in which Lourdes had a cramp. It was the kind of thing, had it been in class, the instructor would have run to her with concern, or the girl next to her would have known, would have grabbed Lourdes' calf and started kneading because they all know what it feels like when your muscles betray you. When that long thin muscle becomes a dense sphere, a filled rubber ball, an anvil.

But it was a recital. If you had looked closely, if you had known what you were looking for, you could have seen it, one smooth, curving muscle and one sudden, relentless round fruit. Lourdes finished. She flexed her foot once but that was her only attempt at relief, her only break. It was a minute or two. She completed the pas de beret, the turn section and the grand jéte. She finished on one knee. And when it was over, she sobbed back stage and clutched first her friend Angie and then Miss Ruth as they rubbed the stubborn mass back from pain.

"How long was it like this?" Angie asked and Lourdes said the last half and Angie said Lourdes was a heroine. They were still clapping out front and it was Lourdes glory and Miss Ruth told not only Lourdes' class, but all the classes except the littlest girls, who might have been frightened, how very brave Lourdes had been.

Luz put her chin on Lourdes shoulder and woke the younger from her musings. Luz looked for Lourdes' eyes so they could stand in judgment together. Zuke was shadow boxing. Zuke was a hero too. *He said Ima buy a Lamborghini. Pow. Boom. Ima buy my mother a fur coat. Pow. Pow. Whatchyou want Grandma? Whatchyouwant Sinbad?* aside: *That's my trainer.* Dulce fluttered. *Whatchyou want Dulce?* He winked at her and paused, posing with his fists up. *Huh? What you want? Channel number Five? Shoes?*

Luz and Lourdes had enough, and instinctively moved together to take their sister lightly by the elbow. Dulce shook them off. Zuke went on, he told Dulce how there was a fighter, he was famous, you never heard of him? He's Puerto Rican—his wife had a shoe collection and she would put sequence on them. That that was what she liked to do, glue those little sparkly things...

Rudy had been staring off somewhere else for a long time. He seemed an ally to the older girls. The whole thing made him uncomfortable. Luz and Lourdes each took an arm and tried to gently turn their sister, the grief stricken mother at the coffin. She didn't know her own mind and should be treated gently yet firmly. Dulce yanked her arms from their touchings.

The breeze came back, stronger yet, lifting Dulce's hair in the wind to black flames, her skirt. They all shivered. Zuke looked down at Dulce's legs. Lourdes bore her teeth. "Dulce it is time for us to go home right now."

Dulce looked at her watch, said no it's not, and made it clear that her sister was lying. Zuke started talking faster. He seemed to feel that if no one else could get a word in edgewise, they wouldn't be able to end the conversation. The girls stepped back and he stepped forward, reaching out and over with that babble one time there was a fighter and that guy was already twenty-three and Zuke himself is only seventeen and he annihilated that old man how old are you Dulce... but he talked right over her answer, let me guess, oh I'm right—I figured. You could be older though, you got that sophisticated look, but I guessed.... There was something panicked in his talking and it gave both Luz and Lourdes the creeps.

Lourdes made Dulce turn to her. She didn't care if it was rude. "We are going home."

"No."

And then Zuke said, let me buy y'all some Italian ice. You girls want some Italian ice, and Lourdes said no, we're going home.

Dulce set her jaw. "Excuse me one second, Zuke," she said, with her shoulders up around her ears, and her spine, curlingcurling. She, Dulce, that little girl, grabbed her sisters by the elbows and pulled them aside.

"I am going to get Italian ice. I don't care what you do."

"No."

"How are you going to stop me?"

"I'll beat you right here, I swear to God." This was Lourdes.

"Go ahead."

"Dulce, are you crazy? Look at him." This was Lourdes again. Dulce looked over and gushed. "He looks like an assassin."

"He's ugly." Luz said.

Dulce's head was shaking something Lourdes had never seen before. She had never seen Dulce so stubborn. She would not admit the possibility of anything else.

"Beat me."

"Ma will beat you when you get home."

"What are you going to tell her? I had Italian ice? She's going to beat me for Italian ice?"

"I *will* tell her." This was still Lourdes, and even Luz was shocked by the proposal of tattling, they were way beyond the years of tattling.

"Do what you want. Go home and tell Ma, or beat me right here, *like you could*, but I am going to get Italian ice with Zuke. You can come if you want." She walked back to rejoin he who was now her date.

Lourdes' eyes darted all over Luz's face. Luz should have done something. Luz was the oldest. Dulce would have listened to Luz. "We have to go with her," Lourdes said. She was about to cry. Luz scrunched up her eyes with more accusation of insanity. Lourdes' desperation was more ridiculous than the whole ridiculous situation. Too much passion for this dumb day.

Luz thought of who might see her. She thought of a boy she liked from last year's biology and she thought of Jenny who was always looking for a good reason to say horrible things. Luz did not want to be seen with that ugly hoodlum. They argued, but it didn't matter, Dulce went for the ice.

"It's just over there," she called as she walked with Zuke and Rudy, it made Lourdes feel better that Rudy went too, and she could see the cart from where they stood.

Zuke didn't touch her. He turned back to wave at Dulce's sisters.

And it wasn't very long that Lourdes took her eyes off of Dulce. It was just long enough to threaten Luz with telling their mother, and complain that Luz could have stopped the whole thing and long enough for Luz to say Lourdes was a big baby and that everyone was acting crazy. It couldn't have been more than a moment but there was Rudy, the embarrassed messenger, talking without looking up, his black glasses sliding down his damp face "Your sister said she'll be home before dark." And Dulce was nowhere in sight.

The breeze disappeared.

The seething sun.

Lourdes took the leadership as they searched, shading their eyes. This was the first time Luz didn't behave as the eldest, it had been stripped of her. Lourdes just walked where she would, knowing Luz would fall in beside her. Knowing Luz should have done right earlier if she was going to do right. They combed the park. They chased a yellow dress, and it was a Filipino girl too, until the wrong gesture cleared things up. You would know from a distance even, your sister's vocabulary of gesture. You would know her pacing. They saw Rudy again, shuffling with his fists in his pockets and he promised to look too, to tell Dulce to wait by the fountain but Lourdes didn't believe him. They saw a kid or two from the neighborhood but no one had seen a sign. Lourdes walked around front of a group, to get a look at a short Mexican in chinos and a t-shirt. She walked to look him full in the face and the guy's girlfriend asked her what the hell she was doing. She kept moving. They split up and met back at the fountain and then Luz said, look we have to go home, if she gets home before us we'll really be in for it.

Luz said we'll tell Ma she went off with Linda, their Mom's best friend's daughter, and we'll call Linda and tell her what to say too. No way Jose, Lourdes said. I am going to tell Ma the truth. I don't care what you say. Dulce can't act like this. She has to learn.

They walked home with their defiant jaws. Nervous and mad at each other. Lourdes' headache pulsed. She had to stop and close her eyes to cool it. They walked by the Chinese food place, where an 'n' had fallen off so that the sign read 'Chinatow.' Luz nudged Lourdes to point it out and Lourdes said so what. Then Luz said "light on-the-heavy-side-not-too-much-mayo weight, itsy-bitsy-teeny-weeny weight." and Lourdes couldn't resist and said "fly-in-the-buttermilk weight, fly-in-the-face-of convention." And then she laughed so hard she forgot her heated brain until they got very close to home and grew at first quiet and then argued again about what to tell their mother.

Lourdes with her *poise*. Her placing one foot then the other on the stoop, the stairs. The toe before the heal. The precision of her fingers on the banister, the doorknob, her nimble darting fingers. Everything always placed, never put.

Lourdes looked very much like Luz, a version wound up taller with posture, but Lourdes' eyes were all her own. Nothing like the rest of her family, with their eyes open and receiving, their *come-what-may* eyes. Lourdes' eyes were always planning, narrowing, focused, her furrowed brow.

Luz knocked. Lourdes' stomach surged. They would all be in trouble but she would take responsibility. Lourdes' prepared herself. She stood up, up. Baning answered the door and smiled. The two came in and Baning looked out in the hallway for the third. Before she could ask, Lourdes blurted "Ma, Dulce went to get Italian ice with a boy she just met and never came back."

Baning's expression twisted. This would have to be repeated.

Luz said "Oh Ma, she just went with Linda and Linda's boyfriend and a friend of Linda's boyfriend. They promised to be home before dark."

Lourdes felt she had been generous because she did not say that the boy was a mash-faced Mexican boxer . Now, if she told, she would make two of them liars. It would be two against one, and Luz and Dulce would be ganged up against her for months. She would have to sleep in the room with Dulce who would be not speaking to her. Dulce with her broad back turned, with silence to Lourdes' stories. Luz should be the wise one. Luz should know right and save Dulce. Lourdes looked to her sister whose expression of defiance was only meant for her. Luz's face was so subtle Baning would never see. Luz would make Lourdes look crazy to save her own ass.

Baning sighed and said nothing. Luz went to the corner store to call Linda from a public phone and then waited on the stoop for Dulce as long as she could, until their mother called dinner. Lourdes clutched a pillow in her bedroom, plotting how to teach Dulce. None of her ideas would take hold. Usually— answers came to Lourdes and stayed. Usually, she would think for a moment and she would know. But on this day, she would decide and then a moment later forget what the decision had been. She was malfunctioning, dizzy. She had to save Dulce, but. Luz was bullying her, but. The phone. The truth.

It was dusk when they ate. It was nearly dark. Usually- Lourdes ate so neatly. Usually, Lourdes was the one who cut small squares of her chicken, or only ate so many noodles and turned the fork over, back up, to place each small portion in her mouth and wipe with the napkin from her lap. She ate more than anybody and took her time doing so. But on this night she didn't eat. Lourdes basically stirred her food. And when the doorknob turned, Luz, thinking ahead, before Dulce even shut the door behind her, Luz, with her mouth full of noodles said "Did you have a nice time with Linda and her boyfriend and that friend of his?" her stern, warning eyes. Baning said she was a bit late. Was she hungry? No, Dulce wasn't hungry and she swooned past them into her bedroom and swooned onto her bed so that she could stare at the ceiling and swoon.

There is a certain way that aunts raise their nieces and nephews. They love them for their missing sister, the dead, ill or indifferent. A double love. Love for a ghost and then some. With weariness and heartbreak and a desire to stave the disaster they could not stave before. Lourdes, years later, she would raise Dulce's son with a bit of restrained madness. She would be afraid to touch him.

There would be other boys for Dulce—worse and worse again.

Some of our sorrows our wistful. These are the best kind. The lost and beautiful opportunity. Lourdes' former life as a dancer would be wistful long into her years as a nurse and wife and mother and aunt.

And then there are the sorrows which are bitter without sweetness. The ones we never summon, but which arise against our will, the wincing, cringing sorrows. The forces beyond our control, or worse, the things we brought upon ourselves. The road we did not take, perhaps, but more likely, the soul we could not save.

from *Rolling the R's*
You Don't Have To Wait

R. Zamora Linmark

You and your son Jeremy are hypnotized by Merv Griffin. Your wife is nap-
ping. Snap out of it, Mr. Batongbacal, you've got work to do. Summon her tuber-
cular body out of the bedroom and into her car.

(Tell her, *Beer!* You've run out of beer) "Lita, drive to Star Market and get me
a six-pack of Bud."

"I just got home."

(So) "So what? There's no beer left in the fridge. I want you to go to Star and
get me my six-pack now, hurry, before..." (Before you lose your temper) "Before
I lose my temper."

"But I'm tired."

(No) "No. When I tell you to do something I want you to do it. I don't care
if you have to sleepwalk your way to get to the market. I want my beer and
that's that."

She looks pissed and tired, but a man's got to do what a man's got to do. She
sleepwalks out of the house and into the car. Switches on the ignition, presses the
gas pedal, and she's off. One down, one to go.

Shut Merv Griffin up, and get rid of Jeremy, quick.

"Go to your room."

"But I want to watch the news."

(Late night news) "You can watch the news later on tonight. I want you to go
to your room..." (Homework) "and do your homework."

"But it is part of my homework, Dad."

(He's got to you)

"..."

"..."

(I got it, the clarinet! He hasn't been practicing the second-hand Bundy clarinet you bought him from Easy Music Store) "Where's the clarinet I bought you?"

"In my room."

"How come I haven't heard you play it lately?"

"Because..."

(Gotcha)

"Cuz..."

"Well, get your skinny ass in the room and don't come out until you can play..." (Gershwin backwards) "Gershwin backwards, you got me?"

"Cheeze wheeze, Dad. I didn't know you knew Gershwin."

(Smart-aleck) "Don't cheeze-wheeze-dad me, wise ass, or I'll kick your butt across the room."

Just a few seconds left. Go run to the bathroom, fix yourself up, but don't take too long.

My, my, Mr. Batongbacal, you look slick. And gee, your hair smells terrific. Alberto VO5? Really? And your cologne, it's so musky. Wait, let me guess. Jovan? No? English Leather? No? I give up. Old Spice? Could've fooled me.

Jing's turning from the corner. Quick, sprint to the floral drapes your wife recently purchased at the Kress 2-for-1 sale. This time, try to be inconspicuous. Do not stick your head out and grin from behind the curtain before Mrs. Freitas, who is watching you from her kitchen window, has a heart attack from seeing your gold-capped tooth, toupee, and fat eyebrows.

Oh, baby, check Jing out. Se-Xy! Brooke Shields, look out cuz nothing comes between Jing and her Chemin de Fer jeans, tube-tops, and thong sandals with the rings around the big toe.

"Good afternoon, Mrs. Freitas."

"Good afternoon, Jing."

She stops in front of two yellow-painted mailboxes and bends to scratch her knees.

"Freaking ants."

(You love it when she swears)

She opens the mailbox marked 1715-A, scans through the piles of letters, shakes her head. Bills, bills, and more bills, except for the brown envelope that says her mother has won another million dollars and all she has to do is subscribe to five of the fifty thousand magazines of her choice from the long sheet of perforated stamps. Jing dumps it in the trash bin marked 1715-A.

She unlatches the gate that protects your one-story house with the three-bedroom extension your wife's family built eons ago. She scratches her knees again, then throws her nose in the air. Sniff, sniff, sniff. She smells something fishy. And it ain't Chicken of the Sea. She stops right below you, looks up into your eyes blossoming among the daisies.

"Fucking asshole."

Ignore her. She's had a rough day at school. Confrontation with Ms. Sugihara, who warned her that if her grades don't improve by next quarter, she can kiss her aerosplit and pom-poms goodbye. So have some sympathy for the poor cheerleader in distress.

What? Your throat's dry? Do you have any Halls? No? How about Sucrets? No? What, Li Hing Mui seeds on the coffee table? Perfect. Go grab some. They're more fast-acting than Halls and you can sleep for hours tonight.

Feel better? Good. Is she still staring at you? Great. Spit the seed out, clear your throat, cross your fingers, spin three times, open the door, and, in your very best Tom Jones impersonation, invite her in.

"Good aaaafffternoon, JJJJJing."

She gives you the Linda Blair look from *The Exorcist*.

(No need to wipe her sandals on the God Bless Our Home doormat your wife bought from the Arts & Crafts Fair at Thomas Square) "Do you wanna ccccome up and watch TV wwwwith Jeremy? You ddon't hhhhave to take off your sandals."

(Quit stuttering and offer her a drink) "Do you want some Kool-Aid?"

(No, not kiddie drink) "Or strawberry daiquiri, perhaps?"

(Something stronger) "How about orange juice and vodka?"

"How about taking a screw and driving it up your ass at the speed of light?"

Aw. Now, Mr. Batongbacal, control your temper. Pretend you didn't hear her. Now, now, lighten up. She's said worse things before. Besides, it's not worth getting all huffy-puffy about. It'll add more wrinkles on your face, and you've already got enough lines to start a Tic-Tac-Toe game-a-thon.

It's not that you're not attractive. You look much more appealing than Lawrence Welk. That's for sure. And of course you shouldn't hold your anger in.

Go vent it out. Go pound on Jeremy's door.

(Tell him he can't play for shit) "Jeremy, quit tooting that fucking thing. You can't play for shit. (Bass, drum, tuba) You should've just stuck to bass drum or tuba."

He doesn't hear you. "Open the fucking door, Jeremy, before I break it down."

He still doesn't hear you. So go ahead, kick the damn thing.

"What's the matter, Dad?"

Give him a couple of hard slaps in the head.

"You stupid fag, didn't you hear me knocking?"

Slap him in the face, too, while you're at it.

"I'm sorry, Dad."

"Sorry what?"

"Sorry, Daddie Dearest."

Is his face red? Good. Now, tell him to stop all that nonsense about current events pop quizzes and becoming the next Benny Goodman before he finds his head inside *The CBS Evening News With Walter Cronkite*.

It's almost five-thirty. Put on your invisible badge and march down to the back of the house, the extension your wife inherited from her grandmother. Circle the house and stop where the bathroom is. Don't whistle or hum, or you won't get a backstage pass. Double-check your watch and make sure you're not too early, or else you'll only end up with Bino.

Is it five-thirty? Are you sure? Shhh, here she comes. Go ahead, press your face against the screen, but don't press too hard or the screen will snap and you'll have to drive to City Mill to replace it first thing in the morning.

What? She's stepping into the shower with clothes on? Are you sure? Are you positively sure? Darn it. Don't worry, patience is a virtue. And like the good book says, great things always happen in the end as long as you slow your breathing down.

Mr. Batongbacal? Hello? Wake up and smell the Folgers, Mr. Batongbacal; that's the shower you're hearing. If you want to whistle, this is the best time.

So, how did your day go? Nothing much? Want to hear a joke? What do you call Portuguese guys fighting in a car? Cabral. Get it, car brawl. How about a knock-knock? Knock knock. Who's there? Boo-hoo. Boo-hoo who? Why are you crying, Mr. Batongbacal?

What's taking her so long? The water has stopped running for a minute now. Don't get all excited, Mr. Batongbacal. Shhh, she's coming out. Shit, she heard you. Back off, Mr. Batongbacal. Away from the screen, damn it, before she snatches the giant can of Raid and wastes it all on your face, like she did the last time and your wife had to rush you to Saint Francis.

Gee, that was a close call. Now, now, Mr. Batongbacal. Don't get all hysterical. Besides, remember your motto: Once you've seen one, you've seen 'em all.

Go home, it's dinner time. Go and have your little *Brady Bunch* dinner. Hang out with the Missus and Jeremy. Watch *Three's Company* and *The Ropers*. Or suggest a board game. Clue sounds good. But not those heart-attack games like Operation or Super Perfection.

Ooops, it's nearing eight o'clock. Say goodnight to Jeremy.

"'Night 'night, Jeremy."

(How cute. Now apologize to him about this afternoon)

"Hey, Jeremy, I'm really sorry about what happened this afternoon."

"It's okay, Dad."

Now say night-night to Missus. Tuck her in bed if you're feeling up to it. No? All right, it was just a suggestion.

"Good night, honey."

It's eight o' clock, pitch-black. Put on your invisible badge and tiptoe out of the house. Watch your step. Are you standing by the malunggay tree overlooking Jing's bedroom? Then what are you waiting for? Stretch out your claws and jump that tree. Not so loud. Stop shaking or all the leaves will fall and there'll be nothing to make that chicken kalamungay soup with. And be careful because the branch is not that sturdy. It might snap, and they'll have to cast up your legs again. Stay still. Shhh. And quit that heavy breathing. Everyone in the house can hear you. You don't want to spend the rest of the evening with Mr. and Mrs. Stanley Roper now, do you? Well, be quiet then.

What time is it? Eight-fifteen? Are you positive? Oh, you're wearing the watch that glows in the dark? My, my, we are prepared tonight. Just don't get carried away or you'll forget about the eight-thirty deadline when Auntie Marlene pulls into the garage to drop off Jing's mother from her night class. But don't worry, that's fifteen minutes from now.

So what is Jing wearing? A pink nightshirt? Does it have a picture of a pony or a little girl wearing a beanie cap? A girl? That's Strawberry Shortcake. Bino gave it to her for Christmas.

Mr. Batongbacal? Mr. Batongbacal? Hello. Earth calling Mr. Batongbacal. What is she doing? Thumbing through *Tiger Beat* or *16* magazine? No? Is she brushing her hair in front of the dresser mirror? No? Trying on perfume? Jontue? Charlie? White Linen? Prince Matchabelli? Yes. Hmmmmm. Stop and smell the air. Makes you want to walk through her bedroom wall, huh? Run your fingers through her hair, sample the perfume on her skin. Closer, Mr. Batongbacal. Come closer... Oh, well, time's up. Sorry. Now, hold your breath, tighten up those ligaments, and one, two, three, jump. Don't look so sad, Mr. Batongbacal. Run to the bathroom, lock the door, turn on the shower, let it all out. It only takes the thought of her and a couple of jerks. Don't forget to wash up. Cleanliness is next to Godliness.

What? You can't wait til tomorrow? Nor can I, Mr. Batongbacal, and you know why? So I can tell the entire valley to wear their invisible badges and come here to this yard. Their eyes will bug out when they see your Mr. Cleanliness body trying to balance on the branch. Oh no, Mr. Batongbacal, don't worry about them shaking the tree. They won't need to. All they have to do is whistle for the branch to snap. You'll fall flat on your fat face and break all your bones. And Jing will have nothing to do with it, because by the time you come back, all cast-up and wearing your shower cap, she and her family will be gone. Yes, Mr. Batongbacal, gone.

What Manong Rocky Tells Manang Pearly About Carmen, Rosario, And Milagros

Eh, how many time I wen' tell you stay away from those three sisters? You deaf or what? Like me clean your ears with one broom? You better watch it cuz the next time I catch you near them, I not goin' regret whatever I goin' do to you. No, no try open your mouth, no try explain, cuz I saw you, stupid. You think I blind? I not blind. I think you the one blind. I was drivin' by and I saw you talkin' to them in front Kalihi-Uka School, so no lie to me before I give you one slap in the head. Maybe that's what you need, ah? Maybe one good slap goin' finally put some sense into your stupid head.

Look at that house, that glass house they go around braggin' to everybody that they, and not their husbands, was the ones who wen' pour blood, sweat, and tears. Blood, sweat, and tears, my ass. Maybe was them the one who had the money, but was their husbands who wen' bust their ass buildin' it. If it wasn't for them, those wahines goin' still be livin' in that grass shack. Who they think them, anyway, buildin' one glass house way on top the mountain? They no more shame or what? Everybody can see what they doin'. Tommy said one time, he wen' watch Mila watch her husband vacuum for eternity and all she did was sit on her lazy ass and chain-smoke cigarettes.

What? What you mean how can Tommy see that close when he lives all the way by the cemetery? Maybe he was usin' his binoculars or somethin'. Shit, I don't know. I no ask him that kind personal stuff. Why you like know for, anyway? That's his business, not yours. Oh, just sharrup and go get me my beer in the fridge.

I tell you, everytime I pass Murphy Street, I like walk up that hill and break that house down, and false crack their husbands, too, for doin' all that housework shit. They piss me off. They piss us guys off. We already wen' warn 'em many times before, we told 'em, "Eh, braddahs, you guys know what you gettin' your-selves into or what? Think hard now, no act irrational, no get sucked by their pretty faces cuz beauty only stay skin deep." But what do those guys do after our man-to-man talk? What do those pussywhip haoles do?

Even Father Pacheco tried to talk them out of it. Eh, no say that. That priest might only care for his red wine and church donations, too, but he get one big heart and he just like one prophet when he stay sober. He knew way aheada time what they goin' end up doin' if they marry those sisters. He sensed it cuz he know those wahines like they was his own daughters. Boy, did he hit the bull's-eye. Oh, sharrup. I said no talk like that about Father Pacheco. Sharrup, I said. You talk too much. Why no make yourself useful for once and go get my packa cigarettes in my shirt pocket. Hurry up.

Eh, stupid woman, you come bring me my cigarettes but where's the lighter? What you expect me to light my cigs with? My fuckin' fingers?

Sit your ass down and tell me what you was doin' talkin' to those witches in front the school? Yeah, that's right, they nothin' but witches. And I get proof, too. Tommy told me that Roberto wen' tell him that one night, while he and Nolan and a buncha other guys was comin' down from the mountain from hunting wild pigs, they wen' spot three women that wen' look just like Carmen, Rose, and Mila. "Had to be them, brah," Roberto wen' tell Tommy. "They was dancin' and screamin' and just like they was speakin' in tongues." Then Tommy told me that Roberto wen' tell him that alla sudden, one of 'em wen' take off her clothes and started rollin' around on the dirt.

Of course, I believe Roberto. Of course, could only be those sisters, cuz, tell me, what women crazy enough for be runnin' around naked and wild in the mountain, and at night? You? Thought so. Shit, all this talk makin' me thirsty. Go get me one 'nother beer.

Why you so quiet alla sudden? Got you all shook up? So, how come you still never answer my question? I said what they was tellin' you in front the school? That they Filipinas and goin' prove to you by speakin' fluent Tagalog? Big fuckin' deal. I could care less if they speak fluent Spanish. I bet they was talkin' stink about me, ah? No shake your head. No make like you was born yesterday. Shit, you can lie better than that. Recipes, my ass. They no even cook, let alone do the grocery. How I know? Cuz Tommy wen' tell me so, that's how.

What? They wen' invite you over their house for dinner? For what? So they can feed you more horseshit about me, ah, like they wen' do to Elwood's wife Marianne? Shit, they was probably the one who wen' tell Marianne that Elwood was foolin' around with Thelma. What do you mean Marianne already knew about Elwood and Thelma way before she went over to Mila's them place for dinner? No, that's fulla shit cuz only us guys knew about Elwood and Thelma, and real guys no squeal on their friends.

So tell me, who get the advantage in the end? You or them? You, of course. You somebody, one wife, one mother, superwoman. But them, they nothin'. All they get is a buncha losers for husbands who walk around pretendin' they don't mind cookin' and cleanin' and bein' bossed around. If you still no catch the picture, I goin' paint 'em for you one more time. They like destroy us, you, me, our daughter Rowena, and everythin' that's special between us three. That's why they like get you into their side of the yard. Right now, they makin' you think you this, you that, one nobody, but the moment you believe all that rubbish, I tell you, babe, nobody goin' give a damn about you. And I mean nobody. Not them, not your parents, your brother, your daughter. And especially, not me. You better believe it, babe. So come over here and give me a kiss.

Jungle Manhood

Michael Sandoval

Jo Jo wonders, between heady bites of human flesh, about the time and location of things.

It is a warm, Sunday morning, he reminds himself. Ten minutes to eight. Advent mass will begin in a few minutes. The synthesized bells of Saint Ignacio church die out in a burst of blue fire, and "Good King Wenceslas" fades into an electronic hiss.

"What? What?" asks Gloria.

From the crest of Plaza de Locos Hill, the honking of the trucks and yapping of the rector's Chihuahua grow suddenly more distinct. The air south of San Francisco hills is thin and dry. A sprinkler weaves arches of water across the lawn; mist floats to the ground in the breeze. The clapboard of a bungalow shines beneath a wavering rainbow, and droplets on the wood sparkle like Christmas lights. Christmas eve is fourteen days away. This bungalow, at the top of the winding street, is Jo Jo's house. The window, propped open by a can of Dr. Pepper, is obscured by dead rose bushes that sag in a whitewashed frame.

Jo Jo's knees grind against the floor. His chin rests on the edge of his bed. In front of his nose knock the feet of a thin, red-headed girl with exquisitely manicured hands, whose name is Gloria Patricaino. Jo Jo is moving his lips, although not in a prayer. He is making love. His lips brush against the girl's soles. A corner of the bedsheet covers her right shoulders. Otherwise, Gloria Patriciano, who is fifteen, is quite naked.

—Sing it, says Jo Jo. Sing "Good King Wenceslas": Bring me...

—*Bring me flesh, and bring me wine....* Gloria chants nervously, her back pressed against the sheets. *Bring me pine logs hither...*

No chimes through the window, anymore; just the wash of sunlight and the flotsam noise of trucks, a sprinkler and a yapping dog. Jo Jo sweats. His damp back gleams like polished copper, as if he has been boating for hours on the surface of a sea. He is eighteen years old. His thick black hair is braided in a single rope that swings as he draws Gloria's perfect big toe into his mouth.

Jo Jo gives a tremendous, vacuum-creating suck. Each hair on Gloria's toe joint sprouts up and is wrenched from its follicle (Jo Jo imagines), the orange fingernail polish peels away like the skin of a cooked shrimp.

—Ow, Gloria says.

His tongue traces the veins on Gloria's feet, which travel like rivers. Rivers of blood, which is what veins are, he thinks, or really pipelines— coursing strength, through the sex connecting up, up to the heart— as his tongue wanders up to the knob of a smallish white ankle and through spinning glass portals, through which the afternoon sunshine and the parking lot of the Shangri-la Cineplex Mall seethe in a blur of pane glass and rising car fumes. The salty licks of Gloria's ankle, the faintly sour smell of her feet and the lint garnished between her toes are, in all semblance of reality, made of vapor, wafting upwards with the creak of new leather and the coolness of new sunglasses, as the Flip boys from Plaza de Locos spin through the door and wag through the mall just yesterday, smooth as cock robins.

• • •

A fuse has burst down Plaza de Locos Hill. The electronic bells flutter, then fade. In the lobby, Rector O'Neil curls his lower lip.

He walks briskly to the back room, where thirteen-year old Nestor lounges in his white altar boy's cassock. The Rector grasps Nestor's earlobe, and twists.

—Check the fuse box, he says.

—Can't you get a professional to do this?

He twists Nestor's ear much harder.

Nestor scampers out of the room, past Rector O'Neil, who smiles and scruffs the boy's head. The children's choir is singing *Good King Wenceslas*, quite badly, minus the camouflage of the bells. The childish voices heckle Nestor through the corridors.

• • •

Nestor is Jo Jo's little brother. Nestor still enjoys Saturday Morning cartoons, although when Jo Jo walks through the kitchen he quickly switches the channel to Mexican professional wrestling, beamed in from San Jose across the bay.

In Nestor's pocket is Jo Jo's knife, which he found hidden in Jo Jo's hoe early this Sunday morning. The knife is a horn-handled *balisong* butterfly knife, which their uncle bought for a hundred and twenty pesos on a visit to the Philippines. The blade is flecked just a little bit with red. Nestor rubs the folded handle with his thumb and forefinger. His fingers slip easily across the surface, as if the horn had been coated with oil from a sweaty palm.

• • •

After returning from the mall the day before, Jo Jo folded the knife's handle, stuffed it into his sock, hid the sock in his shoe, washed his hands twice; called his girlfriend, and collapsed into bed.

The time, this Sunday morning, is now five minutes to ten.

At dawn, Jo Jo helped Gloria in through the window and coaxed her to remove her clothes. The keys of a waxed yellow Nissan— parked in a hidden driveway away from her father's spying— dangled and dropped from a delicate finger. Jo Jo watched, as he lounged on the corner of his bed, Gloria slowly roll her summer frock over her knees, legs, hips. The summer dress was of the finest black silk, resplendent in silver roses; but his hand jerked back when it ran over cottony, pink-flowered underwear, the kind his little sister owned. Nevertheless, Gloria's pearl earrings shifted alluringly in white-pink hues through the window's light. He ripped off the underwear and laid it upon the night stand, then gave the dress a snap to make sure no wrinkles formed. A smell of lilacs tumbled out from between the creases, and Jo Jo felt momentarily at peace.

She had protected her breasts and private parts with the cup of her hands. Jo Jo had grasped Gloria's wrists, moving her arms down to her sides in a gentle motion.

• • •

Now audible with the dying of the bells: the hush of moving sheets, the gulping breath of fear; perhaps ; Jo Jo listens: even the splash of red droplets onto the pillow.

Jo Jo's face stings from the wind in Genaro's jeep the day before, Saturday, fifteen days before Christmas. He glides over a winding highway that follows the curve of the California coast.

Gloria rumbles her throat at the stroking of her hips, although her palms still press tightly against the sheets. A cavernous mall looms up before Jo Jo, a glass and steel castle rising above the gassy sea of cars.

The mall is swathed in polish. Waxed floors reflecting up, candy cane pillars; neon, neon, neon. Twirling, bright oranges above the Orange Julius stand; great, glass windows: a seven-foot mannequin in a silk teddy. Teddy bears stacked in a gold pyramid, a golden wreath of Rolexes, mounds of marzipan on silver plates. Waterfalls. A flight of red—carpeted stairs leading to a jetty flanked by tightly-bosomed elves, a Santa Claus who shouts Ho! Ho! Ho! with a Tagalog accent over a bridge of reindeer-shaped shrubbery.

—Santa Claus is a brother. Big Remy points out. Hey man Santa Claus is a—

—How much you wanna spend? Genaro asks Jo Jo.

—I dunno. What does a thirteen-year old like?

—A video game cartridge, man. Get Nestor the *Gong-Fu Temple* one.

—Naw, that's stupid. You don't wanna have your brother wasting time all day. Get him something educational.

—I'm hungry.

—Get him a hamburger,

—Get him a bag of chicharones.

—How much do you wanna spend?

—Man I'm hungry.

The Plaza de Locos Flip boys call themselves the Jack-U-Ups. Remy, Genaro, Clemente, Rex, George, and Jo Jo. Remy, Genaro, and George lift weights and are very broad. Remy and Genaro sport shaven heads. George and Clemente nurture low Mohawks, carefully starched t-shirts; exercise to develop thick, bull necks. Rex is lean: he has a fade cut and the word, "FLIP!" carved with electric clippers on the back of his head. Jo Jo's thick black hair streams behind him as he walks like he is running on air. The gang knifes its way through the crowd; past the baby strollers, the Chinese grandparents, past a lost, cherubic black girl who wails, "La—la—latandra wh-wh-where are you?" As her balloon bobs at her wrist. They stride and glide into and out of columns of sky light, carried forward by the secure tread-squeak of new basketball shoes. People get out of their way.

Nestor scampers down the rectory stairs. His white cassock gets caught on the handrail, wrapping his arm momentarily around him like a straightjacket. Jo Jo and Gloria are shirtless. Jo Jo slides off his boxer shorts: they are now both pantless.

The day before: Jo Jo, Remy, and Genaro wear uniform black t-shirts, oversized "for big lovers!" shouts Remy, crisp shirts, hanging almost to the knees, swaying against their thighs with each stride. On the back are silkscreens of Diego Silang, an Ilokano warrior who revolted against the Spanish in the eighteenth century. Diego grasps a sword. A fact: he bears no resemblance to the Diego Silang of real life; since the Diego of real life was small and wiry and scarred with experience and the Diego of the Shirt, next to which is emblazoned "Brown Power," and "Diego Silang, Freedom Fighter," has a bulging, vein-popping, body builder arm and looks like a young Schwarzenegger, only with a touch of melanin. Remy and Genaro are not concerned with historical implausibilities.

—Where's the goddamn toy store? says Genaro.

At a kiosk, he finds Clown World Toys at the south end of the mall, past New WΔve° (where all the salesgirls say "it's you, like, it's really you!") two stores up from Aunt Flora's Pampanga Eatery. Mouths begin to water.

They march past the Optical Hut and the cutlery store, which displays in the window a five-foot-high, battery-powered Swiss Army knife whose giant blade, saw, and can opener jerk up, and down. The Jack-U-Ups' knives tucked in their waistbands are six inches long. Clemente wanted the Jack-U-Ups to pitch in a buy a 9 mm Glock—*for real bad-ass firepower*! he had exclaimed— but Jo Jo thought the balisong knives were more fitting.

—It's more appropriate, Jo Jo once explained. These are the weapons of our Tagalog forefathers.

—They got their asses kicked, Clemente said.

—No they didn't.

—No they didn't, fool, said George.

—Yes they did, insisted Clemente. Anyway, family's not Tagalog. They're from Cebu.

—Fuck that jive island, said Jo Jo.

Inside the toy store, a baby is crying. Salespeople are stacking boxes and mopping up. An older woman works the cash register behind the counter. She is peering at Big Remy and Genaro through her gemstone eyeglass. Big Remy and Genaro have placed a Ken doll atop a Barbie and are chuckling loudly.

— I want your best video game, says Jo Jo to the lady.

—That, says the lady, is a matter of opinion.

—Do you have that kind of money?

Clemente, George, Rex, Big Remy, and Genaro stare at the lady with their hands in their pockets. The lady adjusts her glasses.

—Yes, we have that game, she says.

—How much?

—That will be 58.95.

—Shit, I can't afford that.

The lady smiles.

—Are you buying this for a minor?—Yeah, so?

—There are less violent games that I would recommend.

—What else you got?

—We have Melvin in BongoLand, Gumball Alley. Escape from Dooby Mountain...

—Are you crazy?

—How much you need? says Clemente.

—Genaro, Clemente, Big Remy, and Rex press dollar bills into Jo Jo's hand. The lady pouts but accepts the money. Jo Jo purchases Girl Ninjas of Gong Fu Temple with two twenties and a scoop of change and fives and ones.

—Blood 'n slaughter and bam! Pow! Knee kick up her wah-wah and SPLAT! That's what it takes! SLAM! BAM! Jo Jo mimics holding a joystick.

—You're the man, Big Remy says to Jo Jo, patting his back.

As an afterthought, Jo Jo purchases a plastic Revell model Viet Cong-*Punji Stick Patrol* kit for Nestor's stocking, because his younger brother likes to work with his hands.

• • •

Nestor fingers Jo Jo's knife. He has reached the basement, where the air is cool and where the sounds of the children's choir cannot follow. An upright piano sits in the corner. Nestor hits a few notes, then picks out the melody of dance mix he likes. A mirror runs the length of the wall. Reflected in the mirror are plastic toys with teeth marks, and the fuse box. Somebody has placed on it a fish-shaped sticker on which is written, *Love is the way of the Lord.*

Nestor stops in front of the mirror. He begins a *plié*. His arms circle down, he stands on tiptoe and tilts his head back just-so. Then he stops suddenly, and looks back to the stairs. Nobody is there. He smoothes down the front of his cassock and examines himself in the mirror. He wears the loafers Jo Jo bought him a year before. The shoes he purchased, his silver-toed Goaties, are hidden in the bottom of his locker in the rectory changing room. Nestor moistens his hands with his tongue and smoothes down the back of his hair. He hikes up his cassock and tries to stretch out the collar of his hand-me-down too-tight Izod.

—Can you get me one of them shirts? Nestor had asked. One of them Diego Silang shirts?

Jo Jo rolled his eyes.

—You don't even know who Diego Silang is.

—Yes I do! I know more than you! Nestor said.

—What do you know, retard?

—Where did Diego Silang come from?

—He was a Tagalog hero, Jo Jo fired back.

—No he wasn't. He was Ilokano. He was born in Ilocos Norte in 1754.

—Gimme a break.

—Nothing came of the rebellion. He was assassinated, dummy.

—You're making that up. Jo Jo said. He was a jungle Tagalog warrior. He killed Spanish people. Jo Jo glared.

—I can show you the book. If I show you the book, will you go down to San Jose and get me one of them shirts?

—Nestor? said Jo Jo.

—What?

—Shut up.

Nestor switches the knife to his other pocket and trots to the fuse box, then remembers that it's too high for his reach. He grabs a chair from a stack, clambers on the seat, and reaches up to feel the switches; and Nestor stretches high because he is only five foot two.

• • •

Jo Jo is five foot eight and stretches his own hand up to touch Gloria's face, to pull himself into the present. His face nuzzles the inside crescent of her thighs. Gloria's hand clutches at Jo Jo's hair. Her other hand lies across her forehead: the jade ring her father bought her last Christmas hypnotizes him. She is moaning, but not for the reasons Jo Jo thinks. The knot of sheets underneath her hip is hurting and Jo Jo's weight is beginning to cut the circulation in her legs, so she goes up on her elbows, squirms out from beneath Jo Jo, and starts to flip over.

"Hey!" Jo Jo says. One of her legs hits Jo Jo's head. "Don't you like what I was doing?"

Gloria laughs, and looks out the window.

"Yes, of course."

"Then what's up?"

"Nothing."

Her body folds like a piece of origami over Jo Jo's body. Jo Jo grabs her arms and pulls her to the bed. He touches the coldness of her ring.

He notices things. Gloria's dress has fallen from the night table: it now hangs from the edge; her flowered underwear has somehow become entangled with the dress and droops an inch from the floor. Remy and Genaro and Clemente are staring at him with stains around their mouths. The branches of the rose bush move in the breeze outside. Gloria is breathing softly. A yellowjacket is buzzing around the Dr. Pepper can which holds the window open. A short man holds a gun in Aunt Flora's Pampanga Eatery. A slight tan line cuts across Gloria's marble hips. Jo Jo traces this line with his finger.

• • •

The Jack-U-Ups sit around a table and use salt and pepper shakers shaped like water buffalo to season their food. Banana sauce splatters onto the table, but these are quickly pointed out by Aunt Flora, who makes Rex wipe the table off. Jo Jo relaxes against the archway of the entrance. Big Remy has stuffed a napkin around the collar of his Diego Silang shirt. He is reading a comic book on the Chinese pirate Limahong, who, the comic states, attacked Manila with a fleet of 600 junks in the sixteenth century.

Three men in work boots are sitting at the counter watching the television on the wall. The TV is tuned to a satellite variety show beamed in from Stockton, hosted by a mestiza singer name Chica Vanilla Mendez. George is feeding Big Remy a bite of his own pork with a fork. The Jack-U-Ups will smell like vinegar, soy sauce, and onions when they leave the mall.

Jo Jo holds half of a *bibingka* cake, wrapped in a napkin. Nestor's presents rest inside in a ClownWorld bag, the centerpiece of the table. At home, Jo Jo imagines, he will peel off the price tags, wrap the gifts in reindeer bunting and green ribbon, and slide them under the tree. On Christmas morning, Nestor will rip off the paper, he will say "cool!" and "awesome" and will give him a hug. The men in the corner are guffawing over Chica Vanilla's antics: she is hitting a man in a dress with her microphone.

—Chica Vanilla's tasty, says Genaro.

—Man, that girl got the job because of her complexion, interjects Clemente between bites. Probably uses skin lightener cream.

—Oh yeah? asks Big Remy over his Coke.

—Bet her real name's something more native than coconut, Jo Jo adds between bites. Like Netty Magulabnan Dumadago, some shit like that. Old fucks laughing at that stupid show!

Somebody chokes on Aunt Flora's bitter coffee.

—Pardon me, the somebody says in a thick Tagalog accent, but what the fuck did you say?

Jo Jo's head snaps up. One of the men at the counter sets down his Styrofoam cup, and swivels the counter stool to face Jo Jo. His eyes are obscured by sepia-toned aviator glasses.

195

—I said that's bullshit degrading show. Jo Jo's voice rises. What does it mean to you?

—I see, says the man. You don't like Chica Vanilla?

The man has very dark skin, as if he has spent the day working on the highway. His chin is stubbled, and wrinkles run thickly across his face, but his hair is jet black and looks like it has been set with real grease. A rubber mallet hangs from his webbed belt. The sleeves of his Naugahyde jacket are rolled up. Jo Jo's mother gave him a similar jacket a few Christmases ago, which he never wore or even lent to Nestor but simply hid, blanching, in his closet. The other men are silent.

The man's jacket is too tight: his muscles gather the shoulders of the jacket into hard lumps. Jo Jo's knife rests serenely against his stomach. He can feel it press against his skin, underneath his belt buckle where nobody could pat it down. Remy is running his thick forearms. Clemente focuses his eyes back down at his plate of longaniza.

The man rises. He is short, brown, and wiry. His forearms are strung with thin, corded muscle and turns like hemp rope, revealing a blurred tattoo: *Olongapo Rats*.

—You like my tattoo?

—No.

—He did it. The man gestures to his friend. With a needle sterilized in a drop of el Diablo tequila!

—You worked at Olongapo Naval Base? asks Jo Jo. Back in the Philippines?

Jo Jo's eyes shift to the Jack—U—Ups, who have stopped eating, and snickers.

—This mo'fo' shined the shoes of sailors! You one of them male prostitutes? Up the ass. hey?

—Cool it, man, whispers Clemente.

* * *

As Nestor reaches for the fuse box, the handle of the stolen knife digs into his stomach. He takes it out and unfolds it the way Jo Jo showed him. The knife flips out with a double flick of his wrist. His cassocked image, the ugly Izod peeking from beneath, glares out from the mirror. Ugly Izod! Nestor jumps off the chair. He swings the knife in figure eight circles and dances around the toys. Nestor slashes at the figure in the mirror: a young boy with a cowlick. He aims at the wrists, as Jo Jo taught him, takes aim at a jugular: jabs at the stomach of a dumbfounded Spanish soldier. The long sleeves of his cassock whip through the air.

Nestor jumps on the piano bench attempts a flying kick off. He lands, loses his balance, and somersaults, the toys scoot across the floor but Nestor is beyond care. He lashes out to the left and to the right and to the left. A conquistador armed with an AK-47 approaches him from behind. Nestor spins and puts the blade into the man's testicles. Colonial Ninja fall around him.

Then the sleeve of his cassock catches hold of the blade and rips. He trips on a naked baby doll.

Nestor pants on the floor. After a minute, he rises and returns to the shining fuse box, steps on the chair. An enemy—the enemy—stares at him from the metal surface and laughs, hard at his antics. Rector O'Neil's oval mouth wags open and shut. That atrocious Christian fish sticker with its big engulfing lips. Nestor jabs his knife in.

Sparks flies out. It is as if a dozen bee stingers have lodged in his hand. The knife drops. Nestor loses his balance. He shields his face as slivers of electrical current pop out from the fuse box. The main light switch blinks, and fades. The electricity goes out in the basement, now shrouded in darkness.

Genaro is licking mango yogurt from his fingertips.

The man with the aviator sunglasses has moved into the space around the table. Aunt Flora's Pampanga Eatery is a smelly, cheap, fast-food ethnic kitchen. Jo Jo can now smell cigarette smoke wafting from the man's body, smoke and minty deodorant, as if the man had spent his life in bars and used roll-on but never washed. The man has noticed the back of Big Remy's and Genaro's shirt.

—Diego Silang, he says under his breath, and grins. Hey! That's my name! Diego!

His friends laugh.

—Whose bag is that? one of his friends asks Jo Jo.

Jo Jo remains silent.

—*Hoy, Diego! Sa bag mo iyan!* says the other friend.

—That's right! replies the man. Hoy, bata, asshole, my name is Diego! That must be my Christmas present!

He reaches out for the ClownWorld bag. The other two men circle the table.

Jo Jo growls. The *balisong* knife flashes in the air. The blade stabs into the man's hand. Jo Jo feels the give of bone. The man's hand bounces off the table, splattering Big Remy's lechon and rice. Blood and thick, gray lechon sauce spatter onto Rex's Tjon Bone parka. Jo Jo pulls out the knife, and the man's hand jerks up, slightly. Aunt Flora is screaming something in Pampangueño.

Jo Jo holds the knife ready.

He waits for the man to gurgle with pain, to clutch his hand and to run away. Somebody will call the police, in which time the Jack-U-Ups will make a discreet exit. They will skip through the spinning glass portals into the sunshine, pile into Genaro's jeep, and sail off, bass rolling. He will wrap the present up in red and green bunting and stick it underneath the tree.

The man with the aviator glasses grunts.

He keeps his hand on the table for a moment. Then with the same hand, he reaches into his jacket, pulls out a dark-barreled pistol, and levels it at Jo Jo's head. With his other hand, he plucks the bag from the table, looks in, sniffs, passes the game cartridge and model kit to his friends, and tosses the bag onto the floor. Keeping the gun aimed at Jo Jo, he pulls Big Remy's napkin from the collar of the shirt and presses it against the wound. The man smiles.

0, Gusto mo ba magdisco? he says. So. Do you really want to dance?

The pistol aimed at him is a 9 mm Glock. Clemente curses. The man is smiling. Blood is soaking into his napkin. Jo Jo glances at the other men, who are calm, as if their friend has received a paper cut rifling in the junk box of a mother's kitchen. The Jack-U-Ups have not moved. Aunt Flora has stopped yelling.

The man in the aviator glasses cocks the pistol and presses it against the back of Genaro's shirt.

—You want me to make a hole in Diego's head?

—No, I don't, Jo Jo says.

Jo Jo still holds onto the half-eaten babinka cake, although the banana leaf wrapping has fluttered to the ground. Big Remy's mouth is speckled with orange grease stains. Genaro has frozen a sip of Coke in midstream.

—Just keep the toys, man, says Jo Jo. They're yours, man. Keep them.

Jo Jo slowly backs up through the entrance.

—Hey, you fuck!

—What?

—You can't litter at Aunt Flora's, the man says. He points with the pistol barrel at the empty bag on the floor.

—I'm sorry. I'm sorry, really.

He bends, picks up the bag, and shuffles out of the alcove. The Jack-U-Ups remain sitting at the table, staring at the gun. Chica Vanilla has just received a pie in the face. A laugh track roars on.

Jo Jo sticks the knife into his jacket pocket. He treads over the ploshed floor of the Shangri-la Cineplex Mall, stumbles through the spinning glass portals, and is surprised to see how overcast the sky is. The Pacific fog, which usually doesn't roll in until five, has settled over the parking lot.

• • •

Incense smoke floats up, driven by the movement of air through the chapel door. Nestor, wringing his hand, has shoved it open by a crack. The Eucharist is being served. Rector O'Neil is placing a wafer of bread onto the boy's tongue when he spies Nestor and frowns, and gestures with his head for him to take bread. Nestor is relieved: none of the floor lights have turned off, although he wonders what will happen when Rector O'Neil will try to use his microphone. The rector mouths something.

—*Where are the bells? The bells. Where are the bells?*

But Nestor is skipping down the hallway, through the lobby, and out the oak doors.

The breeze lifts his cassock up around his knees, and the sides billow out so that he flies like a dark-haired gargoyle, swept from the pediment of the church. No more altar boy for him, he grins, thinking of hoops and a burger.

He peels off his cassock and runs up Plaza de Locos Hill. The cassock flaps in the wind.

. . .

The dead rose bushes tap in the breeze against the window frame. The crinkled petals fall through Jo Jo's window in a desultory way.

—I want to bite you, too, she whispers.

Gloria pulls Jo Jo's hands away from her face and she presses him down. She kisses his forehead and cheeks.

—*In his master's steps he trod*, Jo Jo recalls the last stanza of "Good King Wenceslas"...*where the snow lay dinted. Heat was in the very sod which the Saint has printed...*

—You seem sadder than me, says Gloria as her hips wrap around Jo Jo's waist.

Jo Jo's hands ternderly cradle her face. He begins to bite, again; first her earlobe, then her chin as he moves to face her, then her nose and then again down to her neck. Jo Jo licks one eyelid and then another. Gloria's mouth, which has remained as still as the statue of Mary, begins to move.

Nestor runs through the sprinklers. He swings by the corner of his house and stops: a strange sound, a buzzing and moan. He crouches on his knees, creeps up behind the sagging rose bushes, and peeps in through the window, past the can of Dr. Pepper.

A black dress hangs from a drawer. An insect alights on the lid of the can. A pillow tumbles from the bed, and a slim, white body, peppered with bite marks, shudders. Gloria collapses onto Jo Jo's body. Her flesh has been picked clean. Jo Jo's face is buried in a thickness of red hair that rises from long, unsatiated breaths.

—Look, Gloria says. There are petals on the floor.

Nestor is wide-eyed. He shoos the yellowjacket away and tries to peek at Gloria's body.

The press of the stolen knife is hurting his stomach. Nestor pulls it out from his pocket. Wipes the grease-like feeling off on his too-tight shirt, which he knows could have been one with picture of a hero on the back. *That stingy motherfucker*, thinks Nestor. *And this bullshit weapon...*

With a yell and a quick swing of his arm, he hurls the knife into the room, over the bed where his brother and the girl sleep. The knife tumbles through the air, bangs against the wall, drops onto the bed. Gloria lurches up. Nestor sucks in his breath; a perfect white figure, small, an obscure diamond spaced by red hair.

—What the fuck! Jo Jo cries.

But Nestor is ten yards away, laughing, dizzy running up over the crest of Plaza de Locos Hill. On the far side, where the sound of the electronic bells of Saint Ignacio Church cannot reach, he will find basketball courts. He will play a pick-up game with some other young men from the hill for an hour, then sneak back into his kitchen to make lunch.

Nestor will fix an egg salad and adobo chicken sandwich. For dessert, he will consume half of a bibingka cake, which he will unearth in the refrigerator; wrapped, strangely enough, in a ClownWorld Toy Store bag. He will not dwell on this mystery: he will simply crush the bag into a ball and toss a free throw into the garbage. Then he will run outside, over the hill: looking for more games, the promise of honey, the feel of a metal pistol pressed against his tummy.

Perished Fruit

Maria Cecilia Aguilar

A mango, a hard boiled egg, a crisp fish head, a bowl of fried fat cut into small cubes, hot dogs, clams, banana ketchup, rice, freshly baked pan de sal dipped in pepsi, milo brand malt flavored tonic drink, and pristine pieces of refrigerated american chocolate were our favorite things to eat when we were seven and eight and knew the joy! of living in a flood-ed house, when we knew the joy! of playing in the darkness between lots where dirt bites.

If I arranged this food for you in a basket, or if I painted pictures of them on the bath-room tile, I wonder if upon seeing and smelling them, you would not then stand up from the toilet, open the newspaper, squat, and go about it this way instead of on a porcelain bowl. And if you heard a knock at the bathroom door, I wonder if you would not let me in. I wonder if you will not have already set out a place for me, an extra page of newspa-per. I wonder because you are my brother. I worry because your hair has grown tense and inarticulate, and your eyes are glossy, cracked, and lost as if a gang of angry girls had broken mirrors over them.

1
What is taken

You've locked yourself in the bathroom for almost an hour now, and unlike our earlier days in this house, neither of us is singing through the door to keep the other company. Instead, we are crouched on either side, banging and cursing.

"Where's my money?" I ask, as I elbow the door. "Where's my money?" I ask again this time quietly, thinking maybe if I asked in a soft voice, you would forget who I am and tell me the truth.

"I don't know, Ate. I already told you, I don't know!" you shout, irritated and worn. I had chased you from the kitchen all the way upstairs to the bathroom to accuse you of stealing money from my room, because I wouldn't let you borrow it.

"I got money of my own. I don't need yours."

"Then why are you locked up in there?" I raise my voice and my fist makes a question mark that is poised for charge. "Why are you hiding, then, if you did-n't steal it?"

"I'm taking a dump, goddamn it, leave me alone!" You give the door a loud kick. This startles me, and for a moment, I believe you. But only for a moment.

"No, you're not. You're smoking !" My voice sounds harsh and the words come fast, but my thoughts begin circling slowly when I think about the pipe you made from parts of a plastic tea set. I picture you holding a bright little cup and tube in your hand and I picture smoke wavering all around you as you sit on the other side of the door. But, it is a picture I can't quite complete in my mind, where does the tube go, and the cup? "You're smoking, " I repeat, more out of wonder than accusation.

"Do I have to fling shit in your face?"

There is silence. Do I say yes to this? Can I help it? I catch a glimpse of the edge of the kitchen table. I catch sight of its rickety wooden leg, the tip of a book, and a piece of one of the plates you broke after dinner. I was helping you write a paper on Hamlet, but whenever I made a point, you cupped your ear and writhed. Then you laughed as you wrote down everything I said, grinning and nodding so much that I had to wonder which one of us really knew the play, which one of us was really the fool. I remember thinking as I looked at you from across the way, that the table between us is not the one we used to know. This table has corners and it sways. It gives when you lean against it. It's only a few years old and already it's beginning to sing. But at least the table is a nice color brown and at least its edges are chamfered. It is always nice to feel wood slope and fold beneath your fingers when nobody has anything to say. And I found it hard to speak even one word when, after all my patient explanation about Hamlet's plot and meaning, you looked up from your book, grinned at me and said, "Isn't Hamlet the guy with the round table?"

Our thoughts bridge incredible distances sometimes—they come so close, then they diverge into what seems like separate realms. Hamlet may as well have been King Arthur, but I couldn't say so, and I told you simply, "No," but then I thought yes, we used to have a round table, and if we were there now we would be speaking the same kind of English. But as it stands, I know thee better than you. How do I love *thee*, let me count the ways I was raised far from you in a land of barns and snow. No round tables there where I lived. No round tables here either, as if the rooms themselves resisted such a configuration. The sharp rectangular walls, the narrow passages displace families like ours and make meals at round tables seem awkward, overdone, as ungraceful as a naked brown belly can be amid lean angular forms.

"Do you remember the table we had in the Philippines?" I ask, all of a sudden hoping that the bathroom door might absorb my strange excitement.

"I don't know. I don't know what you're talking about."

"What do you mean you don't know? "

Before you answer, I hear the toilet seat squeak uneasily and I hear your body shift its balance with my question, as if it were still your feet that bore your weight and not the stoic fixture underneath. "I don't know," you say, "I don't remember."

But how can you not remember? A week before I left for America, *Lola* found us there with *balut* we stole from her room. We were yelled at for stealing it and spanked because we were too scared to finish it. What we wanted was the broth, and the small, hard, white part. We left the rest floating in its shell, while we browsed through a Sears catalog and slammed our hands on pictures of toys. Then we heard a loud, *"Hoy!"* And we knew we were in trouble. We offered *Lola* the rest of the *balut*, the parts we didn't like—the *sisiw* and the yolk— but she was so angry with us for taking them, and then for not even eating it all that before we knew it, we had little duck feet dangling from our mouths. And we almost gagged because we heard the beaks crunch through our tears, and felt duck hairs brush softly against our tongues.

I remember staring at the leg of the round table then too. You had thrown up the *sisiw*, and I followed the unborn bird's flight from your mouth to the table's flourished foot. Your bird lay there unmoving beside a broad column of wood which opened like a hand to support the whole table. You stared at the bird for hours while I helped *Lola* and Mom clear closets and pack suitcases in another room.

"What ever happened to the *sisiw*?" I ask, turning my head in the direction of your sound, lifting my head to where I think your face might be.

"I picked it up and threw it into a tree."

"A tree? why a tree?"

"What do you want? I couldn't leave it there."

"Of course not," I say, thinking about how cautiously you move around the chicks we have in our back yard, how you're always careful to blow on your hands and make sure they're warm before you rotate incubating eggs. "but why a tree?"

"It was better than the garbage."

"Oh—Did you look at it?"

"Kind of."

"Was anything missing? Was it all there?"

"I don't know." The tone of your voice makes a face I know well. It is the face you wore that night at dinner, when our side of the table smelled of vomit and our feet were afraid to dangle over darkness, over parts of a bird that may have been left there, and though I managed to swallow all of mine, I shared your fear. It seems strange to think that our former places at that table are now occupied by the brother and sister we left behind. I mean to ask them in my letters if sadness has ever made them notice the carved base, but I don't know how to ask that question in Tagalog.

The table we have now is so much smaller, and it stands just outside our kitchen like a protruding tile that suddenly became too useful to replace. Looking over there now, through the row of railings, I realize just how short the distance is between our table and kitchen here, and yet how far the kitchen is from the bathroom, a distance which, odd as it may seem, took time to get over. In our old house in Manila, these distinctions were reversed and on occasion they even collapsed. There, eating and preparing meals occurred in vastly separate spaces, but shitting and killing game took place in the very room where we cooked our food.

In our American house, there are about six steps from kitchen to table. Very few memories are allowed to fit between them. In the Philippines, kitchen and table were joined by a long hall and once, when one of our maids—then pregnant with her first child—went into the kitchen to get more rice, she came back with a newborn baby in her arms. If we ever fought in the Philippines, I would not have had to chase you very far, unlike here, in this house, where the stretch of hall that I am sitting in seems inappropriately placed. The kitchen where we would have argued, would have been right next to the bathroom you would have escaped to. And if you were telling the truth about what you were doing there, I would know, for there would be no door between us.

2
What is shared

"Knock knock," the girl says, as she taps the door lightly and presses her ear to it, listening for traces of her voice lost in its hallow. She hears the quiet hum of the tank and the soft hiss of her brother's feet gliding back and forth over the bathroom rug, a hiss that travels from his toes to his throat and comes out in an exasperated sigh.

"Who's there? Why are you bothering me?" her brother asks.

"*Ate*"

"*Ate* who?"

"Your *Ate*."

"Oh—" the boy's voice brightens, "you mean *tae*?...Well, It's about time! I've been waiting for you! Where have you been, you little shit?" He bursts out laughing, and, at the sound of something dropping in water he slaps his thighs in delight and yells, "Oh shit! Did you hear that?"

"Yeah. I heard it," she says flatly, "We have to clean the kitchen before Dad gets in and sees the broken plates." Whenever he calls her tae she stiffens, amazed at how a quick switch of letters could rupture her name and turn it into something spent and wasted. "Get out of there, I'm not cleaning the kitchen alone."

"Are you mad? Don't be mad... I'm just joking, can't you take a joke?" the boy asks bewildered by his sister's change in mood. They haven't shared a joke in years. It used to be that their letters to one another were filled with silly riddles, accounts of all sorts of coincidences. Now he has become the puzzle, and as only his sister's frowns can tell him, he has turned into some kind of trick that's gone awry.

"It's just that the kitchen is so cramped and gloomy and—"

"It's been like that since we got here," he says softly, "get used to it."

"It makes me miss Mom." The words flutter out of her like a dying surprise. Half of their family waits in a wing of a house slowly emptying of people and there they are quartered by a door. Sometimes, the girl tries to picture their mother in the kitchen and when she does, she is again confronted by a dilemma of proportions. Their mother's absence from a space unknown to her impacts the girl in a way she is not always prepared for, like in the moments before dinner when she sees her father standing alone by the stove, or when afterwards she sees her brother sweeping the floor with his head bowed and his body moving as if pulled by an invisible current, as if he thought that at any moment, the kitchen could transform into their old one and his sad head would somehow meet a warm waist and open arms.

The kitchen of their old house in Manila had an inside and an outside. The inside kitchen had a yellow-green stove, big blue tanks of gas, long tiled counters with painted pictures of vegetables and fish, a wide, wooden bench, and a floor that could never look totally clean because of the noise of its design, a design that made your feet unsure if you were walking over tiny stones, bugs, or fragments of watermelon seeds. The outside kitchen had another long counter, a small square area with basins and water, and a ladder leading up to the roof. This is where they saw live chickens axed, their blood drained on shallow bowls of uncooked rice. This is the route they took to the roof top where they flew their kites and beetles. In the final days before the girl fled the house forever, she and her brother sat between the inside and outside kitchen and shit together, their backs and legs hunched over hundreds of words foreign to them, their mother hovering gently above their small bodies, preparing their meal and waiting to see what forms would grace the wordy expanse, their great inky nests.

"Do you remember shitting in the kitchen?" the boy asks his sister.

"Yeah," she replies, astonished by the interest in his voice.

"And how we talked when it was coming out?"

"We talked forever, cause it took awhile, remember? Mom just got out of the jeepney when we came to her."

"Squirming 'cuz we had to go so bad, I remember that."

"And we walked with her all the way from the front gate, through the house and into the kitchen where she expected us to ask her for presents, but instead, we said, we have to go poo, do you remember that?" The girl chuckles softly, and when she hears her brother laugh too, she feels her insides roll. But I need to take care, she tells herself, I can't be too excited or he'll take this away from me. So she tries to float her next words over. She struggles to slow down. "But I told Mom this was a problem, because there was only one bathroom and it was dark and moist in there, and Tita Bingo was using it."

"And the Komics we had were too small to shit on, and they had pictures of people in them." The boy takes a deep breath and smiles. This is the most he and his sister have said to one another in months. It means a lot to his sister, his speaking to her like this. He liked it too, sometimes.

Yet, even now, separated as they are by a household door, both brother and sister are not much more than their usual litany of nervous laughter and halting words Their father once remarked to their mother overseas that their son and daughter had taken on the sounds of different leaves. Their daughter was the sound of a book turning its pages, and their son, the sound of dried foliage blowing outside. How did they get that way? their mother often asked. Will they ever get back to the way they were? The way they were, as their mother knew, was the way they were that afternoon in the kitchen of the old house— two children hanging playfully on her arms, two children going on and on without knowing that that day would be the very stem of their bifurcation, without knowing that they were fruit that had slowly begun to perish.

While the boy and the girl complained, their mother calmly unfolded miracles on the kitchen counter. It is hard to say which were more miraculous: The fruits, cakes and vegetables she uncovered or the sheets and sheets of crisp newspaper they were being unwrapped from. The children grabbed the newspaper, but they both knew it was not a question of choice. Choice divides, and even as they took paper and pulled off their underwear, they knew they would eat fruit soon. The paper they squatted over told them that. It was the one afternoon of their lives when words had a scent other than of newly ground ink. Her section of the paper smelled like garlic, mango, and papaya, his of cabbage, lime, and sesame. If they were stranded together somewhere, they would have the starting ingredients for *Pancit*. All they would have to do is tear out the words *law* and *beauty*, *queen* and *Pasig*, to taste it for themselves.

They talked and talked. About *jolens* and rubberbands, chinese garter and plastic balloons, about playing *Tex*, *pico*, *tumbang preso*, and *patintero* which they were never very good at. The boy told his sister about a girl in his class who swallowed a jack and about a boy who had hair down to his ankle. "He keeps it in a bun and nobody makes fun of him.". The girl brought up piano lessons "Will you come to my recital?" The boy brought up something about learning to draw. Then he went on to talk about planetariums and the stars on people's faces when they opened the door, and his sister laughed out loud at the thought of it. They added and subtracted page numbers and multiplied letters and paired them into words, *na-is*, *ta-gum-pay*, *at-in*, hardly remembering where they were and what they were there for until their mother, who was chopping vegetables, came over to them, rubbed their backs gently and whispered, "Chocolate," feeding them two small squares of cold Hershey's miniatures from her small fingers which smelled like washed onions.

The suggestion of brown in their mouths made their stomachs turn a little and the boy and the girl smiled anxiously especially when they caught sight of each other with only their shirts on over sheets of paper still blank in the middle. They had stayed in the kitchen where it was lively and bright rather than risk darkness and unseen ipis in the bathroom. Nevertheless, it loomed in front of them and they stared at its door, wondering why anyone would want to go it alone in such a scary and lonely place. The sunlight, which hit their eyes when their mother returned from the market, soon sat between the third and fourth wrung of the ladder outside, dimming slowly into the ladder's bark. It was getting dark, the words on the paper began to disappear along with their little feet and legs, but not before they saw each other's scars and sang so loud they almost collapsed onto the small pile of shit which finally managed to coil out of them.

On the inside edge of the boy's thigh, just beyond his knee was a perfectly round peklat he got from playing with a hot iron the year before. He looked at it proudly, he liked it. He called it his "third eye". His third eye winked as he squatted adroitly like a frog. The boy's feet were grounded, and his shit came out straight, while his sister's fell in broken curves because her ankle could not stop jiggling from the strain.

The girl had a scar too, shaped like a centipede, a scar that crawled up her left ankle. She brought it home as a souvenir of her first trip to America. She'd had an operation there to fix the tip-toe that made her so ashamed of walking. On the way back to the Philippines, the girl carried her cast on the plane and at the airport, she handed it as a gift to her parents. But long after the operation, there were still moments when the girl worried over her leg and hoped it would grow as strong as the other. And though she was no longer ashamed to walk, at times she was still afraid.

Her mother kept the cast in a plastic bag in the cabinet. The boy and the girl used to take it out from time to time and have a look at the piece of gauze which had clinging bits of dried blood from the surgery. Then afterwards, they'd read and run their fingers over names and words inscribed on the cast by the girl's American classmates: Get well soon. Love, Heather, Steven, Patti, Christy, Arthur, Johnny...her brother liked the name Johnny, he settled on it. He would often say that when he got to America he would change his name to Johnny, to Johnny Jones. Whenever he said that name aloud, he sounded like a revved up motorcycle.

When the girl left the Philippines for good, she took the name with her and looked for Johnny everywhere, a small quick boy with a bright blue jacket, a helmet, and a slim speedy motorcycle. She never found him. In his letters to her then, the boy did not know the difference between periods and question marks. Every sentence ended uncertainly. *Miss na miss kita? Umiiyak ako? Sino ang katabi mo? Hinalikan ko ang sulat mo?* When he came a year later, he was brown and frail, so easily lost among the colors of toys and candy. The boy was afraid of the shower. He used to have his sister stand outside the door of the bathroom and sing to him.

"Saan ka pupunta?"
"Sa Amerika."
"Anong dala mo?"
"Maleta."
"Anong laman niyan?"
"Gitara"
"Patugtugin mo nga"
"Timpalok, timpalok"
"Tae ng manok"

The boy liked the song because it was true and kept coming true for a long long time. He and his sister used to sing the song over and over until each of them had several turns answering the question, until eventually, they arrived in the same place. The song had echoed out their mouths the day they rocked back and forth over their own childish wastes. They made so much noise that the house recoiled, grew dim and demanded silence. At the end of the song, their mother stood still and began to weep without them ever knowing it.

3
What is refused

The door isn't locked as you say it is and for awhile now, I've been wondering whether or not I should tell you, whether or not you'll figure it out. All it would take is for you to wrap your hands around the door knob and give it a twist. Then, if you nudged the door gently, it would open and you'd see me, shitting like I told you, and smoking too, which I never denied. Maybe if you opened the door, I'd show you my pipe and tell you how it works. Maybe since I made it, you wouldn't be so afraid to try it for yourself. Maybe If I opened the door now, it would save us all this trouble, but I'm stubborn, and I want to see if you'll remember that locked doors aren't my nature. But in all this time, you've not tried once to reach for the door knob and now I want you to go away, so that I can keep my secret.

"You can go down to the kitchen now, Ate," I say, in as steady a voice as possible. "I'm almost done. I'll be there soon."

"No, I'll wait for you."

"Why?"

"I want to."

"Just go. Please..." Our voices rise and fall with truth and still we have no faith "You don't like to wait. Just go"

"I'm fine. I'll wait," you say, insisting on patience.

"Who left for America first?"

"I did. I did" This you say without thinking, as if I were still competing with you, as if I still wanted the honor of being the first to leave.

"See? So—go." I hear you trying to get up and then you stop.

"Wait. What did you say?"

"Nothing."

"You're playing with me again, you're tricking me."

"No, I'm not," I say plainly, but you stay, and the shit keeps coming. Dad doesn't know we're fighting. He is in the back yard, feeding the chickens and weeding the flower beds around the swing set we built for our brother and sister, a swing-set they've outgrown but never seen. It's hard to believe we live in an American city, especially when the rooster crows and Dad plucks fresh eggs from a coop he built himself, and kalamansi from bushes planted just a few feet away from the pool table. "Where are we?" you had once asked aloud, while we sat on the rafters above our unfinished patio. The view from the back of our house could have just as easily been of a squatter in Manila. Small houses dotted the horizon, tires held some roofs in place, and I couldn't help but think of how this image holds its own truth for us. "Who ever thought we'd go from interior decorating to teaching people how to drive?"

"What?" you ask, as if I don't make sense.

"When Dad worked for American Driving School, he used to always wear suits and every morning, in front of the mirror, when I ran to get him his shoes and coffee, he practiced saying, ` Good Morning, Mrs. Jones, my name is Dante— dawn-tay—if you're ready the training car is waiting at the curb.' But in the Philippines, just a couple of years before that, people paid him lots of money to make their houses look good. It's interesting how things change, that's all."

"It's okay now," you say, trying so hard to reassure me. "Now that we run our own driving school, he doesn't have to talk like that anymore. Practically all his students are Filipinos and in the middle of the lesson, if he feels like it, they could go to the turo-turo joint on Plaza boulevard and have merienda." Your voice is slick and makes my meaning slip like a haphazard step.

"You say that like it was easy and that's not even what I'm talking about."

"I know what you're talking about, I was there."

"Only during summers, remember?" I like making you eat your own shit. "Or did you forget all about New York?"

"No. No, I didn't." When you say this, I hear your shoulders slide along the face of a cabinet and I hear the hinges squeak against your slouch. Sometimes I think you ask me if I remember just so I won't find out what you forgot.

"You said you didn't want to change schools to live with me and Dad. You liked being in the country, you liked eating snow. You liked living with Tita Mercy and Uncle Joe. You liked that he was American, that your English got good with him, that you were the only Filipino in your class. You hated California, you hated the city. You hated locking doors at night. You hated the sound of kids crying in Spanish and you hated keeping an eye on everything you had. That's why you didn't stay with us, remember?" These words roll off my tongue like drowned things heaved to shore by storm. All this time, I've tried to keep my mouth shut but I can't, not when I get this feeling that you think you've won me or saved me or kept me safe.

"I never said I didn't want to live with you. I'm here aren't I? Why do you think I'm here?"

"I don't know. Why are you here?"

The first time you left for America, Dad hoisted me on his shoulders so I could see you board the plane. I saw you limp along beside Lola in a blue checkered dress covered with small flowers. As she turned the both of you around to take one last look at us, the metal brace on your leg twinkled and gleamed. When Mom, Dad, and I saw it, we waved and shouted goodbye. The second time around, I was too old for shoulders, so I had to stand behind a fence and watch you leave through rusting wire The day Dad and I left, Mom cried alone.. In her arms she held a sagging bag of butong pakwan that missed our carry-on luggage.

I thought that once I got here, there would be no more of this. I thought America was just one place. But every fall, for three years, you left Dad and me. "For snow," you'd say, "For snow." as you disappeared down a bleak jet-way. Now that you're with us to stay, you're crying and kicking at the door, and your voice is engulfed by the sound of my hand tugging furiously at a roll of toilet paper. If I didn't feel so terrible, I would laugh at the coincidence, and at the fact that I've never figured out a way to tell you that it snows here too...

...Because you'd visit us in summertime, I never thought about snow, only about our tape recorder and where we'd go with it. When we rode the bus through the city on our way to see water, we took the tape recorder with us and pretended that its slowly spinning eyes were Mom's. We told her: *I got lots of hundreds on my spelling tests/ I did real good too/We have a swimming pool at my school in New York/ The church next to my school burned down/I saw deer last november/ Last week, I saw a black man at an intersection selling pies.* One summer, while you and I fished at the edge of a pier, we met an old Filipino man on a date with a redhead. When he saw our tape recorder, he asked if he could borrow it, and we said yes, Lolo, you can. Then from one of his dozens of plastic bags, he pulled out a dusty cassette, and played tango music. We wrote about him in our letters.

In letters home, we inserted two dollar bills for our brother and sister. I'd put my initials on one of the bills and you would put yours on the other, so that they would know which particular dollar was sent by their kuya, and which one was sent by their ate. In exchange, they slipped us paper cut-outs of fruits and stars. You glued fruit to the spines of books, the stars I painted and pasted to my ceiling.

Every Sunday, Dad called Mom and she'd cry at having to wait so long to come. *When* and *If* were said a lot then, *Hintay* and *susunod*, hovered over all of us. "We'll be together soon" Dad would say as he got off the phone, then he'd take us out to fly kites. The first time we did that, our toes couldn't help but curl around grass, because we were so used to having them grip the ridges of a roof... Because you'd visit us in summertime, I never thought about snow. I only thought about it when you left, when you wrote me letters about cold. You said though cold makes you stammer and shudder and crack, it gives you the feeling that you're fighting. Heat just makes you falter.

"*Tahan na,*" I say. "Stop crying."

"Why are you always so pissed off at me?"

"I'm not pissed off. I was just trying to call you on some shit, that's all."

"What shit?"

"Your shit. You're so busy digging around in mine, you don't notice yours is stinking up the place too."

The one time I let you dig around, you didn't want to. The year you finally came to live with us, Dad and I had begun breaking up dirt in the back yard to grow flowers and build a patio. Once, I found a hammer and an orange buried out there. The hammer's wood was brittle and fell apart in my hands, but the orange lying at the hammer's head, had grown hard. I told you about the orange and left it there for you to find, but you never found it, you never even looked, you just stared at the plot from the window. Don't you know? It was when you doubted fruit that our arguments began. It's hard to say now what those early fights were all about, though they always seemed to happen when I'd call you to come out and you'd wave a book in my direction, as if everything we were standing on and building started with words and not the other way around.

This house looked abandoned when we first got here. The backyard was nothing but dirt and a drooping lemon tree that stood on the rim of a canyon. To plant anything, Dad and I had to level the ground, but its slope resisted our shovels. When we cut into the canyon's side, our shovels met snakes and rock and roots of trees that had once grown there. Though at first we scrambled at the sight of snakes, flinched at striking rock, and tripped ourselves over roots that were so deeply entwined, eventually the earth gave way and formed a horizontal path before us. When the ground was finally evened, we marked and measured plots, and turned soil into rows, taking care to preserve the width between the flowers. Roses, poppies, and marguerites were sown into the ground and followed by timed rounds of watering and weeding.

When Dad I worked out there, I thought about the house which stood right next to ours in the Philippines, the house with a giant hole in its lot, the hole that lost our things until some men came, fished them out and returned them to us broken: bicycle chains, slippers, headbands, marbles, my sling shot and the cracker tin that held our dead pets. I remember having asked one of the men what they were doing in the hole, what they were doing with such big pipes. He said that the hole was the hole where shit from the bathroom was going to, and he said that the pipes were the pipes it was to going to come out from. And did I want to see it happen? Yes I said, I would come back later with my sister to watch it happen. You and I returned and peered into the hole but found nothing. We returned when the men were gone and bent down to look into a pipe, but nothing stared back at us. No oozing something, no petrified, stinking pebble. The following morning, the hole was sealed And you did not talk to me for days.

"Are you okay, Ate?" I ask a decade later.

"I'm alright," you say, tracing circles against the bathroom door.

"Are you going?"

"No, I'm still waiting"

"Me, too."

The door between us is one we've come to know, tall and wide and hollow. Words are lost here, suspended in the air between wood. At times, it is the closest thing to us, even as it keeps us apart. That's why I ran here, that's why I let you follow. Tonight we played a fool's game: which one of us is mad? who is to know? If I were to have told you I once saw Jesus while I drove, would I be evil then? If I told you, clouds shaped into His arms, would you call me a liar? If I told you I tried to take His picture, would you say I was a thief? If I died then and ran right into Him, would I still be your brother? And I wonder what people would think if they knew I had broken plates tonight on purpose, if they knew you had thrown a glass in my direction? What would Dad have done, had he walked in from the yard, lemons and roses in hand, as you chased me up the stairs? What would our mother, brother, and sister see if they were to appear at the front door now and surprise us all? If that were to happen, who among us would have the courage to say, Welcome home?

4
What is offered again

The toilet flushes and the door creaks open, the boy walks past the girl. His hands toss money on her lap, but the money he throws isn't hers. The girl searches the borders for her initials and finds her brother's instead. Before her mouth can utter a word, the girl's knees take her to the corner he has just walked around. Her body aches from this sudden movement, but her eyes stay steady, following him as he makes his way down the hall to his room. He opens the door slowly, tentatively, and for one brief moment, as she struggles to get up, she catches sight of his small brown body against a ceiling full of stars. And before they are eclipsed by yet another closing door, the boy looks back to meet his sister.

Before we left for America, before we folded up soiled newspapers and threw them in the garbage, before we even finished going to the bathroom over fading ink and letters, our mother gave us a mango, sliced into halves and shaped like boats, one with the seed for a sail, and the other without. We ate the mango slowly as our last meal slid from us. Later, when we squatted by a shallow basin of water to wash ourselves, we didn't bother to rinse the pulp from our hands. We simply cupped water and pressed flesh to flesh, fruit to fruit, soiled and unsoiled. We didn't stop to think about what we were doing, we didn't stop to wonder what we were capable of.

Poems

Sunset and Evening Star

Carlos Bulosan

Winter and sublime terror to the immigrants...
And my gentle brother who was sick in bed
Turned to the small window and the thick fog
That weakened the sun, twisting visions
Of our early days in the little grass house.
He spoke of our other brother, the one who died
Hating greed and money; the native village
And the foreigners who went to settle there.
I sat and listened. Sometimes a bold image
Evoked complete surrender; and I would scream
Fearing the lost was lost forever, till the noise
Submerged the trembling voice and fear reigned again.

About this dreamworld of our early long days
The October dreamworld of our builtup future
Gained bolder reality; the wonder of new friends.
The convulsive joy they manifested; the new life
That new thoughts and livingways created
To face the revolving crisis of the years.
While my brother dreamed, memory of pain
Explored the streams of our new relationship;
Our dispassionate arguments, our hurtings at times,
And, because we felt our imprisonment, our lives and deaths.
But I waited and watched the cold sunset and evening star
Embrace in light and darkness the heart of America.

All the Living Fear

Carlos Bulosan

You did not give America to me, and never will.
America is in the hearts of the people that live in it.
But it is worth the coming, the sacrifice, the idealism.
Yes, it is worth all these—and the loneliness at night.
The bitterness of prejudice, the sharp fang of hunger,
The terror of rootlessness. It is significant that I found
You after the cold and filth in the long naked streets.
After the screaming voices buried in lost corridors
That encompassed the shouting in the dark continent.
But it is significant only that I found you in America.

You did not discover America for me, and never will.
But it is significant to know that this body, foreign
To all traditions, is not foreign to sun and rain.
It is significant to know that the life in this body,
Your life in another body, is the undying life
That was sacrificed to make the wide American earth
A living example of man's democratic institutions.
Yes, it is significant only that I found you in America.

You did not make America for me, and never will.
You are stranger to that land of mind and heart
Where I travel dreaming of the future of the soul,
When the secured piety of one man is every man's
And none evolved from it, when the blood's desires
And the flesh's renascence are simple for everyone,
And the center of heaven a legend for children's laughter,
And affinity starred, handshake a manifest of tenderness,
None may be severed from the joyous human bondage

That wheels history like a shocking nakedness
Of anger and fear and pity—all the living—

But it is significant only that I found you in America.

The Last Trip

Carlos Bulosan

Rushing in the dark that pushes the searoar
Against the cold wind, feeling the nearness of home,
Climbing the last known hill that stands between
The wide plain and the ocean time's seamless print,
Reaching the crown and the first tree with surprise.
The sudden brilliance of the city strikes me with fright,
And I pause and wait for my heart to cease fluttering.

This is the last trip homeward. Neither war
Nor disease is here to annihilate the truth.
I watch the continent's edge lift up like a huge hand
To fill the great darkness beyond, and disappear behind
The last ridge of earth, beyond the last star of vision.

This is America   a sudden rush of machinery above
The savage lip of the sea. Kingdoms under the waves,
Vast shattering domes of tearless glass aging enormously
Are myths only. None lived to prove the sea's secrets.
Atlantis is a word only. The ocean's floor is reached.
This is America. —the last furious stir of life,
Whirling like spears of light above distant cities...

And I rush homeward through the last mile
Of pink advertisements and known places,
Warming a simple thought for you,
Thinking: This is our America.

The Living Hour

Carlos Bulosan

When there was nothing to see,
I see you. We are boundless but incomplete.
When there is no private war the mind is complete.
And we can find the lost staircase of the city
That led to paradise...
And we are not alone
in the heartless rooms
and death-cells

Whenever we are bound to each other,
We are boundless. We hear angel words
In each other's words, and nothing more.
Whenever there is nothing to hear, I hear
Your hair sing and all is complete in touch.
And I expect you to unfold like a budding rose,
And you expect me to fall like a soft star.

Whenever pain is complete, we are complete.
Whoever is incomplete will find completeness
In the boundless music of our touch.

From a Window In An Old People's Home

Edith L. Tiempo

Things had been ample in the old place.
A large life really, although
One would say painted on a small canvas;
Her children and children's children fell
Into change before her eyes, born,
Grown, and leaving, the changes
Seldom intimate- as people then,
And nations, coups and wars just
Were or happened, all things
Settling into their ordered places.

Here it has been the other way,
Perhaps because the little window daily
Gives the same little fragment
Of a scene. The frame does not show
The house across the street, only
The lawn beside it and the redbud branch
Hanging between the grass and the sky:
A green strip, a purple-red smear,
A shred of blue; although sometimes
The dog comes out to stretch,
The man trundles out a mower, and
The lawn becomes something more.
It is the window's fault
The dog and mower crowd the frame this way.

Though of course it isn't just the window,
It's her eye also; the cramped view wants
The picture larger than the life,
And that's never comfortable, something like
Trying to weave flesh and bone
Outside one's womb. Really a blasphemy,
A window without the person, or rather
The person without frames, seeing all
That peaks or wall-eyes wee until
There was nothing more to see.

Now it's a shrunken focus and
Things must be looked at, often
Idly, but sometimes the brightening glance
Falling on a sinner, each time maybe
A Magdalene, a Thais full of sorrow,
A desert woman at a well
Where water lives. There's the window
To see the stretch of green, the purple
red swinging in the wind's blue breath
To construct her vision, and let her
Sin no more.

Manhattan Rain

Carlos Angeles

for Con

Walking down Lexington Avenue
beneath the rainlashed canyons of Manhattan,
you by my side, umbrella-less,
your eyes misting like dark welling pools,
how can we survive the autumn pall?
As we turn left on 43rd Street East
towards La Biblioteque on a dead end street,
in the wet panic of a sudden down pour
I cry: "Run, we'll make it!"

We'll make it, as we made it years ago,
remembering that trek to Tubao in Luzon,
to flee the fire-gutted mountain city
and disemboweling bombs of friendly forces,
the rain drenching the thin shreds of our escape,
and you, heavy in the womb
with our first-born-to-be,
clinging to rope I tied around your waist
to hoist you up through mud-slicked steps,
clinging to hope the way
the despairing clutch at and claw
the dank unreachable
nothingness that's everywhere,
the way the drowning strangle
in the airless deep... "Hang on!"
"We'll make it," I cried, "hang on!"

And we did make it, across full forty mountain tops,
lands' curves and arcs crawling with refugees of war
fleeing under a cannonade of rain
in unseasonable punishing frenzy that frayed thin
the weathered starving skin
under the breakable fabrics of our escape
onto the foothills of refuge
onto the liberating arms of G.I. Joes—
those mightily from green-eared lads transformed
to fighters of the noble cause—
those who had been blitzed by fire and then like us
drenched to the bone with storm blows raining
raining everywhere
until we unrelenting refugees
descended on the final slope toward the final easement
rapturous in the respite of the ended rain.

What are coincidences but reflexive imports
of the time of incidence of place?
In biblical times rain pummeled earth in apocalyptic torrents
the way it plummeted on those mountain crests.
Tell me it was some such precipitation poured then held afloat
the weighted ark on Noah's drowning land....

Con, my wife and mother of our seven joys,
how long ago since last we shared
the fled persuasiveness of panic in the rain?

Walking crosstown to Park Avenue
under a steady drizzle of the ended day,
you hand me the evening paper to cover my head
and protect me from remembrances.

Jacaranda Trees

Carlos Angeles

Cool mornings. Skies the color of bruised plums.
May and its promises of rain. Uncertainties
of spring weather that let no rain fall free at all.

But let me tell you about the jacarandas
that line the streets on my block,
from Chatterton Street to Turk
and all along the bend on Wegman Drive,
then on through Main—full-blooming now
their violet clusters cresting treetops
and cascading down like collapsed bouquets
along the widening sides of tenting foliage,
the heady crushed-grape scent of wine
flooding the noonday air.

And let me tell you that throughout the day
jacaranda clusters drop their velvet petals
onto deep shadows of the trees
to overflow a spill of royal blues
and imperial purples.

At nightfall, phantom emperors and kings
walk the earth around the block
their footfalls treading the flooded streets
of bruised blue and purple colors.

Crossing 14th St. and Avenue A

Luis Cabalquinto

I nearly get bumped by a speeding
Red Apple double-decker charter bus
filled to its open top with tourists,
their wide-eyed vacationing faces
melting in the sticky-hot July afternoon.
They all look in my direction. No one
waves. No one smiles. All is well.

Sunday with the Smiths

Luis Cabalquinto

The pond fish have been caught & cleaned
    & I have left their heads on
& Bob says "Ugh!" as Kathleen prepares to
    bake them.
Steve is doing the chickens on the
    outdoor grill
& at a table on the grass in front
    of this white farm house
Vicky & I lay out stuff on the cloth.

When everything is done after an hour
    we all sit down for dinner,
Having earlier begun our wine
    & fruit.
"A fine day for a barbecue party,"
    Kathleen says,
& we pause & Bob says grace.
    I sit sharply aware: I feel & see
Us all, as if apart: I watch from a
    point just above my head in space.
Beside the blue spruce alive with needles
    of light
We quietly pray, & the bees come to us for
    the wayward wine on our lips.
The sun's long lukewarm rays—
    & the smell of apples in the yard
& of pears on our clothes
    & of "Shaggy" chasing shadows
Among the yellow lilies

bring a small quake rushing
Towards the end of my fingers.
I pray that something gentle
& old, involving all of us, should often
come true: something like today,
Something after this Sunday's mold.

Dragon (Winter 1994)

Rene J. Navarro

Snow is falling in transparent
sheets across the garden
of lilacs into the woods
beyond. The dragon is out
there, his tail whipping
the wind in gusts along
the rhododendron path.
He has been out since
dawn, tasting the melting
snow on his tongue. He hears
the elegant explosion
of snow vaporising
in an instant: it recalls
other quiet revelations
of the quotidian. A flute
music rising with the mist above
the darkening canopy
of trees in a deep
valley in the Catskills where
Rip Van Winkle slept
for twenty years. The morning
mist in Chengdu wrapping the sun
in haze as the rays hit the cold
wind from the foothills
of the Himalayas. The taste of cold
ripe cherimoya: sweet,
sour, bitter at once, flavors
of a childhood in a tropical
town north of Manila. The moaning

echoes of a frozen Waban
Lake as ice pushed
against ice. All the seasons
of his lifetimes
he has heard
this earthsong
of white cranes that take
him as far
as the North
Star, his senses
waking him
in small
satoris to the
presence of God.

An Imaginary Letter to My Twin Sons

Gemino H. Abad

Dear Davie, Dear Diego,

I am on an island called Oahu.
Here there are many white people, they are called Haules.
There are also Japanese, Chinese, Filipinos.
I have seen the fields of sugar cane
Where the Ilocanos worked when they first came over.
How poor they must have been and lonely;
No one could follow their speech to their own island home.

There are very few native Hawai'ians;
Their words which are the names of streets and buildings
Outnumber them. "How could happen this be?"
A long time ago, they had a queen, but soldiers came from America
And took away her throne, and then all the land.
Those who fought were killed, and then many more died
Because they did not know the diseases that the soldiers brought—
They were never so sick before on their island.

But it is a beautiful island
Perhaps because nature's story is so different from ours.
Trees and mountains and falls and beaches are her speech.
And perhaps, because our own story is dark,
We see only half her beauty, and only dream of good will and peace.
I cannot fathom the human sadness that infects our sense for beauty.

Let me just tell you now
About the Chinese banyan tree by my window.
Tonight it is my father because his love
Was like a great tree, but without speech.
Every morning on that banyan tree
Many species of birds are in full throat,
So that now I wonder: would my sons, years from now,
Gather from a tree's silence my own heart's affection,
And in that moment know that once, while I made their world,
I had deeply wished, when they shall have left that world behind,
I would be the tree to their morning?

Andy Warhol Speaks To His Two Filipino Maids

Alfred A. Yuson

Art, my dears, is not cleaning up
after the act. Neither is it washing off
grime with the soap of fact. In fact
and in truth, my dears, art is dead

center, between meals, amid spices
and spoilage. Fills up the whitebread
sweep of life's obedient slices.

Art is the letters you send home
about the man you serve. Or the salad
you bring in to my parlor of elites.
While Manhattan stares down at the soup

of our affinities. And we hear talk of coup
in your islands. There they copy love
the way I do, as how I arrive over and over

again at art. Perhaps too it is the time
marked by the sand in your shoes, spilling
softly like rumor. After your hearts I lust.
In our God you trust. And it's your day off.

Filipino in Frisco

Alfred A. Yuson

In their dreams the old-timers
pawn themselves no farther than a push,
taking the measure of affectation
from the higher pieces. This city,
this hilly chessboard, is after all
no larger than Geary Square, where
the brown and the yellow rule
the diagonals.

Mang Kardo basks in the sun
mulling over his privilege to castle,
were it as good to know which tenement
goes under and which the safer...
Chinaman before him hurries off
his peril, has to see to market
freshness of bass and grouper,
as well to the public burning (such
small feet for an effigy) of the
mainland countryman.

Da Flip tosses a mental coin
a la old cara y cruz, opts for the shorter
distance of convention. Kardong Kaliwete,
Super Southpaw, they called him all that
time before the last great quake, when
punchdrunk he gave it to the white
woman at Ka Mario's quilted four-poster,
time he stroked the bottom most.

Now with this game good as done
he'll take Da Chink's quarter to parlay
for a minute's video—his king
for a peepshow! Else hustle the day away
with boardcraft for a prize glimpse
of Carol Doda, Da Dyoga. That is,
if one got lucky.

Jumping his knight for tempo Kardo
thinks of the double-leap the brown
young lovers took from Golden Gate.
A first! Did him proud. Three more moves
and love's erection is assured. No risks
now, the dream takes off on tightwire
(by cable car all the way to Noveleta,
hazard of a hometown). Time now to wave
antenna of the race, get cocky.

America

Simeon Dumdum

I listened to him speak
of West Virginia
(he was born in Leyte
but was living
in West Virginia).
He spoke as they do
in the movies,
and as Ronald Reagan does
on the radio.
Even the way
he said "Virginia"
was better than the way
Hinying, a girl I knew
whose hair fell down a shoulder
like the tail of a bird,
said her name,
which was "Virhinia."
And on that warm evening
I told myself,
That's where I want to be,
in West Virginia, or New York,
or San Francisco,
because cousin says
everything there is big
and cheap—big chickens,
big eggs, big buildings,
and big flowers.
Cousin looked at me
and said, Yes, big roses,

tea roses, and he was
about to name other roses
but the moon was rising
and it was bigger than in
America.

To a Friend in Autumn

Simeon Dumdum

And I thought I had done with leaves.
It came pressed, hand-like, extra-territorial.
Is it maple? Did it mark a passage
In your anthology?

The leaf lies on the grass
Safe and yellow. (The exile shivers on the subway
Far from warm-weather dictatorships.)
Is Li Po in your anthology?

"And you have been gone five months."
Sunlight comes in through the window.
We're both safe and unsafe from our versions
Of the New York City winter.

A Snail's Progress

Luis H. Francia

Who is the god of snails
But Speed?

I have seen them on a
Summer night shuck their shells

And whirl around the park
Dervishes of the dark.

I have seen them naked in races
Their shiny-brown bodies
Putting the fleetest of
Olympians to shame.

The hummingbird pauses, impressed.
The turtle smiles for they
Are brothers under
The shell.

The hare harrumphs but
Bleeds in envy.

Greyhounds of the garden
And all in adoration of Zip

Streak Flash Dash!
The thousand sacred names of their

Secret god.

Applauded by worker ants
Sighed after by ladybugs
They bound across hillocks, swing from

Bougainvillea and jasmine, and
In a cathedral of star apples and
Mango trees

This congregation
Chants hymns lustily
Of poetry and love,

Of Eros and Thanatos—

Then as the curious sun comes
They veil their blinding limbs

To once again become a tribe of
solemn priests
As I become one
Brown thoughts concealed in the morning
to walk and work in a

White world
Aleck smart, monk furtive
Wanderer in this
American wonderland

Frocked, stately, our shells
Both cross and armor

This band of faux conquistadors
Readies itself for the rocks
Of infidel boys

Who have no patience

With us who do not
Run at first sight
Or sing hosannas to
The west

Who are Wildmen and
Conspirators at night
Martyrs by light

Catholics Anonymous

Luis H. Francia

Don't even
look, don't even
move your head half an inch
I remembered the group's advice
to stare straight ahead

It was difficult doing so
passing by this cathedral on Fifth,
spires ready to slice the
belly of heaven like a blue piñata and
let all those good boys and girls
with wings come fluttering down (oh yes,
come on down my darlings and let me
knock you up)

my knees started to bend towards
accustomed prayer
and at that instant the church spoke
just at that moment
right on the sidewalk
my body smack in the
the line of fire from
the altar down that polished aisle
straight to me

the voice and the bells and the
cardinal spoke that instant

my knees bent further
towards the ground
my mouth opened
ready for holy utterance, prayers
amassed in memory, a vowel
for the holy ghost and consonants
for the rest
but I remembered the group's advice

My mouth opened and I put an
apple into it and bit, I remembered a
garden and exile
remembered bamboo man and
bamboo woman emerging
I remembered the love of
priestesses
my mouth opened and

I stuffed a city
into it, and seven thousand islands full of
palmyras, rhum, fish, warm-blooded
women, a canoe circling in a
sky of water content with
the sun's benediction

my mouth opened
ready for holy utterance
I remembered the group's advice
and placed it on the nearest stranger
a veiled houri who turned the other
cheek and looked at me spiritually

my mouth opened

school prayers waving their banners
in my throat
I remembered the group's advice
and wrapped my lips about
my knees moving still between
bend and not-bend
I shook, wiggled, rattled them

arms flung straight up behind me
spires of flesh
mimicking sanctified battlements
on the avenue
the trembling became a dance, crouched there
passers-by throwing me coins
thinking I was break danc
ing yes I was dancing to
break a two-thousand-year spell

I danced to be a naked brown god, not
Him, that humorless old fogey
whose Latin had nothing to do with
congas and timbales and a
beat better than religion

whose good was bad, whose
bad was good

now my new dogma, damnation be

my salvation, my
Inferno my Paradiso

yes, I was turning and turning to
make the world stop

the church stop
the past stop
the bus stop (it

did) and I got on
having remembered the group's advice
to get the hell out of there

Walls

Luis H. Francia

I know about laws
how well they set up walls

Do's in a small room
Don'ts in a labyrinth of huge halls

I know about
official trust
how they apportion it
Like chunks of bad
meat for the hungry

I know all about the smooth
wall in the law
difficult to see

but I keep bumping
against it

how it hides what's true
By telling me I'm a
swell fella
Filipino brother
(no you're no bother at all)
but it's the other way
around

I know its surfaces
very well

How when you try to
climb it you
find you've
fallen farther

than before

A Philippine History Lesson

Alfrredo Navarro Salanga

It's history that
moves us away
from what we are

We call it names
assign it origins
and blame the might
That made Spain right
and America—bite

This is what it amounts to:
we've been bitten off, excised
from the rind of things

What once gave us pulp
has been chewed off
and pitted—dry

They Don't Think Much About Us in America

Alfrredo Navarro Salanga

Q. Do you feel you are free to express your ideas adequately?
A. Of course, yes. I live in America.

—From an interview with an exile

The only problem is
they don't think much
     about us
in America.
     That's where Manila's
just as small as Guam is:
     dots
on a map, points east,
     China
looming up ahead. Vietnam
more popular
     (because of that war).
They don't think much
     about
expats, either:

Until they stink up
     their apartments
with dried fish.
     Or worry those
next in line at the fish shops
—that's where they insist

on getting
fish heads
Along with the fillet: "They're good
for soup, you know."
        But distance helps—
all the same.

That's what it is—it's all the same:
so we hit the New York Times
        and get
a curdled editorial.

        Who cares?
The Washington Post can say as much
and the Potomac still
        won't be changing course.

It's here, back home,
        where the curdling
begins; where minds can melt
        like so much cheese.

War, Like Fever

Alfrredo Navarro Salanga

Our long-term goal is to be
able to meet the demands of world-
wide war, including concurrent re-
enforcement of Europe, deployment
to Southeast Asia and the Pacific
and support for other areas.
(US Defense Secretary
Caspar Weinberger, 1984)

They must imagine that wars
break out swiftly
       like chicken pox,
faster than pins can be stuck
on strategic maps fevered
with the colors of allies,
friends and neutrals.

       Only chicken pox
globules vary with pigmentation:
darker on darker skin but the pox
all the same. If unserumed,
the pox kills swiftly—and as quietly
as the first rush of jets across the sky.

The sonic booms come later,
floods of sound that blanket
the ear and brain, globes that burst
when the meaning of it
descends

to shatter all meaning
like it was glass.

So must you clinic the world
and make us patients of your peace,
a strange love that breeds sanitation
but without sanity, the last physic
gulped by the physician, the majesty
of his cure more fearful
than the pox itself.

I, in America

Ruth Elynia S. Mabanglo

My mind recalls the flight of dreams
From the land of its birth.
Sight and touch mount the streets:
Perch on the whiz of gaits in New York;
Cry with the bawl and howl of hagglers
In San Franciso Chinatown;
Pierce bruises on my hands
As I erase the grimes of bathrooms in Waikiki;
As I rinse my wounds with the bubbles of Miami.
In Alaska, I brave the gnawing colds as I jerk tunas.
In Seattle, I hum with the crescendos of sardine cans
As I snag my throat dry with the foreman's blasts.
Ay, I balm my pains with the spins of blues and jazz,
Celebrate the assaults of misfortunes
As my children cultivate a new tongue.
Here, there, I join the race of speed, brain and brawn—
As I burst to oblivion,
As I sink to extinction,
Unnoticeably giving birth to a new
ME.

Autumn in Vermont

Rene Estella Amper

The woods are being mantled for Fall.
They set ablaze the whole world
from Vermont to the skies. The sun
stands upright between the maples and the elms
deep in the gasps of its wintry chill.

There is a cataract of gold as leaves leap
from fall to fall; as it closes
about the fading green I am overwhelmed
with Autumn fever, diffused, misshapen,
tumbled into the crook of noon, like a pebble thrown
against a pond breaking with ripples
at broken intervals heavy with wonder.

There is a closeness as wide as a front porch
and the wind lisps through the boughs of afterthought,
teasing out Autumn's tatters
from Otter Creek to Gifford Woods;
it lights on the crannies of flame, spills
the blossoms of fire, ready for the gathering frost.

Where the aspen and the spruce scatter the shreds of stones
at the juncture of road and path,
pursuing their stifled needs
of roots and stems and twigs and flowers,
the fires of home come cornered at the bend.

I must be homesick as a loon even
with Autumn fever! The early-morning smell

of riceflowers; the gray dawn breaking
before a storm; the little brown farmer
tending his stunted corn; all the barren hills
of home where Spring is a stranger and Winter and Fall.

My Worst Fear

Cyn. Zarco

is that one day they'll win
one day those people
who always get in my way
will all get together in one room
and have a good time
for the first time
in their lives
all my enemies
those smiling men and women
in unimaginative attire
will win the lotto
and spend it
on promotional materials
besmirching my good name
they'll have the last word
'cause i won't be there to defend myself
or ignore them
or listen to their noise
their petty envies
all my friends will be out of town
or worse
they won't speak up
they'll sit on their asses
and order another drink
go shopping
or something

my worst fear
is that one day they'll win

i'll be a 400-pound couch potato
in a room with no window
only cable tv and cheap ice cream
i'll be watching reruns of old movies
'cause by this time
i'd have seen every movie ever made
even the kung fu flicks
i'll be talking to my imaginary spouse in my sleep
and wake up as marlon brando
with no tarita or tahiti to come home to
i'd be alone
and i'd like it better
than sex

once upon a seesaw with charlie chan

Cyn. Zarco

i think i was three
beneath the guava tree
next to the doghouse in the front yard
with the crisscross bamboo fence
the seesaw was pastel
pink green and yellow
and i a nut brown child with black hair
i had the up-and-down-of-it down pat
as i straddled the wooden plank with chubby knees
facing a boy nicknamed charlie chan
it was a slow afternoon
wives winning at mahjong
maids eavesdropping
i may have been daydreaming
of the other playground
the one with the swings and silver seesaws
the one that survived the tornado
or maybe my mind lingered
on the fingering of a piano
a blue dragonfly whizzing nearby
i soared above it all
above the red hibiscus flowers
and the sweet banana tree
above the bougainvillea and the gardenia
charlie had beads for eyes
that was how he got his name
he was smaller than i

and i was the girl
i don't know what got into him
as evenly weighted we swung side to side
he jumped on my seat like satan
up smack between my legs
a wooden whack drew blood
i searched for the trickle's source
no wound or cut
no sign of origin
i ran to mother
she swabbed me with alcohol and muttered
no explanation
the bleeding stopped
there was no pain
and i never seesawed with charlie chan again

I Remember Fermin 1930

Jeff Tagami

The old man remembered that year
Because it was the year they grew
Too many potatoes. "Dump 'em,"
The boss said, simply.

So all of September was spent
Lugging them on his back
In burlap sacks down the dirt road
To the Pajaro River.
Under a cotton wood
He met an Okie woman and her two sons
Who had been fishing. Loosening
His sack, he let them pick
A few good ones, then freed the rest
Into the calm mirror of water.
They floated, bobbing into one another.
He thought, then
Of his family in another country,
Of the small garden
Shaded by fronds of coconut palm
Where there grew the green tops
Of sweet potatoes called, camote.
As always,
He wondered if they had enough to eat.

Later, going back for another load,
He imagined the waterlogged potatoes
Beginning to sprout
And how, from a distance,

They resembled tiny islands
Before they drifted upriver, finally
Toward the hungry
That was the sea.

Without Names

Jeff Tagami

In the yard choking
With weeds
Near the picket
Fence unpainted
Father slits the jugular
Of the goat drunk
On vinegar, hoofs
Wired together
Like a bundle of firewood.
The cry it makes
Is no louder than Elvis
Crooning off the needle,
Or the sigh sister gives
As she hugs herself,
Imagines her bed
Is a ship sailing
To Blue Hawaii.
She can't hear
My giggling on the porch
At the puppy lapping
My ear, or brother saying,
"Let it lick your dick."

Back of our farmhouse
Filipinos hunchbacked
From a lifetime of hauling
Irrigation pipes,
Squeeze goat entrails clean,
Sticking their fingers
In places I think
Not possible.

Around the fire
They squat and eat
With their fingers
The sweet meat
Dipped in blood,
Drink the green bile
For long life.

Night
And what it uncovers
Is this:A smouldering pit
And the charred horns
Of a goat.
Sister rolling down
her bobby socks.
Myself and my five
Brothers bunked
In one bedroom.
Father undoing
His trousers.
Mother slipping off
Her dress, hoping
For another girl.
The ripening strawberries
Surrounding us like an ocean,
To drown us in work
The next day.
And my father whispering
Above it all,
"It is so good, so good,
I forget my name."

Fly-Over Country

Rowena Torrevillas

This is the famous nothingness
That lives between Des Moines and
Denver at night: you see it peering back
At you from the plane-window's
Oval eye—spans a dog's bark in length,
One light, two, measuring a straight line
Across ten miles of no-name.

Nothing to hold back
The nothingness but
That prick of light, the needle-
Point into the numb heart
As you sail through black
Space, from "here" to "there"—
Unwalled, yet squeezed breathless
By the empty dark. The earth rides
Through a long dream of stars, knowing
Light only as differences of darkness. So

Sing for the lights that cling
Along the hillsides of Nepal,
Wicks sputtering in rancid butter;
For the charcoal burner's torch,
The pressure lamps flickering
Along the coves of Santander; the flap
Of a tent blown back in the desert,
The gaudy necklace of Brooklyn Bridge

That catches at your throat

On the approach from LaGuardia; sing
For the face behind the window
Waiting for Papa's footfall though
It never comes, and for the hand
Cupped round the candle: here

Is where the ocean ends, where
Blood and salt part ways, and
Mountain holds up the sky, and the inland
Sea that once rolled below turns only
To prairie grass. So wrap the night
Around you; don't be afraid
To be afraid. The kerosene lamp behind
The bamboo shutter is the planet's
Beating heart: most triumphant
in the unnamed, the unseen
Spaces, each light a name.

Nightfall, Angeles City

Jaime Jacinto

Tonight a woman will sway her hips
beneath the sallow neon light,
her lips a red purse opening for the eyes
of soldiers following the line of her thighs,
the trembling of skin that rises and falls
with every hot breath.

Tonight a woman will turn her back, squatting
and bending as lyrics drift out a jukebox

Oh baby love, my baby love, I need to hold you
once again. Why do you treat me like you do?
Don't throw our love way, oh baby, love...

Tonight a woman will dance while
her children sleep. She is pay day for
the boy soldiers who sit slackjawed on barstools,
fingering the swelling inside their khaki trousers.

Overhead a fighter jet creases the sky,
its streaking lights bright as neon.
In the bars of Angeles City, it is the night
of the paycheck when less is more
than soldiers could ever want from a woman.
They will only take her if she is like the sign says:
Topless and Bottomless. No cover charge.

While back home, ten thousand miles away
with snowdrifts piled outside their door,

good midwestern folk, someone's papa and mama
watch the six o'clock news and think of their son
and his mission to protect the peace in another country
where now a soldier's wallet opens, deadly as bullets.

Airport Lounge , Manila

Jaime Jacinto

For Luz

What I cannot remember
I'll pretend instead.
How the boy was dressed
Like a missionary's son,
Wearing a bow tie and
Starched white collar,
Listening to the drone of
Airplane propellers from
The airport tarmac.
What I cannot remember
I'll pretend instead.
How the man lit another cigarette,
His face disappearing in a blue curl of smoke
Until he posed for a relative's camera,
Taking his place in a farewell portrait
Silent in the dim shadows.
What I cannot remember
I'll pretend instead.
How the woman stood in line
And waited for the customs man
Who inspected the passports,
Not a word coming from her
Until he asked if they would return.
No, the mother said, there we'll
Go to live, there we'll go to stay.
But this I do remember.
How the boy never returned

To that street where he once lived.
How the man worked at the
Same desk until he died,
How the woman counted the years
Since his last embrace, a feeling
She remembers like smoke
Curling between light and shadows.

Room for Time Passing

Ricardo M. de Ungria

Winter's all spirits and unwarm coffee,
Schoenberg's String Quartets and Late Beethoven,
Utamaro, Dostoevsky, Rumi,
like bread just taken out of the oven,
the kitchen fragrant, the apples and the cheese
cut shortly. When it's sunny I work in the sunroom
where the light is light and the sun a true fishwife.
In the swabbed air of this almost Yugoslav
naif landscape, I chart paths on crunchy snow.
I hum a Beatles tune and even a refrain
from a kundiman I can remember, half-whistling
to see the spirit shapes my breath will take.
A sudden crow and a spiral of chimney smoke
my only company. The rest is epoch.

Starlight by the old museum, and then
past the audible indrawn breath of the park,
past the zoo where the silence of the beasts
is one with the silence of the Old Masters,
the thought that I am bundled up head-to-foot
in my own understanding and alienation.

We went on exhibit here in 1904.
A scaled-down Intramuros and Laguna de Bay
dotted with Moro and Bontoc villages
condensed the first view of the new territories.
The natives were let loose among the Kaffirs,
the Esquimauz and the hairy Cocopas.
"Great pig with two tails" was what the Igorrote

said the first time he saw an elephant.
And Antaero, another Igorrot boy
in a suit of white duck on a visit
to the White House boasted, "Mr. Roosevelt,
I will return to the Philippines
and whip all your enemies." Sank yoh, sank yoh.
Sometimes I feel the show never really closed.
See me march with the little Macs in khaki.
Watch me hit a penny with an arrow
from twenty-five yards. Listen, I'm Miss Zamora's
pupil: "Four chairs minus three chairs are one chair.
No: is one chair." We may not hear until now
what was being said, but we understand English
enough to laugh with everyone at the same time.
There's really no lack of trees to climb
faster than monkeys along the great white way.

It must also be true for everyone
who goes about his business every day,
who has worlds to mind and worlds to take for granted.
Every man's a poor native in this regard,
his mind a mere guest, his heart an itinerary.
When it's over, his last words will be few,
if any. The Mississippi. The Arch.
The jazz. The Beer. The Hill. Church's. Amvets.
He was tucked in bed or he was lent a shawl of love.
There was this, there was that, they don't add up.
It almost makes one stay up late and say
the obvious: Life is short, eat dessert first.
Of course, there's no other body to spare;
but the mind has gods to put in order,
lives to lose, and a few worlds to make plain.
How can one be human at the same time to all?

Sometimes I talk to words, and I catch them
whispering about steeples at sunset, flywheels,
cut hair and clearings dissolving into countless
butterflies, the light gray from a habit of waiting.
It all seems otherworldly, but in fact
it is. Only receive and give back—
there's the marvel and the power, like money.

Whichever side of the ocean I'm on,
completeness will seek me and the world exceed
the surprises I spring on it with these same words.
No more playing with broken pieces not my own,
no more sentiments with needless omniscience
nibbling away at the stealth and wonder of moments.
Let an ethnic moon have its way with time.
Let sad fruitions ghost another paradise,
let absences seek their own level.

Now the old dances like a gypsy inside of me.
Now through the manholes I hear wind move
the bones of the buried River Des Peres.
Now the great divide between the apartments
and the gabled houses with the lawns and the dogs.
Now lamplight and lamplight and lamplight.
Broken bottles spangle the streets, the windows
curtain half-heartedly, or the blinds drawn down,
streaked with shadows of plants and the cat on the sill.
I'm walking the angel home to its body,
one still possible to hold in unburrowed light,
at ease with my turns of mind and the course of things.
From the roundness of worlds meridians away,
I chart the points of balance and equivalences,
the representations and the sides to take.

But the laws of emotions make no promises.
In from the snow I always find the islands
at low tide, urchins picking up pebbles and shells,
and on the table between the bookshelf and the waves,
grilled fish and a bowl of steaming white rice.

Avatar at the Gas Station, Lower East Side

Ricardo M. de Ungria

Half-mad in half-illumination
lives the city's unborn portion.
I could turn into a sparrow,
or a peel of paint, or a body adrift
on the Hudson. Such bounty of acts here.

But the way out is the way in,
moving up and down unrented beings.
I have come this far from all
gradations, my heart pried open
and precise, draining its poisons.

Each turn I took gave way to more
corners and roads where tenements and men
stood, no, flexed in secret strobe light,
each to his own fix leashed, lulled out,
of contention by their shine-chewed eyes.

From the grid of these dark avenues
I mapped a labyrinth of my own,
its walls propped up by old church hymns,
its turns abrupt, sharp with the seethe
of ravening ravenings, thrills, near-deaths.

No one tracked me down here but the sense
of old desolation and collapse
breaking into flower between

the obscure dirt of these walls and the
headlights of cars battered like egos.

Free to be my own waste-winding
strip of empty synagogues, I rest
my orbit here awhile and run
my fears across familiar dread.
I will be reading poems and defying deaths

Before these implements and faces
of familiar strangers, great bridges and
cathedrals, and unconsoling squares and parks.
Embossed among these future souvenirs
I feel less hurt than proud and lost, intimate.

Carillonneur

Ricardo M. de Ungria

I took the thought
of going back to New York
for a walk at dawn
before the fruit vendors
set up their stalls
and while the she-wolf next door
is still making love
loudly for the good of us all.
Wind-whipped trash bags
winging down empty streets
still remain the sure signs
of the city's nursery of speed.

Someone must be keeping count
of what is yet to come.
So strong is the feeling
some long-overdue debt
is being paid me
in installments.
When I look at my photos and postcards
I know I have been somewhere,
and everything is still taking place
long enough for me
to move from here to there.

Making a home for absences
restores to the self the true
magnificence and pain of presence.
It gives me confidence

and drives me out to seek
inclemencies of love.

As long as I can keep from talking
to myself too long,
as long as passion kills
mutely and obscurely
I can live here.
But this can be anywhere,
the tambourines higher in pitch,
the bed harder.
And I find myself again
out of the A train
in the middle of nowhere,
ready to begin again
with slick black hair.

Manila

Pancho V. Lapuz

I remember your sunset from here,
even the stone where you sat,
beside the sea, with the hot day gone,
& the city cooled salt breeze,
& you making light of my heart, always,
& the evening shone like a lucky tooth.
Suddenly I remember how good.
Outside my world, it is a gap older,
& the same car keeps going by now,
rumbling its curse at the years
like a sidewalk toy,
& the day pulls the light out of my heart
like a tooth.
It is the night that needs me now.
Manila, your sweet memory is
spit out of me like a baby tooth,
blood salty painless clink
into an empty rose glass.
The same sun sets to me here,
but down into the night
that embraces me like gravity embraces distance,
like a python embraces its prey,
& I disappear like a feeling
into the smell of its dark wet toothless
clutching swallowing oyster mouth,
& here the night shuts over me
& leaves the rest open to dust.

Echo

Pancho V. Lapuz

I will wipe my shoes on Wednesdays because Wednesday
is the middle of the week.
I will shave on Saturdays because Saturday
is the last day of the week.
I will place my heart
on the stone of Grace Cathedral
on Sunday mornings before light
because Sunday is the first day of the week
of the world I was born into.

My heart is made from the leather of amputations.
My head is a bell. My head is a stray bullet shell.
I hear the chime of dropping digits.
Their sound is polished to a summons.
I will stay in my room forever
so the world can include me.

I will never come out again.
I will go to church with my gun.
I will die with all my might.
I will live inside
the stain of light.

Effect of Distance

Francis Macansantos

That scraggly wood my window framed is gone.
Perhaps some arctic birds worked overnight
To gild the branches with spittle nacre-white
That now are wands translucent in the dawn.
Twined like a nest, or bower, of bright bone,
Is it to a house a Being of frigid might
Coming to claim a primordial birthright?
Some icy phoenix? Some Leviathan?
But a window keeps at bay what it shows
(Or, so the mind assures with sage advice
In a heated room.) That orb that now grows,
Snuggled in the frozen grove, cannot entice
To vagary the sober mind which knows
The sun as ornament: pure joy, pure ice.

Till Death

Francis Macansantos

The hours are dollars, the minutes cents,
Time being money and money, time.
Your heart ticks away the pennyseconds
As you say Have a nice day, and they reply,
You, too. But will there ever be, really,
A day when, pressing the right key,
You finally ring yourself quite out,
Out of this place-time prison?
Somewhere buds are stirring
Out of warmed branches.
Here nothing happens but time
Ticking out your life
In some strange coinage,
Where you are frozen in time by Time:
By the silent, quick-silver accumulation
Of freezing upon frozen rain.

Parallel Universe

Eileen Tabios

for Arthur Sze

I

A shadow slants in different ways:
felled by a steeple, dappling a waterfall,
blocked by your knee against a hovering sun.

I see a woman push a baby stroller,
bow my face to hide a premonition:
the skeleton of an infant, its skull a grimace.

An amber footstep of old cider
refuses to evaporate, a hint
of the universe vinegarizing invisibly.

Winter has liquefied to gray slush
clinging at the soles of strangers
hurrying to boil water. Steam a mint leaf?

How often do Eskimos change clothes?
Beneath their layers, can there ever be
taut flesh an infinite span of honey?

But if one is awake to witness the aging of midnight,
Do not unexpected revelations occur through trumpets:
that there is a cycle of life—

and, consistently, spring then summer begin?

II

From Indiana, he sends a postcard depicting a kiss.
I wonder if I read beyond a thousand words.

My mother is extremely enthusiastic over my new career.
I wonder if she had not wanted to be where she is.

Joyce Carol Oates is fascinated with serial killers.
I wonder if she will write a second book on boxing, or owns an axe.

He poses for a street artist who sketches a mole I have never seen.
I wonder what else I do not know about him.

I hear rain end, feel a sun fall behind a dormant volcano.
I wonder what black lightning looks like at night.

My editor says he agrees with the message, but disputes the style of its delivery.
I wonder why I engage in love affairs with lawyers.

I fall in love with a painting in an art gallery in SoHo.
No, I tell the dealer, I do not consider it necessary to meet its creator.

III

Before the hurricane there was an island,
a house overlooking a bay with dragons
content to skim the sharp bottoms of corrals
until their green eyes and fire breathing
became mere folklore. The house trapped
rainwater for flushing toilets and washing grapes.
In one bedroom, a ceiling fan lazily circled
over a man suckling on a woman's breasts.
After the hurricane, everything is folklore.

The short man says he was a revolutionary
leading a band of guerrillas in an Andean hamlet
before he started arranging flowers
for Koreans at street corners. I see my
dilemma mirrored on his face: whether to laugh
or weep.

Grandfather recalls he did not want to be a dead cat.
It's kapu, he excuses himself:
      a line that cannot be crossed,
      a body that cannot be held.

I stand in a desert searching the seam of the horizon.
Foolishly, I failed to pay attention
to earthly things. I ran out of gas.

IV

An adolescent boy walks calmly down the street.
The daisy grows from his hand, hides a pimple on his face.

She shows me a thin wrist dangling a wool bracelet.
The orange and red strings hearken the sunset
      over the mountain where black
      -hatted Peruvians sit impassively knitting.

The rain falls like massive sheets of gray glass.
I am dazzled by the cranberry sheen of a toddler's raincoat.

I bow to tie a shoelace and notice a perfect snowflake
An inch from my last step. I learn to consider what are trodden.

I watch in slow motion a black dog bite a girl in a summer shift.
The beauty of her naked limbs is heightened by the mouth of a bleeding scar.

A truck floats across my vision. On its side clings a sign announcing
    "Emergency."
I am reminded of my first love—how I have never felt again

that certain pain that cloaked me at passion's end.

American Beauty Roses

Maria Luisa A. Cariño

It's Thursday morning and you're
tightening your bathrobe sash.
You forget about yelling at me
for the fiftieth time because I left
the water boiling on the stove.
Your eldest son the banker's
just left after admiring your ability
to swear loud, Filipino-style, because he has
no time to drive you to the supermarket.
"Gaddemmet sanammabet! I help
finance your house and you can't
even take me to the store?" You shake
your broom at his retreating figure
even if he's clutching the bag of egg
rolls you folded all night for him
with your arthritic fingers.
You come to sit beside me in the back
room where I had cha-cha music going,
to tune out your daily program.

But on the radio
someone's reading this story of a shootout—
just like in "Bonanza,"or in those movies
where they fight "to the bitter end—"
six bullets? no, nine? and still shooting
from the floor. Two Pinoy cops
dead at the center
where on Friday nights we go
to eat dinner; Kamayan,

they call it, but still
nobody uses their hands
except maybe if it"s the Fourth
of July and we're having
a barbecue. You drop your dish-
cloth and clutch the edge
of my sleeve. We don't know them,
neither what they fought about,
so terrible. It didn't matter it was at
a Sweet Sixteen party, but it's all too
familiar. I know how it must feel:
the blood rush, sweaty fingers tight
around the neck of an empty
bottle or dancing around
a trigger.

      I'm thinking
the same thing. We're back
in that billiard hall. The room's
hazy with cigarette smoke;
there's a honky-tonk tune on yellowed
keys and the smell of frying onions.
The inescapable vapor of shrimp paste
rising from rusted skillets
clings to our coats for weeks.
There was a little card
on which you wrote
my name, Gaudencio. Ten
cents a dance and three
days' pay so I could smell
your sweet perfume and see,
close up, the creamy skin
they called American
Beauty Roses.

It was the closest
thing to kindness and I tried
to keep from weeping
into your generous hands.
I knew then I could swallow
hunger, the insults and jeers
that followed us when we walked
in the streets, enough to make you
want to kill a man. I'd dribble leftover
wine from the moon's unwashed
glasses, lay my meager
possessions at your feet: you
who listened to my vagabond dreams
and believed in a world festooned with goat
meat, rivers of blood stew and crossed
consonants.

We're a here
and a there still walking through
the constantly reassembling rubble
of this century. Sometimes I quake
at the thought of how thorough
has been your scrutiny of me.
You know my deepest secrets,
how fervently I exclaim my thanks
to St. Jude, St. Martin and the Santo
Niño when I break wind into the pot;
how I lick the tips of my thumb and
forefinger when turning the page of a book
or a newspaper, and how lately I've reverted to
my old habit of drawing up my knees
in the chair at mealtimes. We walk
to the corner church on Sunday so I
can give thanks that we still link hands

despite my weaknesses and your
predilection for swearing. Afterwards
we'll walk home in the gathering dusk,
careful not to be in the way of large
children zipping by on skateboards
or rollerblades. We'll turn on a lamp,
sip tea or laxatives, take out the grandchildren's pictures and argue over who has
our features. I'll tell you those old
stories you like, of my island home
whose name you can say as wistfully
as I, as we stumble upstairs into archives
of dreams backlit by fireflies' lights—
tiny and accurate, a morse code
blinking out calls for rescue
over a photographic horizon,
grass houses blanketed
and heavy with sleep.

from *The Book of Exile*

Maria Luisa A. Cariño

...I will be then no more
than a calm spin in a tomb of water.

—Claribel Alegria

1. The Gathering

This is the body I bore
through the gates of your cities
Heading west in the shadow
of the sun I saw fields
written over with hieroglyphs
of plenty Clusters of red
and gold made visible in distant orchards
Blessed by the psaltery of billboards
those who trail in the wake of this
ripening collect the fruit in eager
baskets In stores across the land
fish and loaves multiply beside the mustard
greens and wintermelons A miracle
repeated once each day before sunrise
Surrendering the knowledge of water
Surrendering the knowledge of yeast and loam
Surrendering the cry ripped from the flower
field and the ritual breaking of the stalk
The eye of round and the slender spears of asparagus
are gathered here The crowns of roses

and the wandering desert blooms The Persian
melon and the small-hipped fig The mullions
in this rich mosaic raising a landscape
warm with heat and color to eye and hand
Everything here has been gathered so even the thin
scrolls of food stamps grant communion
and the marbled fat melts from the roof
of the mouth its common prayer
Meanwhile the doorways sheltered and gave sleep
The poor roamed the streets with their shopping
carts of debris and refuse
Leaves burnt their sonorous anthem of decay
And thus it came to pass

2. The Arrival

At the gates of this city
there was no one
to meet me though the air
was filled with sounds
of expectancy and welcome

An unseen voice guided my every
step and handhold telling me
how many layers of air to descend

A warning bell sounds
when the ground begins again
and when it is safe to trust
my weight to the moving walkway
When to plunge into the flickering
embrasures of light and rise
to the fractured surface of the dome

I carried a bag of clothes and books
Letters Things I imagined I would need
for the winter Next to me on the plane
a man from South Africa narrated
the contents of his luggage An epic poem
Twenty-five ceremonial
robes a pair of leather sandals
jars of pounded yam and sweet
saffron flowers In the next
cabin a traveller moaned
dreaming his way through the lost
gorges of Azbhekistan

Beyond the steep embankments
the steel supports of bridges
the girders and pediments rising
above the river declaimed the passing
of their origins and mine
Their gestures go out of themselves
in search of history
In the sleeping city the buildings inclined
their throats toward silence
They stood without moving their spines
engirdled by light The asphalt thrummed
with strings A thousand
glowing bars The fretwork
for tires gliding away into more
darkness

In the atriums and lobbies false
palm fronds parted and rippled
The air echoed with others' reunions
A current of kisses surged
toward their compass points

I spin
A needle suspended in a vacuum
Embolus in the commerce of grids
Beacon and breakwater
Isthmus and island
Rubbing the knobs of weary
joints I light a fire
I train the body to inhabit
its places of rest

Here is where I mark the end of the book
of companionship Where I take up
the beginning of this
my text of exile

Her First Night Away

Fidelito C. Cortes

At 4 AM the lights still burned
in the apartment. Seen from the air
they were very bright and they guided
the red-eye jets to Oakland. Not yours,
of course, because you were in Detroit
and it's just your first night away.
For once in this marriage, more than
darkness separated us, more than sleep,
though it's now daylight where you are.
To the east, the dark forms of the
sleeping hills of Berkeley, barely
visible, not even for the runway
of streetlights leading here, to home.
I opened the refrigerator, and its light
—the last remaining unlit beacon—
clicked on: ever brighter no, Oakland,
but still not as bright as day.

English as a Second Language

Fidelito C. Cortes

Today I tried to give a talk about
Philippine history to a bunch of
Americans and ran into a wall
of language. It was a white thing,
really, that room of Americans
doing good for their fathers' sins,
and I thought I saw the chastened
ghosts of McKinley and Bell, and
Otis and Howlin' Jake Smith, walk in.

I started with the Spaniards and had
no problems there. I got an attentive,
even sympathetic, hearing. But when
history turned, as it always must,
to the Americans, the ghosts stirred
uneasily and the wall slammed back in place.
It was formidable and tall, bricked with
impregnable verbs, impossible idioms.
On it rested the ruins of foreign accents

used as scaling machines. At its feet
the foiled battering rams of gutturals
and sibilants. Caught on its barbed wire
of nuance: truth. But history heeds more
than language, and I brought blood and gore
of my forebears, marrow of their crushing,
spit of their muzzled insurrection.
Let Americans play deaf behind walls.
I will not give comfort to their ghosts.

Letter to Home

Fidelito C. Cortes

I would write about how cold and bleak
it is right now, the end of fall, the oak
and maple dead of self-burning, dull
embers scattered on the sod. How full
the air of chill and mournful birdsong,
before the silence. And how merciless
this shift of seasons, this headlong tumble
into melancholy and distress.
Yet this is California, and there is mercy
in the rains that fall endlessly
on the still green hills of Berkeley.
Rain, not snow. So I walk to the bus stop
to meet my wife, solaced and wrapped
in this knowledge, in mist and the bright drops.

Casting Call

Fatima Lim-Wilson

My wife...she also used to be...some kind of entertainer.

—An Australian speaks of his Filipino
wife in the film *The Adventures of
Priscilla, Queen of the Desert*

The woman they are looking for
Is a well-proportioned dwarf.
Madder than a dingo, she salivates
At the sight of dog meat. She slithers,
Much of her seen under fake leopard skin.
Curses leap like fish from her foaming
Mouth. She keeps her husband,
Who towers over her, tame on a leash.
A true artist on stiletto stilts,
She also can do magic tricks
Like making things pointed or round
Appear and disappear from her
Spangled orifices.

They could not come to the audition,
Those same women who were once
Lured by photographs of bearded men
Posing by their desert kingdoms.
Ana sends her regrets:
Her husband has scattered
Her body parts
Throughout the sand.
She is busy, as she was in life,

Making handicrafts,
Turning her own bones
Into bird cages and wind chimes.

In her final scene, they'll have
The men jeer through beer-haloed lips,
Their applause sounding to her like
Unseasonable rain or welcome gunfire.

The Resident Alien as Acrobat

Fatima Lim-Wilson

Seen upside down, my smile's a frown
How polite I am even as my heart pounds
A wolfpaced beat. When I turn around,
I unclench my fist, releasing arrows
Of curses, silently. I walk in a crouch
Disguising kings in my blood and the wings
Fluttering beneath my thin coat.

I have learnt to say "love"
Without wincing, hearing myself
Tossing cheap syllables
Clanging against fancied objects.
No longer will I stop to save
Each snowflake, a miracle
Melting into tears in my cupped hand.
When my throat rages dry,
I recall the dozen ways to say "rain."
Now and then, I let my tongue swim
Against the tide of names: my brothers
And sisters leaping wordlessly
Out of my sight, our likeliness
Blurring into a muted darkness.

But, I survive, you see. Even thrive
Here is this jungle of damp noises.
I bare my teeth, twist my jaws
Like a well trained chimp. Watch me
Blow cartoon bubbles, form frothy
Lace at the corners of my mouth.

Pardon that strange cry I make.
It is just our way of saying
Both "joy" and "pain."

A Sestina Written in a Cold Land
(Or, There is No Word for "Snow" in My Language)

Fatima Lim-Wilson

I come from a land of saints.
We kept jars of their tears and bones.
Rooms filled with the scents of their wounds.
Warned and warmed by the holiest book,
We remember how martyrs sweated naked in snow
Or roasted over flames, singing in tongues.

But here, I wake, with a slithering snake's tongue.
Please save me, my mother's candle honored saints!
False promises spill like steaming guts upon the snow.
My venom makes acid of my blood, chalk from bones.
I wilt like a pile of trodden leaves, molding book.
My words fester, yellow as losers' wounds.

Prettiest phrases axe the air, leaving sapping wounds.
I always slip away, barebacked, on the fish of my tongue.
How I lie, blank-faced as the pages of a dull book.
Swearing on my father's grave, invoking a virgin saint,
Arms wide open as a windswept book.

If I set to flame my borrowed books,
Perhaps I can loosen the grip of snow.
How the fire will halo me, a repentant saint.
The smoke of strange words will clear my wounds.
The ashes of a puppets accent fall from my tongue.
O, to feel the rush of childhood rhymes in my bones!

But, I have gotten too used to softer bones
And the absence of muchthumbed books.
I wear quite well my secondhand tongue
And can now even walk upright on snow.
Newfound friends, charmed by my wounds,
Tell me I smile just like a carved saint.

It is easy to break a child's bones, smashed saints,
Tear final chapters from books, grow flowers from wound.
But how to sweeten a stale tongue, how to find maps in snow?

Palm Sunday

J. Eugene Gloria

Always the sky keeps expanding.
Wide as America's brave margins,
wide as my loneliness in the Middle West.
I lean against a dust cloud behind us,
the glory sinking into a muted timberline.
I am drunk with longing. The wind is singing—

my drunken friend the wind hurls
sweet curses at my face.
We have learned to love
this road, which lies down like pythons,
refuses to forgive our excesses,
refuses to consider us kin. Our driver's

sign overhead reads, *Jesus is my co-pilot.*
Jesus who crossed the city
gates of his ancestors
on a road carpeted by palms.
Our goodtime driver must know this—
he drives with abandon,

despite our fragile cargo: scholars and accountants,
prophets and exiles all the same to him.
The road, which suggests things, is tired of ceremony.
It lies down to sleep like the snow.
Lie down Tall Mountain, lie down
Serafin Syquia, lie down Li-Young, lie

down Divakaruni, lie down Eman Lacaba,
lie down pilgrims of the open road.
Shameless, we gather our light
jackets in balls. We rest our heads,
our faces upturned to a squall of stars.
I near the end, my soul recites.

O loneliness, my body responds.
This empty road is a house
where no one lives. What strange fire
we bring when we come to this house.

Washing Rice

J. Eugene Gloria

When our plane landed in San Franciso,
I looked down at my shins ashen
from the cold, believing that in America,
my skin would soon turn white.

I wash the rice five times,
measure moonwhite water
by the first crease of my middle finger,
imagine families doing the same ritual.

Fog from our pots surrounds the city
Across miles of ocean, morning
smoke burns thick with sadness.
My cousin is singing my return—

singing like the cliffs of Pacifica,
which call out to cars and tract homes
lanky palms nose-diving like gulls
into the dark and ancient ocean.

Carlos Bulosan

J. Eugene Gloria

I am through with you, Carlos Bulosan—
tired of listening for the footfalls
of light leading toward
this switchback of words for you
string like a necklace of *Ling Ling; Os.*

I am through with you Carlos Bulosan
clambering at the door
only to find the ghost of your lost
manuscript scattered on my floor.
I didn't make it to Mangusmana,
but found my name along the Dinalaoan

where a dirt road elbows
into another
and a row of nipa huts active
with kilns burning wood
beneath houses on stilts,
smoke seeping through wide slats
of bamboo where my cousins
spread their sleep
mats and drape clouds

of mosquito nets at night.
Clear through the haze below,
where pigs and chickens
reign, my aunts and their daughters
busy themselves with banana leaves,

separating them sheet by leafy sheet
for the tiny white moons

sweet and abundant as love
my small nieces showered when I came
to visit and brag of my country
that denies me
and has denied you, Carlos Bulosan,
brother of dirt
and the Imperial Valley Asparagus.
Lover of fat hips and all
that is sensual in the white women
you loved when they held your face.
in the dull light
of a Delano bunkhouse,

or was it in Turlock or Tacoma, far
from the country of a thousand smiles
and the strongly devoted,
far from the palmsap wine the rebels drank—.

Tonight I recall the song
of the old woman combing the thick
hanks of her daughter's hair

remember only the part
about the greeny water where
the village mad woman,
fatigued and lovelorn, bathed

one night in the cool Dinalaoan
beneath the new moon in March.
She dies, the old woman sang,
because the river took pity on her.

Here is my hand, Carlos Bulosan,
I make this pact with you.
Let no anthem well within us,
let the moon which owns nothing
have our names. Let this
common face we wear, dark
and inconsolable be our only cargo.

Beetle on a String

Vince Gotera

When I was a kid, I walked bugs on a leash.
This was in the Philippines, where my parents
and I moved when I was a toddler, trading
foggy San Francisco for Manila's typhoons.

Actually, it was an idyllic place for a child—
warm evenings drenched in the sweet scent
of sampaguita flowers, but most of all,
a huge universe of enthralling insects

filling the night with buzzing and clicks, strobe
flashes of their glow-in-the-dark wingflicks.
It was my father who showed me how to catch
a scarab beetle in the cup of your hand, wait

for the wings to subside and close, then loop a thread
between thorax and carapace, tying it off—
not too tight— to allow the insect to fly
on a two-foot-long lasso. I remember

how I would smile and laugh, maybe five
or six years old, as a beetle would circle my head
like a whirring kite, iridescent green in the sun,
the thread stretched almost to the breaking point.

At night, I would tie my beetles to the round knobs
on my dresser drawers and be soothed to sleep
by a lullaby of buzzing. By morning, the beetles
were always dead, weights hung on string.

Those long nights must have been horrible.
Straining your body to shift an immovable weight,
unable to evade the swooping flight
of predators, banging again and again hard

against the dead wood, brought up short
by that unforgiving tether, cutting off
your pulsing blood every time, the long tube
of your heart quivering. It makes me shiver now

to wonder what thoughtless boy holds my string?

Ang Tunay na Lalaki
Stalks the Streets of New York

Nick Carbó

looking to harvest what makes him happy.
The AA meetings have thrown
him to sacrilegious jousts with Titans
and Gorgons with glowing snake eyes
and leather pants. This is life
without the Filipino bottle,
without the star fruit boogie,
without the bomba films. He wears black
Dr. Martens boots because slippers
would expose his provinciano feet
to the snow. He wants to ride
the back of a carabao and bolt
up Madison Avenue screaming
like Tandang Sora or shout
hala-bira! hala-bira! hala-bira!
like his Isneg cousins in Aklan.
Ay, susmaryosep! Such bad behavior
from the "true male" of Filipino
advertising. He looks at his reflection
on a book store window, notices
that his hair has grown shoulder-length—
like Tonto in the Lone Ranger
he would watch on TV. Turns to the right,
his profile now looks like the young Bruce Lee
as Kato in the Green Hornet. Yes,
he realizes it will always be the face

of a supporting character. Rejected
from the Absolut Vodka ads, he decides
to change his name for an upcoming audition
for a Preparation H commercial—*Al Moranas*,
American but in a Filipino flare.

Ang Tunay na Lalaki
Realizes He's Below Average

Nick Carbó

from the American male's six inches
and orders vacuum pumps, every sort
of penis extender offered in the back
of the dirty magazines he has in his closet.
It all began when the sixth blonde he was dating
walked into the bathroom, found him squatting,
his toes curling on the rim of the toilet bowl—
as he had always done back in the provinces.
"That's disgusting!" was the last thing she said
before storming out of his apartment. He thought
she was referring to his penis which was small
and retracted whenever he took a dump.
At night, he was visited by Long Dong Silver,
John Holmes, and Sylvester Stallone in his dreams—
all of them leering and laughing and whipping
him with their elephant length penises.
He was too embarrassed to ask his friends
about his problem, so he went to all
the adult movie places on 42nd Street
and the inches on the big silver screen
kept adding up. The final insult
came when he received a package from
Penis Enlargers Inc. and pulled out
a shiny new magnifying glass.

La Reina

Maria Lourdes Antenorcruz

The woman I remember who
gave of herself so totally
before those sappy love songs
was the Aztec whore, Cortez' woman

By her will an empire fell
500 years of darkness began
madness grew

Why is it
I cannot remember
your voice's light caress
along my neck
"querida, Mi mujercita..."
as
your palm connects
hard
upon my cheek
my eye
your mouth
grinding passion
and then another twack!
The wall
I'm pushed towards the
echoes of your accusations of whowasIwith-
whowasItalkingto...
You bastards
rhyme and ebb to the flow of my tears

Mi muñeca, mi reina

A ranchero song fills the house where
you command
the beans weren't cooked
my lack of womanly talent
itches your fingers
A man has to do things
machismo
my silence your victory

A stranger in this land of the free
for others
But of course, things are bueno now
big man
Nothing left to you but pride
and women
and even men with their extravagant promises

your job may suck, but you still have your machismo
intact
but my virginity wasn't

your reina spits blood
your mother's scream follows you
as you climb higher and higher
the garbage mountains of Mexico City
slipping on American leftovers, dolls, cans

your rubber shoes sting and burn
like your father's strap across your back
and your mother's black eye
to prove He had control and so will you

My mouth open
you kiss
you hit
for my own good

Machoism-my place in the universe
America is your woman now
my body the price for what Cortez' whore
did

Password

Noel Abubo Mateo

to be allowed into
america
I had to utter
the all-American passwords
took the flag and wiped it
on my tongue

I began to taste
my words
my first was
"AIN'T"
I lost my virginity to
"AIN'T"
it was indeed truly american

I slowly added the other classic
softly at first
I said "ssshhhSHIT" (there I said it)

then one day
somebody gave me a gift
the biggest one
the all american "fuck you"

I was cleared for take off

it was like a gun
I held it up
aimed

and pulled the trigger

sometimes it put holes through people
sometimes I got return fire

I knew other curses
before this came along
in a different tongue
but they were nothing
compared to the one and only
fuck you
"puta ang ina mo" was powerful
it talked about your mama
"oki ni inam" was quite graphic
it was gynecological
but these were hit or miss
sometimes they mocked
sometimes they just joked along

but when I heard the sweet sound
of my first "fuck you"
it was like hearing a profound idea
I wanted to explain it
analyze it
trace its origins
it came from somewhere
like the other classics
this was pure american
short and sweet
direct and efficient
deliver its blow and get out
I discovered "fuck you"
and I was going to use it
I claimed it like I invented it

after using it countless times
it got old
like all things american
it clichéd itself
the power was gone
everybody was using it now
even four year olds

I needed new ones
bigger better faster
by this time I was now
a real AMER-CAN
and like all red blooded americans
I looked to japan, beijing, or taiwan
when I needed something better made
I wonder if they have
"the Zen of cussing"
what convinced me
was getting the Beijing flu
knocked me off my feet
even the viruses are better in Asia
maybe their cussing is just as good

So now I have to return it
thanks for letting me
use it for so long
it served me well
but you can have it back now
so thank you for your
fuck you

Dora Ty in Kansas

Noel Abubo Mateo

don't be so proud of
having had a maid
in the Philippines
it's not something I
would brag about

don't be so proud of
your stonewashed skin
or your chaperoned walks
in luneta

your ya-ya
trailing behind
with the umbrella
so your light skin
won't get as dark as theirs

lamenting a time
when things were given to you
when things were done for you

my forefathers were your houseboys
my great grandmothers were your
maids
you who had maids, houseboys and
drivers
you who they called señora
and señorito
we were your trapo

the rags wiping your ass
we were your katulungan
you were the owner, jailer and
master

keep it to yourself
in da peeleepeens
we had many maids
what is it that
you want me to say
oh how wonderful
oh wow you must have been
rich

you're homesick
you miss some
good ol' fashion
slaveownership

guess what doring
you ain't in makati anymore

Jeepneyfying

Noel Abubo Mateo

there you go again
lowering that Dodge Colt
must be in the blood
turning anything on wheels into a jeepney
buying rims at Price Club
a Blaupunkt
deck with the ultimate Alpine Amp
speakers costing more than the car itself

there you go again
tinting all your windows
getting stopped in Oakland
you're too dark
your windshield or your skin
he didn't say

there you go again
putting on that spoiler
who you think you are
Filipino Al Unser
I'll answer dat
my other car is also a piece of shit
friends don't let friends drive
hyundais
signifying through jeepneyfying

your dad bought a van
he couldn't leave it alone
hung a rosary on the rear view mirror

Baclaran candle on the dash
six lace curtains on the windows
sea shells all around

bumper to bumper
full of disneyland stickers
small world you see
hologram of magic mountain
shallow grand canyon is deep very deep
tahoe and vegas dreams of hitting it big
very superstitious
blessed by Father Pol
covered his plastic rear seats
steered the wheel with imitation leather

there he goes again
backing up
annoying the neighbors
tweet tweet tweet like a garbage truck
announcing the arrival
I shall return to mcarthur
jeepneyfying to signify

Cadenza

Jose Wendell P. Capili

I lift an obsession
of many years back:
to fold up the universe
shutting in grandfather.
His first family buried him
beneath an earth
so far away from the hue
that my family had skirted on.
They say we didn't belong
so I climb churches
surrendering to God
whatever remained
of the man's old form,
old figs, old anything
that restores
my image of home
without grief or vastness,
a grimace of flesh,
sweetness where cherry trees
twist on grandfather's will
to heal and return.
I settle on crypts
waiting for a tinge of faith
to chill on my lips
breathing the end
of pain, memory and cinders
from the sea, gesturing in.

Notes from a University Writing Group
(Or, "From the Woman Who Told Me to Write White")

Emily Porcincula Lawsin

Well,
I liked the *universality*
of the story,
she said.
I could really see
this *little*
family,
see their *dinky*
kitchen,
smell the ginger—
root, is that right?
Hear   *Na-NAYYYYYYY*,
the mother.
Oh, sorry,
it's pronounced
Nan-EYE?
Oh, didn't know that.
Well, I even liked
the dialogue,
I could say.

BUT

I
don't think
I
would add
any more.
I
found the
foreign words
distracting.
Well, maybe it was
the *italics.*
And is this really
how life in the,
in the,
in the,
well, *ghetto,*
e-hem,
really is?
Wow.
Wouldn't have known that.

Geez, Emily,
how did
you learn to write *English*
so well?

Home is a Temporary Thing

Jody Blanco

On my way home
is such an easy thing to say
But when you start doing it
you can say I saw
what I saw, but then
you're doing it. Tell me,
which of these
is a temporary thing? Or are
both of these a temporary thing?
It's important, sometimes these
temporary things
on your way; your way
a temporary thing.

On my way home I saw
no one special, no one
whom I see from time to time.
It's such an easy thing to say
such an easy way to see.
We meet people like this
on our way home
all the time: the time
empty questions. It means
nothing. But I was relieved;
I passed through
and came out on the other side.
Someone, no one special
spoke behind me. I was angry
that she was looking

for someone else.

When I turned around
there must have been a hundred
stars in the sky. There must have been
a hundred skies too. There was
an afterglow
which I can't explain. We talk a lot
about the sky; about things
we can't explain. About as much
as war: we walk out
into the cool evening
and there it is.

Between the rituals of work
and nighttime prayer, I
don't know. I'm walking
down the street, my street
a temporary thing. These dogs,
of them I can say two things:
they don't remember
but that doesn't mean
that they forget. And they will get me
one day, I know. You don't
have to remind me
I tell you, I know.

America from a Plane

Jody Blanco

Living
was yesterday. Today
was something else again: it was

a free-flying image
that lost its way, wanting

to commit to so many causes
dance with so many clients
the same night

and couldn't stop lying
for the life of me.
Here were all these

lovers, looking for the key
or right combination
to send themselves
through the blue-gray wash

of monitor screens, thin
tireless hum
and no trace of ink
for a memory

held fast upon cynicism's
vigilance, thin and tireless
light
the desert that constitutes

most of America
from a plane.

What you hear
for a moment
is the roar: and you wonder

if the rip in the sky
or day
will take you out of orbit
for awhile, give you coffee

brief you
on how Earth has changed
since you've been gone.

you,
who's been lost in the stars
for so long

and never thought you'd return
to get up, take a shower
kiss the you that might have been

goodbye again
and hello:
let's get to know each other
while we're waiting

for a stupid
but proud and innocent future
to make sense
of the dust, burn and tarnish
that calcifies what belonged

and belongs and how we tried

not to hurt each other
too much along the way.

from *Grace's Poems*

E. Eng Bueng

I. Waiting for her stillborn to make a fist

This city is a huckster
with the charisma of Jim Jones,
coarse with cheap, hasty sex and wild
as weed at heart.
      Eyes of homicidal
neon, gaze of ground prism,
to recompense, to manumit
without blinking.
      I have loved, idled,
thieved, killed for Miss Liberty
among a jury of clowns
seated in indecorous
wheelchairs and pushed across
the quicksand of life.

XL. Because

Liking the pattern of our days
in this land of soluble families.
Our English bodily feigned against
an early winter hooked on indecision.

In the eyes of a feverish stranger
I gleaned an anecdotal existence.

My seeding patch of boneset cringed
and held the sigh of a token breeze.

I felt the climate shift its weight just then,
and raise semaphores clumsily.
The thought of us snowed in at home
dragged reassurance over my skin.

Hungry

Jessica Nepomuceno

We are speeding on I-95, my
eyes absorbing the cheap Florida night.
My father's eyes are grim and constant scopes
for the road. I watch the drooping heavy
hoods above his eyes that his fellow aging
surgeons cut, tuck, tighten, so that their own
skin does not blind them as they cut into another
       human being.

We're on our way in the family four-
door through sunny states traveling to a
snowless Christmas vacation in Disneyland—driving because it's a small world. Days
later, at the hotel with the Mickey
Mouse phones, I breathe in a chlorine breeze that
comes off the glowing pool. I examine
      my toes which are

pale and huge underwater when I meet
him there—the minor star, the half-man. His
face was familiar from dog-eared 'zines full
of young demi-gods clutching skateboards. I
was hungry for toughness, I wanted the
freedom of wheels. I wanted to sail up
smooth curves of concrete and watch trees float by
      as hard as scars.

Remember: I was hungry for scars. We
planned a party in the nearby sauna

whose lock was easily forced open by
young muscles. I was the only girl but
then wasn't I always, when the boys pulled
ollies off the tops of ramps straight into
the sun? And we all know: being a girl
              means witnessing

all the fun. He and three friends of his
arrived clutching a case of beer, icy droplets
dotting the fuzz on their young bellies.
Some beers: a game. The tallest boy with the
laziest smile wanted to validate
a story his sailor uncle had told
him—Oriental women were built side-
              ways, see. Our twats

looked like a smile: friendly, not like the school-
girl slits of sweethearts back home, brushing back
bone-blond hair. I giggle, thinking, tough talk,
I can take it. Then they decide to prove
it by stripping me naked. I struggle
for real now. I cry. I gasp. I choke
on my tongue, cannot speak prayers. I'm flat on
              my belly in

a second: some body pressing on my
back and, God help me, all I can feel are
the slats of the wood bench. Shut the fuck up,
bitch, we just gotta check this. I did not
know how flesh can be sharp as a knife, then.
I did not know a cock could cut, that I
could stretch taut as dry bone. They knew. The heat
              all around me,

the heat all around me, and I can't breathe
for the heat. I count four cocks—they are beer-
bravado bloated. One like an anvil,
one shrinking already, one consuming
my prayers, one asking the riddle, "What
is there more of the more you take away
from it?" A hole (which means I am not
      holy any-

more.) When I awake or when my eyes open,
he walks me back to my room, puts my
hand on the doorknob, kisses a bruise on
my cheek, says thanks, and is gone. The car ride
home the next day, sore, I sleep and face away
from my father, who had worked his fingers
to the bone so we could enjoy this
      Christmas vacation.

Vacation: examine the word.
Vacating: I am: alive
as long as we keep moving
and the cool glass of the car
window presses into my cheek.

Drinking Milk in the Dark Kitchen

Jessica Nepomuceno

The kitchen is so dark that it
could easily be mistaken
for someplace else, perhaps a wheat
field in Kansas, perhaps a bus
stop in Times Square. In the night
time, when all things lose their shape in
the masking darkness, does the milk
stay white? What does it become?

The cool fluid passes through the
man's lips and slides slickly down his
throat. He wonders what it is he
has drunk. It could have been blood, or
freshwater rain. Who's to say, he
thinks, that it was white? Maybe it
was purple, maybe it was green.

The man pads through the darkness, past
rows of wheat and leering hookers,
past Kansas on tractors and New
York marquees, into the shadows
that could be his bedroom. He
lies on his bed, which may be a
coffin, or a park bench. Closing
his eyes, he falls asleep almost
instantly. He does not see through
the thin blue cotton of his
pajamas the outline of a
glowing trail of milk flowing into his stomach.

Months

Irene Suico Soriano

for Napoleon Lustre: 'dong, to keep you going in my head

I.

Essex said it perfect:
"It is easier to be furious than yearning."
You do belong to tribes of warriors and outlaws.
Many of whom are now dying or just waiting like you.
As I sit here by your bed looking at your sleeping body,
I wonder how long your fury can sustain you.

II.

This is a love song to a friend
whose remaining time with me
is determined by facts and figures
from studies, accounts and tests.
"Many have lived over 10 years since diagnosis."
My friend, it is your tenth year
and you are getting so sick so much more frequently now.
I am finding out that nobody really knows.

III.

As I drive these freeways and reach the golden hour
I will remember you and what I said about the beautiful color
this time of day gives the earth.
Healthy, vibrant, and new.
It would hit your dark skin and make you golden

healthy, vibrant and new.
If I could only make you
healthy, vibrant and new
with these words, I would.
I remember afternoons in your room over
Italian Roast and Benson & Hedges
and talk of cinema and discussions
about the fascinating curl of your spine.

IV.

You are brown, like me
coming from tropical islands we both
dream of going back to.
Do you know that after
leaving you each time
to go home to
my own life,
I am reminded of typhoon season
and the green spread of luscious cogon
in the mountains of Badian.
You bring me back
and for this exile,
lonely and wanting of things familiar
you give me sustenance.

V.

I look at your hands and see monkey hands.
I look at your arms and see how thin they have become.
I see you from across a crowded room and see your dark brown skin.
I see you dance and know we may never be able to do this again.

VI.

You were born somewhere else, not here,

not in this country where you found the gay ghetto.

Eleven years ago

you were somebody else.

When I asked your mama

What did he lose?

She wailed and said

His life! His life!

You are scared that

she will see you die,

I am scared that I will see both of you die.

VII.

I dreamt of you a long time ago,

in my dream you weren't as you are now.

You would inhabit different shapes

and wear different masks

but you were there with that stare

and presence that told me

you are not alone.

I am here and will always be here.

I am scared of growing old and not being able to tell you

I love you everyday.

I have to remind myself that when you are gone

what that woman said,

about you leaving your mark on her skin forever.

You are in blood, bone, and marrow.

Burnings

Ruel S. De Vera

1. Washington

Walking
to this city of stone
plumaged by mists,
you are surrounded
by streets which,
like you,
remember nothing
about the city's
proud dead,
save for their names.
Your new feet carry you
to where the obelisk
stands swathed
in its iridescent halo,
sharp
against the dome of sky,
immutable
against the vicious light.

But none

of these stone-silent
statues notice you.

None

of them even bother
to turn and look
at you.

2. New York

A light rain keeps
you company
as you walk
to the Met
amidst a gallery
of many turned faces.
If Gauguin was here,
or Van Gogh
or Cezanne,
he would paint
this scene
post-haste,
post-impressionist
in hazy hues,
watched over
by a cold, cold sun.

But in this geography
of your short,
short histories,
you are met
by an uncertainty
sharper
than a sheerest skyscraper
more beautiful
than St. Patrick's
shimmering spires.

3. Manila

Looking out the window,
you impale your words
on the tip of the hooked moon.
But while trying on
this coat of memories
you've outgrown,
never look away
from the familiar
caliber of night.
You might see something
you have never seen
before.

Look: There.

A shooting star,
the heart's glimmering ghost,
silently scars
this smoke-filled sky,
heavenly body falling
to this waiting earth,
carving out one maxim

and one maxim only:

In that final falling,
in that last homing,
there must always be
the quiet purifying
and the brightest of
burnings.

Imaginings

Lucille Rigor

"We wonder if she called out to us before she died."

With the curve of the highway in a town
in Spain as your black Nissan two-seater
careened off the road, skipped a boulder
crashed a fence, was the sun setting in Cordoba?
Was it orange or purple? Streaked or muted?
What was the music you were listening to
did you close your eyes to feel the measures
Were you scared? As you opened your eyes
to the fence, did you see the color
of your own aura? Were the windows rolled down?
On impact, did you hold your breath or exhale?
Did you think—this is only a dream, I will wake up.
Did Kelly's face, her raven hair, alight from nowhere?
Did you run a European marathon or eat beef stew?
Did you see Mom and Dad posing as you sketched them?
Did you see me an Atlantic Ocean away
standing in New York at dusk with a strong wind
blowing even the hair on my arms.
I looked up at the trees. They were so green and full.
I was thinking about being alone.
When did your glasses crack to shards into your face?
When did your blood spray on your books and journals?
At last. At last. Did you die a good death?

Peggy Lee

Elda Rotor

breasts
small cups
dark brown nipples
full of cancer
knock off the whole Philippine Islands
floating this five-block radius
from the hospital where our mothers,
nurses, make a living
for a family out of an American
death

their own mothers live
almost to 100,
straight-backed, crude
selling vinegar and candles
in the market of the villages
where they were born

our mothers
plain, plain women in their
early fifties
save new Gucci bags in plastic
small expensive perfumes, and
very real jewelry
diamonds, emeralds, and gold
from pilgrimages to Italy where
they attend mass
with the Pope

while their daughters have mouths
and sex like the sailors
from Subic Bay
cover their baby faces
with mud-brown lips,
perfect English
they think is beautiful

mothers' round bodies
once petite and hour-glass
like young Hollywood in the sixties
darlings in nursing school
courted by sweethearts
and learning early to work fourteen
hour shifts, to send money
back home to poor family and
pregnant nieces

our mothers were pretty
like Peggy Lee
swooned at Johnny Mathis
now replaced by Julio
who's third ex-wife was Filipino

mother's photograph
a chorus line of student nurses
waists as small as reeds
dark black curls lacquered and sprayed
low pumps show the line of leg
pastels and chiffon
move with the warm bay breeze
sweet with the smell of something
burning in Manila

these bits of lives wrapped
in tissue paper and put away
like gold jewelry and small rubies
for daughters to find in the closet
when they are older and curious

this plague we blame
on too much red meat
the asbestos in the hallways
or the coffee they drink
in the eleventh hour on duty
turns nurses to patients

makes daughters unlearn
the rules of sweetness of modesty
and rush to take what is theirs
smoking a pack a day
standing in front of microwaves
correcting the accents of their
fathers

this is a mother-daughter story

Plugging the Basketball Diaries
for Leonardo Di Caprio

Regie Cabico

two hands hung on the naked rim of a hoop

blonde christ finding sanctity in the company of boys
idle time is the devil's plaything

so you trample psychedelic poppies
leaping high as you shoot
smack

The thought of your limber body
curved over
the camera

dribbling those Spalding balls, shirtless, Mr. Di Caprio
steams the milk the depths of my dark cappuccino

So I turn on the tube hoping to catch
you mooning the Circle Line Cruise or jacking off
on the roof

Instead I find you flashing smiles for that
crosslegged MTV bimba named Daisy.

Enamored by your bashfulness she uncrosses her legs,
leans towards you like an awkward sunflower
in heat and asks:

You're the hottest actor right now
which girls are after you?

> You remain silent, a femme little thing
> in a butch leather jacket.

I'm asking about your love life,
but you say there's no one.

Walking past Tower Records, I freeze in my tracks
at the sight of your stance:

> a savage cheetah   w/ a crimson smile
> catholicism's leash   tied'round yr virgin neck

You may be too young
to catch my entendres 'Nardo

but I'd like to give you
an Oscar.

You Bring Out the Writer in Me

Regie Cabico

Your breasts are couplets
Your body is a sonnet
Your thoughts share my soliloquy
Your kiss is imagery
Your eyes are iambic
Your tongue is trochaic
Your touch is stream of consciousness
Your complexity is Eliot
Your neck is Steinbeck
Your stubble is cacophony
Your presence is from fantasy
Your brilliance is Ashbery
Your ass is assonance
Your penis is epic
Your torso is a tanka
Your rambling is a renga
Your fucking is a foreshadowing
Your sighs are the climax
Your orgasms are onomatopoeia,
      onomatopoeia,
         onomatopoeia,
Your clinging is Sexton,
Your ejaculation is sprung rhythm,
Your testicles are testaments
Your backbones are stanzas
Your view is omnipotent
I see you in epilogue
Going
Going
Gone

The Trick

Regie Cabico

three forty-seven a.m.
Last call for drinks
I stumble to his motorcycle
Ride the wind
behind his back
My hair plays—
Born to be Wild

four a.m.
Inside his apartment
is an enormous
       —tank of goldfish
       anthropology books
spill over a desk.
(I'm glad there are
no dogs)

four twenty-one a.m.
He unbuttons my shirt
licks my tit
slams me eagle
on the mattress

five-thirty a.m.
I stare at his body
with my stain on his chest
"You're my best geisha-boy!"
He whispers, turning the halogen off

six thirty-three am
The sky turns from purple to orange
as I walk home from the East to the West
and roll back on my bed

seven-ten p.m.
he doesn't know that i compose
poems on keyboard   that i wear
eyeglasses to work   that i spell
my name with one "g"   that i
am allergic to cut grass

this is the vanishing act of the year

Tales Told by Eye

Maximina Juson

A fear of my own people
HINDI KO ALAM TALAGA
Whatever is myself
I see too much in them
While most other times
Their sight is not my own

A photograph of a Filipino girl
Placed on my father's wall
An American hymn
Rings loudly when I sing

In the land with four seasons
Mutants are created
My eyes tell a story
Which my voice cannot speak

When I return to the sea
Of brown hair and brown skin;
ANO'NG GINAGAWA MO SA AKIN?
ANO BA NAMAN?
There's a chill in the heat

The illusion of my indigenous shroud
Dissolves with my alien words
A visitor at home
Foreigner to the familiar

A war between hate and love
To both I surrender

Outside

Lester Salvador

for M.A.

it is harder on the nights
when you are caught between worlds

when you are battered within
a vast and mapless raging

scanning the unseen horizon
for the fire of her eyes

and while navigating by
the lingering smell of incense

you move fast over black waters
in a Malay pirate vessel

your sails swell full to bursting
w/ the voice of the autumn storm

destination

somewhere

forward

home

Nanay Lumen

Patrick Pardo

my grandmother lies in a coffin
like some strange cargo, crated
and resting alone on a pier, or
perhaps an unmarked package awaiting
inspection at a foreign airport hangar.
she will confront neither dock workers
loading the sea-bound export, nor
suspicious customs agents surveying
the new arrival, but instead:
the employees of Whitman's Funeral
Home of Long Island preparing her
for the flames of the crematorium.
unknown doctors, coroners, and morticians
have already examined and interpreted her,
and we have come here to a stranger's home
to bear witness to their work, to observe
the body, as best embalmed, groomed,
dressed, perfumed; her final expression
a fiction, re-configured, re-expressed.
we have bought a casket from among the
models displayed in the basement showroom.
we have selected the box with her needs
in mind: roomy, utilitarian, handsome,
but not showy, noble, yet combustible.
and so, she acts the hostess
in a home that was never her home,
in whose living room she had never lived,
until today; looking at her,
i recall the nights she spent

in our house, when i would
find

      my grandmother asleep
with the television on again,
a judith krantz novel by her side,
reading glasses on the tip of her nose.
johnny carson is on only his second joke
when my grandmother begins to snore.
initially every third breath a snore,
then every other, then when she achieves
a rhythm, i put away the book, her spectacles,
turn off the set, and before closing
the light in her room, watch as her
73 year-old body rises then falls;
for a brief instant, i feel she
may levitate from her fold-out bed
the dessert cart of Waid's cafeteria,
but tonight she will not resist gravity.
i shut off the light, shut the door
on her nasal monologue,
leaving her to the things
envisioned in her
sleep.

Notes on the Authors

Gemino H. Abad was born in Manila in 1939, was educated at the University of the Philippines and received his MA and Ph.D. from the University of Chicago in 1970. Together with four other poets, he co-founded the Philippine Literary Arts Council (PLAC) which publishes *Caracoa*, the only journal in Asia devoted to poetry in English. He currently teaches at the University of the Philippines where he is University Professor and Director of the UP Creative Writing Center.

Maria Cecilia Aquino Aguilar is from San Diego California. She will be graduating from Sarah Lawrence College in May 1997.

Rene Estrella Amper was a fellow of the National Writers Workshop Asia Foundation in Silliman University, Dumaguete City, Philippines, and recipient of the Palanca Memorial Award—the highest literary award in the Philippines—and the Cultural Center of the Philippines literature grants for essay and Cebuano novel. He has been municipal mayor of the town of Boljoon in Cebu since 1992.

Carlos Angeles has won the Palanca Memorial Awards as well as the Republic Cultural Heritage Award in 1964 for his collection of poetry, *A Stun of Jewels*. He recently published another collection, *A Bruise of Ashes* (Ateneo 1993). He lives in La Puente, California.

Maria Lourdes Antenorcruz was born in Seattle and raised in Hawai'i and currently lives in Queens, New York. As a journalist and poet, she plans to create a series of articles and documentaries on child prostitution in the Philippines and in Asia. She works in the public affairs office of the Statue of Liberty-Ellis Island Foundation, Inc.

Gina Apostol grew up in Tacloban, Leyte. She has an A.B. in English from the University of the Philippines and an M.A. in Writing from Johns Hopkins

University. Her stories were published in *Catfish Arriving in Little Schools*, an anthology of contemporary Philippine fiction (Anvil 1996), *The Gettysburg Review* (Pennsylvania), *Taipan* (Manila), and *The Evening Paper* (Manila). Her novel, *Bibliolepsy*, was recently published by The University of the Philippines Press. She lives with her husband and daughter in Makati, Philippines.

Peter Bacho is a teacher, journalist and attorney who lives in Sacramento, California. His novel, *Cebu*, was published by the University of Washington Press in 1991. He is working on a collection of short stories.

Jody Blanco grew up as the second of four boys near Blank's pond and Wing Lake in Detroit, Michigan. After college, he spent a couple of years in the Philippines. Since 1993, he has been based in Berkeley, California, where he is pursuing a Ph.D. in comparative literature.

E. Eng Bueng was born and raised in Caloocan City, Philippines and studied chemistry at the University of Santo Tomas. He received citations in the Scottish International Open Poetry Competition twice, and his works have appeared in *Hawai'i Review* (University of Hawai'i at Manoa), *Manna* (Fishdown Press, UT), *Plainsongs* (Hastings College, NE), *Orbis: An International Quarterly of Poetry and Prose* (UK), and *Sandman* (DC Comics, NY).

Carlos Bulosan (1911-1956) immigrated to the United States as an eighteen-year-old. A largely self-taught writer, he supported himself working on the farms and helping organize farm labor. Some of his stories appeared in *The New Yorker*. He is the author of *Voice of Bataan*, *The Laughter of My Father*, *America is in the Heart*, *Power of the People*, and *The Philippines is in the Heart*. He died of consumption in Seattle in 1956.

Luis Cabalquinto writes poetry, fiction and non-fiction. His work has appeared in numerous journals, including *The American Poetry Review*, *Prairie Schooner*, *Manoa*, *Trafika*, *Asiaweek* and *International Quarterly*. His fourth book-length collection of poetry, *Depth of Fields*, is scheduled for publication in 1997. Born in Magarao, Philippines, he currently resides in New York City.

Regie Cabico's work appears in numerous anthologies including *Aloud: Voices From the Nuyorican Poet's Cafe* (Holt, 1994), *The Name of Love* (St., Martin's, 1995), *On A Bed of Rice: Asian American Erotica* (Anchor, 1995), *Eros in Boystown* (Crown, 1996), among others. He was the winner of The New York Poetry Slam, a Road Poet on Lollapalooza and the opening act of the MTV Free Your Mind Spoken Word Tour.

Jose Wendell P. Capili studied at the University of Santo Tomas and the University of the Philippines and is currently taking his Ph.D in Social Anthropology at the University of Cambridge. He was also a Mombusho research scholar in comparative literature and culture at the University of Tokyo and received a Korean Foundation Research fellowship in Korean Studies in Seoul.

Nick Carbo is the author of a collection of poems *El Grupo McDonald's* (Tia Chucha Press 1995) and the editor of *Returning A Borrowed Tongue: An Anthology of Contemporary Filipino Poetry in English* (Coffee House Press 1996). His poems have appeared in such magazines as *Asian Pacific American Journal*, *Green Mountains Review*, *Western Humanities Review*, and others. He is married to the poet Denise Duhamel.

Maria Luisa Aguilar Cariño recently fulfilled a Fulbright fellowship in the Ph.D. program of the University of Illinois in Chicago. She won the Manila Critics' Circle National Book Award in 1993 for her collection of poetry, *Cartography and Other Poems on Baguio*. Her fourth book of poetry, *In the Garden of the Three Islands*, was published by Moyer Bell in 1995. Her poems have been published in *Black Warrior Review*, *Folio*, *Journal of American Culture*, *Bomb*, *TriQuarterly* and *the Asian Pacific American Journal* and in the anthologies *Returning a Borrowed Tongue* and *Premonitions: The Kaya Anthology of New Asian North American Writing*.

Linda Ty-Casper has published numerous books of short stories, novels and historical fiction in Manila, London and the U.S., most recent of which are

Kulasyon: Uninterrupted Vigils (Quezon City, 1995), and *Dream Eden*, a novel (University of Washington Press, Seattle, 1996). She holds a master of literature degree from Harvard and has received grants from Radcliffe Institute, the Djerassi Foundation, the Massachusetts Artists Foundation, Wheatland and the Rockefeller Foundation in Bellagio, Italy.

Fidelito Cortes was a Wallace Stegner fellow in poetry at Stanford University in 1985. His first book of poetry, *Waiting for the Exterminator* (Kalikasan Press, 1989), won the Manila Critics' Circle National Book Award in 1989. He is currently living in Berkeley.

Ruel S. De Vera is a poet and journalist in Manila. He is a staff writer for the *Sunday Inquirer Magazine* and teaches at Ateneo de Manila University. His first book of poetry, *The Most Careful of Stars* (Anvil, 1996) was recently published in Manila.

Ricardo M. De Ungria received an MFA in Creative Writing from Washington University in St. Louis and is Chair of the Department of Arts and Communication at the University of the Philippines, Manila. He was a writer-in-residence at the Rockefeller Foundation in Bellagio, Italy, and a Fulbright fellow in 1987–89, and has published four collections of poetry, including *Body English* (1995), *Decimal Places* (1991, winner of the Manila Critics' Circle National Book Award in 1992), *Voideville: Selected Poems* 1974–79 (1991) and $R+A+D+I+O$ (1986).

Simeon Dumdum is a practicing lawyer in Cebu island in the Philippines and has published two collections of poetry, *Third World Opera* and *The Gift of Sleep*. His poems are included in the anthology *This Same Sky* (Four Winds Press, Macmillan, 1992), edited by Naomi Shihab Nye.

Bataan Faigao holds a master of arts degree in social psychology from New York University and an MFA in writing and poetics from the Jack Kerouac School of Disembodied Poetics, The Naropa Institute in Boulder, Colorado, where he is currently on core faculty teaching ta'i chi ch'uan. His poetry has been published in *Festschrift for KGB*, an international anthology of poetry, (Lyrebird Press, London, 1972), as well as *Bombay Gin, New Blood, New York Underground, Ningas*

Cogon, Human Means, The New Savage State, Brown River, White Ocean (Rutgers University Press, 1993). He is a recipient of awards from the Boulder Arts Council (1982 and 1984).

Luis H. Francia is a New Yorker, a Manileño, a poet, critic, and teacher. He has written two books of poetry, *Her Beauty Likes Me Well* (with David Friedman) and *The Arctic Archipelago and Other Poems.* He edited the seminal *Brown River, White Ocean*, an anthology of Philippine Literature in English. A Palanca Memorial Award winner in poetry, he has had his work published in numerous literary journals and was writer-in-residence at Columbia University and at Asian Cine-Vision. He writes for *The Village Voice, A. Magazine*, and *Asiaweek*, and teaches Asian American literature at Sarah Lawrence College.

M. Evelina Galang is the author of *Her Wild American Self*, a collection of short fiction from Coffee House Press. Her stories and essays have appeared in magazines such as *Mild American Review, The Crescent Review, Amerasia Journal, Riksha, Special Edition Press, Calyx, American Short Fiction, Quarterly West* and *New Voices.* In 1993, she won the Associated Writers Program Intro Award in non-fiction and in 1994 she was the John Gardner Scholar in Fiction at Bread Loaf Writers Conference. She received her MFA from Colorado State University and a BA in Radio, Television and Film from the University of Wisconsin-Madison. An assistant professor at Old Dominion University, she teaches creative writing and literature and in the director of the university's 19th annual literary awards.

Eric Gamalinda was born and educated in Manila where he published three novels, *Empire of Memory* (Anvil, 1992), *Confessions of a Volcano* (Anvil, 1990) and *Planet Waves* (New Day, 1989), a short story collection, *Peripheral Vision* (New Day, 1992), and poetry, *Lyrics from a Dead Language* (Anvil, 1990). He was writer-in-residence at the Rockefeller Foundation in Bellagio, Italy, and a participant in the "Poets Among Us" program of the Geraldine Dodge Poetry Festival in 1996. His work has been published in *Harper's Magazine, Frank, International Quarterly, Forkroads, The Asian Pacific American Journal, Columbia: A Journal of Literature and Art, Oxford Magazine* (Oxford, U.K.), as well as the anthologies *Brown River, White Ocean* and *Returning a Borrowed Tongue.*

J. Eugene Gloria received an MFA in Creative Writing from the University of Oregon and spent a year and a half in Manila as a Fulbright Exchange Scholar. His poems have appeared in *Mid-American Review*, *Parnassus*, *Quarry West*, *The Asian Pacific American Journal*, and in the anthology *The Open Boat* (Anchor Books, 1993). He currently teaches at Holyoke College, Massachusetts.

Vince Gotera teaches at the University of Northern Iowa, where he is professor of creative writing and poetics. He has published a book of poems, *Dragonfly*, and a critical study, *Radical Visions: Poetry by Vietnam Veterans*. His poems were published recently in *Premonitions: The Kaya Anthology of New Asian North American Poetry* and *Returning a Borrowed Tongue: An Anthology of Filipino and Filipino-American Poetry in English*.

NVM Gonzales is emeritus professor of English literature at California State University, Hayward, and international writer-in-residence at the University of the Philippines, Manila. His many novels include *A Season of Grace* and *The Bamboo Dancers*, as well as *The Bread of Salt* (University of Washington Press, 1993), a retrospective selection of short stories from the early 1950s to the present.

Jessica Hagedorn was nominated for a National Book Award in 1990 for her first novel, *Dogeaters*, which was also voted best book of the year by the Before Columbus Foundation. A well-known performance artist, poet, and playwright, and formerly a commentator on "Crossroads," a syndicated weekly magazine on National Public Radio, she is also the author of *Danger and Beauty: Poetry and Prose*, the editor of *Charlie Chan is Dead: An Anthology of Contemporary Asian American Fiction*, as well as the screenplay for the film *Fresh Kill*. Her new novel, *The Gangster of Love*, was published by Houghton Mifflin in 1996.

Jaime Jacinto was born in Manila in 1954 and studied at the University of California, Santa Cruz. He teaches at San Francisco State University and is a founding member of the Bay Area Pilipino American Writers' Workshop as well as co-editor of the anthology of Filipino American poetry, *Without Names* (Kearny Street Workshop Press, 1985). His poetry has also been published in *Breaking Silence* (Greenfield Review Press, 1983), and *Premonitions* (Kaya Productions, 1995). His translations of poems from Spanish of Asian South American poets have appeared in *This Wanting to Sing, A Collection of Asian South American Poets*. A collection of poems, *Heaven is Just Another Country*, was recently published by the Kearny Street Workshop.

Maximina Juson is a poet and musician and has played bass on tour, television and radio with Natalie Merchant, formerly of 10,000 Maniacs, and Ras Eddie-I, in which she performed spoken word. She has also performed with Blueprint from The Black Rock Coalition and Sunchilde of Sony Music during The New Music Seminar.

F. Sionil Jose is a bookseller, editor and publisher of the journal *Solidarity*, as well as founding president of the Philippines PEN Center and an author published in twenty-four languages. His novel, *Sins*, was recently published by Random House, which is also readying for publication his five-novel *Rosales* saga.

Pancho Lapuz wrote the poems included in this anthology in San Francisco, where he lived and worked until recently. He now lives in Baguio City in the Philippines, where he oversees a book and music store.

Emily Porcincula Lawsin is from Seattle, Washington. A trustee of the Filipino American National Historical Society, she now teaches Asian American Studies at California State University, Northridge. Her poetry has appeared in *Homegrown 3*, *Forward Motion Magazine's Asians in Struggle*, *Seattle Arts*, *The FAHNS Journal*, *The International Examiner*, and *The Seattle Times*. She has read at various events at UCLA, Bryn Mawr College in Philadelphia, University of Washington, and the Broadway Performance Hall in Seattle.

Fatima Lim-Wilson's second poetry collection, *Crossing the Snow Bridge* won the 1995 Ohio State University Press/*The Journal* Award in Poetry. Her first collection, *Wandering Roots/ From the Hothouse* received the Colorado Book Authors Award and the Philippine National Book Award.

R. Zamora Linmark lives in Honolulu and recently published his first novel, *Rolling the R's* (Kaya Production, 1995).

Ruth Elynia S. Mabanglo is well-known and much awarded for her Tagalog poetry. Originally from Manila, she now teaches both the Tagalog language and Philippine literature at the University of Hawaii in Honolulu.

Francis Macansantos resided for five years as a househusband in the United States while his wife was on a grant to finish her Ph.D. in Mathematics. Originally from Dumaguete in the Central Visayas region of the Philippines, he now lives in Baguio City.

Noel Abubo Mateo is a poet and painter living in Southern California. He holds degrees from the University of California and Yale University. His poems have appeared in *Bamboo Ridge* and in the anthology *Returning a Borrowed Tongue* (Coffee House Press, 1996).

Rene J. Navarro is a licensed acupuncturist and herbologist based in Greater Boston and has been a martial arts master in Shaolin Temple boxing, ta'i chi ch'uan and arnis de mano since the 60s. He is a faculty member of the New England School of Acupuncture where he teaches Taoist energetic medicine, Qigong, meditation, Taiji, internal alchemy and abdominal massage. "Dragon (Winter 1994)" is part of his collection, *Du Fu's Cottage and Other Poems.*

Jessica Nepomuceno graduated from Barnard College, Columbia University in 1996 with a major in English and a writing concentration. She was published in volume 31 of *Quatro,* the literary magazine of Columbia University's School of General Studies, and in *13th Article,* Barnard College's literary magazine. She is a member of Native Souls, a multicultural writers' collective based in New York City.

Patrick Pardo was born in Kansas in 1969 and was educated at Vassar and Sarah Lawrence College. His poems have appeared in journals such as *420* as well as the anthology *Returning a Borrowed Tongue* (Coffee House Press, 1995). He lives in New York City.

Edgar Poma won the Galbraithe Prize for Poetry in 1983 while an undergraduate at the University of California at Berkeley. His plays, *Reunion* and *Little Train*, have been produced in San Francisco. He was selected for HBO's first annual New Writer's Project and recently received a California Arts Council grant to develop new work.

Bino Realuyo was born and raised in Manila in 1967 and studied International Relations in the U.S., and South America. He has finished two books, *In Spite of Open Eyes*, a poetry collection, and *The Umbrella Country*, a novel, from which *States of Being* was excerpted. He has published widely in literary journals and anthologies, and participated in the "Poets Among Us" program of the Geraldine Dodge Poetry Festival in 1996 and has been a guest lecturer for a literature and creative writing class at Yale University.

Ninotchka Rosca has written two collections of short stories, *Bitter Country and Other Stories* and *The Monsoon Collection*, two novels, including *State of War*, and a journalistic work, *Endgame*, on the events of 1986 that forced the Marcoses from power.

Elda Rotor has published work in The *Asia Pacific American Journal*'s *Engendering Visions* issue, as well *off our backs* magazine. She is the publisher and editor-in-chief of *New Digressions*, an art and literary magazine.

Alfrredo Navarro Salanga (1948-1988) was a newspaper columnist and editor and a founding member of the Philippine Literary Arts Council. He wrote a novel, *The Birthing of Hannibal Valdez*, and a collection of his poems, *Turtle Voices in Uncertain Weather*, came out posthumously in 1989.

Michael Sandoval has an MFA in Fiction Writing and has taught as a lecturer in the Department of English at The University of Michigan for the past year. In 1994, he traveled to the Philippines on a research grant to investigate native responses to the Philippine War for a novel-in-progress. He is currently on a Creative Artists Grant through the Arts Foundation of Michigan.

Bienvenido Santos (1911-1996) first came to the U.S. in 1941 and held Rockefeller and Guggenheim fellowships and was awarded the Republic Cultural Heritage and Palanca Memorial Awards in the Philippines. He is the author of several novels and collections of short stories, including *You Lovely People* (Manila, Bookmark Press) and *The Scent of Apples* (Washington University Press), which received the 1980 American Book Award from the Before Columbus Foundation.

Lester Salvador is a poet, essayist, short-story writer, and part-time journalist, a member of the New York-based *EXCURSUS* literary collective, as well as the New York-based multicultural writers and artists collective, Native Souls.

Irene Suico Soriano was born in Zamboanga, Philippines, in 1969 and immigrated to Los Angeles in 1981. She established the Asian American Reading Series, *Wrestling Tigers: Asian American Writers Speak* for the Japanese American National Museum and coordinated this series from 1994–1996. She curated a Monday Night Reading for Highways 1995 Women's Festival as well as the literary component of the 1994, 1995 and 1996 Los Angeles Festival of Philippine Arts and Culture. Her articles and poems have been published in *Clamour-dyke 'zine*, *DisOrient*, *FLIP Magazine*, *Philippines Free Press*, *Solidarity Journal* and *The Writer's Guild Journal*. She is a founding member of the Los Angeles Pilipino AIDS Task Force and a board member of the Asian Pacific American Literary Arts Organization and program coordinator for Asian Pacific Health Care Venture's Asian and Pacific Islander Women's HIV/AIDS Prevention Project.

Lara Stapleton is a Filipino-American, born and raised in East Lansing, Michigan. Her work has been published in *The Asian-Pacific American Journal*, *The Michigan Quarterly Review*, *The Alaska Quarterly Review*, *Another Chicago Magazine*, *Columbia*, *the Chatahoochee Review* and *Glimmer Train*. She currently resides in New York City, where she teaches composition at the Pratt Institute and Long Island University in Brooklyn. She was a two-time winner of the University of Michigan's Hopwood Award for Fiction and received an honorable mention in *Best of American Short Stories 1991* and in the Master's Literary Award organized by the Center Press in Los Angeles.

Eileen Tabios received a B.A. in Political Science from Barnard College and an M.B.A. in Economics and International Business from New York University's Graduate School of Business. Editor of *The Asian Pacific American Journal*, she switched careers in 1995 from international banking to full-time creative writing. Her poetry and fiction have been published in numerous journals and anthologies and her collection of poetry-in-progress essays, *IN PROGRESS*, will be published in 1997 by the Asian American Writers Workshop. In 1996 she received *Poet's* Iva Mary Williams Poetry Award and a fellowship from the Virginia Center for the Creative Arts.

Jeff Tagami was born in Watsonville, California, and is the author of *October Light* (Kearny Street Workshop Press, 1990), a collection of poems. He co-translated the chapbook, *This Wanting to Sing, Asian American Poets in South America* (Contact II Press) and co-edited *Without Names*, a collection of poetry by Bay Area Pilipino American Writers (Kearny Street Workshop Press). He lives in San Francisco.

Joel Tan is a widely anthologized writer, poet and spoken word artist. His short stories, poetry and non-fiction essays have appeared in *Asian American Sexualities* (Routledge), *On a Bed of Rice* (Anchor), and *Maganda Magazine*. He has performed at several universities, performance spaces, and conferences nationally, including Intersection for the Arts, Howard University, UCLA, and Creating Change '92. He is HIV Project Director at the Asian Health Services in Oakland, California.

Edith L. Tiempo, along with her late husband Edilberto Tiempo, is the guiding light behind the Silliman Writers Workshop in the Philippines. Among her published works are *The Tracks of Babylon and Other Poems* and a novel, *A Blade of Fern*.

Rowena Torrevillas is a poet and short story writer originally from Dumaguete, Philippines, and is currently managing the International Writing Program in Iowa. Her books include *Upon the Willows and Other Stories* and a collection of poetry, *East of Summer*.

Marianne Villanueva is the author of *Ginseng and Other Tales from Manila* (Calyx Books, 1991). Her stories have been in, among others, *Charlie Chan Is Dead: An Anthology of Contemporary Asian American Fiction* (Penguin Books, 1993) and *Into the Fire: Asian American Prose* (Greenfield Review Press, 1995). She lives in Redwood City, California with her husband and son.

Alfred Yuson has received the SouthEast Asian Writers Award and various national and international distinctions for his poetry and fiction. He attended the International Writing Program in Iowa, the East-West Center International Poetry Conference in Honolulu, the Asian Poetry Conference and the Chikyu Poetry Festival in Tokyo, the International Writers Reunion in Finland, the World Poetry Congress in Bangkok and the World Poetry Reading Festival in Kuala Lumpur. He received fellowships from the British Council and Hawthornden Castle in Scotland. He has published three collections of poetry, *Trading in Mermaids*, *Dream of Knives*, and *Sea Serpent*, a novel, *Great Philippine Jungle Energy Cafe*, short fiction, *The Music Child and Other Stories*, as well as essays and children's fiction.

Cyn. Zarco is a Filipina-American poet-journalist whose work has appeared in *US*, *Elle*, and *Interview*. She was born in Manila and raised in Miami, and studied at the University of California at Berkeley and Columbia. She has published a book of poems and short stories, *cir'cum nav'i ga'tion* (Tooth of Time Books, 1986) and co-authored a book on Eighties pop fashion, *Wild Style* (Simon & Schuster, 1986).

About the cover: V.C. Igarta finished painting "Manong" in 1996. Born in Sinait, Ilocos Sur, in the Philippines in 1910, he emigrated to America in 1932 and worked as a farm hand and in factories, moving up and down the Pacific West Coast with hundreds of immigrant workers. During the Depression, he moved East where he attended art school in between jobs in New York. A retrospective of his work has been shown at the Metropolitan Museum of Manila. He continues painting in his apartment in New York's Lower East Side.

Acknowledgments

Grateful acknowledgment is made to the publications from which some of the works in this anthology were chosen. Unless specifically noted otherwise, copyright of the poems and stories is held by the individual writers.

Gemino H. Abad: "An Imaginary Letter to My Twin Sons" appeared in *Philippine Studies 43*, 1995, and in *Father and Daughter: The Figures of Our Speech* (Manila: Anvil, 1996). Reprinted with permission from the author.

Maria Cecilia Aquino Aguilar: "Perished Fruit" appeared in *The Sarah Lawrence Review*. Reprinted with permission from the author.

Carlos Angeles: "Manhattan Rain" and "Jacaranda Trees" appeared in *A Bruise of Ashes: Collected Poems* (Ateneo de Manila University Press, 1992). Reprinted with permission from the author.

Maria Lourdes Antenorcruz: "La Reina" appeared in *The Asia Pacific American Journal*. Reprinted with permission from the author.

Carlos Bulosan: "Sunset and Evening Star," "All the Living Fear," "The Last Trip," and "The Living Hour" appeared in *Carlos Bulosan and His Poetry: A Biography and Anthology*, Susan Evangelista, ed. (Manila: Ateneo de Manila University). Reprinted with permission from the University of Washington Press.

Luis Cabalquinto: "Sunday with the Smiths" appeared in *The Dog-eater and Other Poems* (Manila: Kalikasan Press, 1989). Reprinted with permission from the author.

Regie Cabico: "You Bring Out the Writer in Me" appeared in *Pennsylvania Review*, "The Trick" appeared in *Red Brick Review*. Reprinted with permission from the author.

Fatima Lim-Wilson: "Casting Call," "The Resident Alien as Acrobat," and "A Sestina Written in a Cold Land" appeared in *Crossing the Snow Bridge* (Ohio State University Press, 1995). Reprinted with permission from the author.

R. Zamora Linmark: "You Don't Have to Wait" and "What Manong Rocky Tells Manang Pearly" appeared in *Rolling the R's.* Copyright © R. Zamora Linmark. Published by Kaya Production, New York City. Reprinted with permission.

Noel Abubo Mateo: "Jeepneyfying" appeared in *Returning a Borrowed Tongue*, Nick Carbo, ed. (Coffee House Press, 1995). Reprinted with permission from the author.

Patrick Pardo: "Nanay Lumen" appeared in *Returning a Borrowed Tongue*, Nick Carbo, ed. (Coffee House Press, 1995). Reprinted with permission from the author.

Bino Realuyo: "States of Being" appeared in *Caliban*, Fall 1995. Reprinted with permission from the author.

Alfrredo Navarro Salanga: "A Philippine History Lesson," "They Don't Think Much About Us in America," "War, Like Fever" reprinted with permission from the estate of Alfrredo Navarro Salanga.

Bienvenido Santos: Excerpt from *The Man Who (Thought He) Looked Like Robert Taylor* reprinted with permission from Doreen G. Fernandez.

joel b. tan: "Night Sweats" appeared in *On a Bed of Rice*, G. Kudaka, ed. (Anchor Books, 1995). Reprinted with permission from the author.

Edith L. Tiempo: "From a Window in an Old People's Home" appeared in *Caracoa* (Manila: Philippine Literary Arts Council). Reprinted with permission from the editors.

Rowena Torrevillas: "Fly-Over Country" appeared in *Caracoa* (Manila: Philippine Literary Arts Council). Reprinted with permission from the editors.

Alfred Yuson: "Filipino in Frisco" appeared in *Sea Serpent* (Manila: Monsoon Press, 1980), "Andy Warhol Speaks to His Two Filipina Maids" appeared in *Trading in Mermaids* (Manila: Philippine Literary Arts Council, 1992). Reprinted with permission from the author.

The editors of Flippin' and the board and staff of the Asian American Writers' Workshop would like to thank the following persons for their assistance, generosity and goodwill. Many of these people helped us type, edit and produce the book, others gave financial support, and still others attended or helped us organize our benefit reading in New York City in the summer of 1996. To all of them, maraming salamat.

Maria Cecilia Aquino Aguilar

Sarah Alvarez

Melanie Apostol

Sean Arce

Louis Avenilla

Jodi Barias

Philippe Berckmans

Amy Besa

Jon Bidso

Jed Bolipata

Plet Bolipata

Nerio Brillantes

Cielo Buenaventura

Nancy Bulalacao

Luis Cabalquinto

Hannah Cabili

Nick Carbo

Robert Carnevale

Cendrillon Asian Bar & Merienda Grill

Sam Chang

William Chang

Christine Chao

Calvin Chin

Curtis Chin

Paul Chung

Josy Cobb

Melissa Contreras

Sandra Corpus

Rosanna Cruz

Rowena Degorostiza

Romy Dorotan
Alisa Dror
Denise Duhamel
Dante Fabunam
Ria Fabunam
Rusty Fabunam
Lambert Fernando
Midori Francia
Alberto Florentino
Angelie Florentino
Eva Florentino
Sonya Florentino
Gisella Galang
Feliciano Gallardo
Manjon Gillespie
Tita Gillespie
David Glaser
Winston Go
Katrina Gomez
Miriam Graece
Reme Grefalda
Dr. Hugo Halo
Jessica Hagedorn
Michael Hoffman
Maria Hudson
V.C. Igarta
Vladimir Immanuel
Scott Ito
Parag Khandhar
Angela Kim
Jeannie Kim
Wan Leung
Lea Liwanag
Lisa Ko
Ken Loc
Kathleen Mangunay

Fred McConkey

Bob Messineo

Meryl Messineo

Ravital Naveh

Michael Offen

Peter Ong

Mina Park

Susan Park

Michael Perez

The Philippine Literary Arts Council

Thomas Pollock

Janice Pono

Eugenio Pulman

Rayner Ramirez

Bino Realuyo

Ed Reisner

Archie Reyes

Ninotchka Rosca

Gary San Angel

Maureen Seaton

James Shaver

Joan Shigekawa

Stuart Solsky

Dora Stanfield

Lorna Sumarga

Filamore & Beatriz Tabios

Eileen Tabios

Renee Tang

Julman Tolentino

Angela Tolosa

Ching Valdez

Alan Vilamore

Manda Weintraub

Bonnie Wong

Alfred Yuson

Titles from The Asian American Writers' Workshop

The NuyorAsian Anthology: Asian American Writings About New York City
Edited by Bino A. Realuyo

Black Lightning: Poetry In Progress
By Eileen Tabios

Watermark: Vietnamese American Poetry & Prose
Edited by Barbara Tran, Monique T.D. Truong & Luu Truong Khoi

Contours of the Heart: South Asians Map North America
(winner of the American Book Award)
Edited by Sunaina Maira & Rajini Srikanth

Flippin': Filipinos on America
Edited by Luis Francia and Eric Gamalinda

Quiet Fire: A Historical Anthology of Asian American Poetry, 1892-1970
Edited by Juliana Chang

To purchase any of these books, please contact Temple University Press,1601 N. Broad Street, USB 305, Philadelphia PA 19122. Call toll-free 1-800-447-1656 / fax 215-204-1128 or visit us on the web at www.temple.edu/tempress.